Heart
in the
Right
Place

**Center Point
Large Print**

**This Large Print Book carries the
Seal of Approval of N.A.V.H.**

Heart in the Right Place

Carolyn Jourdan

CENTER POINT PUBLISHING
THORNDIKE, MAINE

This Center Point Large Print edition
is published in the year 2008 by
arrangement with Algonquin Books of Chapel Hill,
a division of Workman Publishing.

The text of this Large Print edition is unabridged.
In other aspects, this book may
vary from the original edition.
Printed in the United States of America.
Set in 16-point Times New Roman type.

Because this book depicts real events and actual medical
situations, some characters have been altered for the
purpose of protecting their privacy and certain
chronologies have been altered for simplicity.

ISBN: 978-1-60285-336-2

Library of Congress Cataloging-in-Publication Data

Jourdan, Carolyn, 1955–
  Heart in the right place / Carolyn Jourdan.
    p. cm.
  ISBN 978-1-60285-336-2 (library binding : alk. paper)
  1. Jourdan, Carolyn, 1955– 2. Medical assistants—Tennessee—Biography.
    3. United States. Congress. Senate—Officials and employees—Biography.
    4. Tennessee—Biography. 5. Large type books. I. Title.
CT275.J88A3 2008
976.8′053092--dc22
  [B]
2008029211

Heart in the Right Place

PROLOGUE

"You'll never see anything like this again," Daddy said as he stooped to hold an x-ray between my face and the sunlight streaming in through his office window. He pointed to a shadowy gray blob near the center of a small rib cage.

"See?" he said. "This little girl's heart's on the wrong side. It's on the right."

I stared at the film, trying to appreciate what I was seeing. The silhouette of a little skeleton surrounded by vague swirls of silver mists and fogs looked okay to me, but I was only ten years old and trusted Daddy, a family doctor, to know which way the picture, and the heart, should go.

When I didn't say anything, Daddy said, "You could go a whole lifetime without ever seeing this even once, because it's so rare."

I wasn't sure, but I suspected this would be a good thing not to ever get to see again, because even though Daddy hadn't said so, I got the distinct impression that this was a very bad thing for the little girl. I touched my own chest as I struggled to understand what the backwards configuration meant. But all I could think to say was, "How does she say the Pledge?"

For days I wrestled with the girl's problem by asking Daddy variations of the same question, "What does she do when they play 'The Star Spangled Banner'? . . . Where does she cross and hope to die?" I couldn't get over it. Left was right and right was wrong. What did it mean?

Thirty years later, the image still haunted me.

What point was God trying to make with the little girl's life?

He'd been more merciful with me. Despite my early fears that my destiny was to spend my entire life as an utterly powerless witness to one medical disaster after another, I'd eventually grown up and landed a good job in a city far from the mountains of East Tennessee, neatly sidestepping my role as spectator to any more catastrophes. Or so I'd thought.

Fall

ONE

As I unlocked the front door of the office I could hear the phone ringing. I hurried inside and stretched across the reception desk to answer it.

"Dr. Jourdan's office," I said, out of breath.

"Do y'all wash out feet?" a woman shouted.

I considered her question. Although I was accustomed to the local dialect and even to garbled medical terminology, I had no idea what she meant. I said, "Excuse me?" and quickly moved the earpiece a safe distance away from my head before she had time to respond.

"Wash out feet! Do y'all wash out feet?" she screamed.

"I . . . I don't know." I sent up a silent prayer that we did not.

"Well she needs her foot washed out! How much do y'all charge for that?"

If I was unsure if we even did such a thing, how could I know how much it would cost? "I don't know," I said.

In the ensuing silence I managed to add, "I'd ask the doctor, but he's not here yet. I'll find out when he comes in and call you back and tell you what he says. Okay?"

I fumbled through the piles of paper on Momma's desk until I located a pencil and a blank scrap of notepaper, jotted down the woman's name and number, and then hung up. I stared at the phone warily. Working as a temp for Daddy might be a little harder than I'd anticipated.

I hurried around to the other side of the reception desk in an attempt to put a bit of Formica between myself and the medical world. But before I'd even gotten seated atop the wooden stool that was the main feature of my new domain, I heard the front door open and then the unmistakable sound of elderly ladies, their voices worn out from too many years of use. One squeaked like a rusty hinge and the other crackled in an unpredictable jumble of soft and then suddenly loud sounds, like a radio with bad reception. The ladies were advising and encouraging each other in an effort to negotiate a small step at the front door. I turned and saw that it was the Hankins sisters, Herma and Helma, and their friend who lived with them, Miss Viola Burkhart.

I'd known them all my life. They were in their nineties. The Hankins sisters had never been married. Miss Viola was a widow who had come to live with them after her husband died. She was ninety-eight, weighed about seventy pounds, and had an advanced case of what the sisters called "old-timers." Somewhere along the way she'd lost the ability or inclination to speak and now she wore a perpetual vacant smile.

Helma was ninety-five and also weighed less than 100 pounds. She was extremely stooped, bent almost double from osteoporosis, and her eyesight wasn't good. Herma was the baby at ninety-one and probably weighed more than both the other ladies combined. She was still sturdy but deaf as a post. So there was one who could hear and see, but not think or talk; one who could think, hear, and talk, but not see; and one who could think, see, and talk, but not hear.

The ladies were inseparable. Helma did the cooking and talking on the phone and Herma did the heavy work and the driving. Both of them took care of Viola.

Helma wore a faded green polyester leisure suit with an oddly intriguing assortment of safety pins arrayed along the edge of one lapel, while Herma had on baggy sweatpants and a misshapen sweater. Miss Viola was wearing a demure flowered dress. All three ladies wore shiny brown Naugahyde coats that had been fashionable in the sixties.

When they moved, they shuffled along together, holding onto each other for support and navigational assistance. They made their way carefully to the reception desk and Helma said that it was Miss Viola who needed to see the doctor today. Herma said, "Hey there, girl," and smiled. "We was sorry to hear about your ma. How's she doing?"

"Pretty good. She'll be back Monday."

13

Herma looked at me in confusion. "I thought she had a heart attack."

"She did."

"Ain't she in the hospital?"

"Yeah, but she told me she'd be out by Monday."

I was relieved when Herma decided to leave it at that. The story sounded a little thin, even to me, but I desperately needed to believe it.

Then, without even a hint of foreboding, I made my first executive decision in the health care arena. "You ladies can come right on back to the examining room," I said. I figured it would be easier to get all of them up and down just once instead of twice; and waiting in the back would protect them from exposure to whatever germs the other patients might bring in. It seemed like a good idea at the time.

As I helped them through the door that divided the waiting room from the rest of the office I said to Helma, "You ladies are lucky to have each other."

She smiled. "Oh yeah, we got enough spare parts between the three of us to make one whole person!"

I took them back to Room 3 because it was the only room with enough places for all of them to sit down. Room 3 was used for surgery and contained Daddy's pride and joy—the hydraulic surgical table.

Thirty-five years ago, when he couldn't really afford it, Daddy had bought the special motorized table that would raise and lower, so he could lift patients to a comfortable height while doing surgery. Even now the table still occupied a special place in his heart, like his Leitz microscope. No one was allowed to touch either piece of equipment but him.

The table was controlled by four pedals that lay flat on the floor. The entire table could be either raised or lowered, or it could be tilted by raising or lowering either the head or foot.

I seated Miss Viola in the middle of the table and told the ladies that the doctor would be in in a few minutes. Then I returned to my post at the reception desk. While I waited, I retrieved my phone messages from voice mail in Washington, D.C. My boss, Senator Hayworth, was conducting a series of hearings on corruption in the nuclear power industry, and I expected most of the calls would be related to that.

There were eleven messages. I sorted them with respect to time zone and then numbered them to indicate the order in which they should be returned. First came the calls to people on eastern time: government affairs representatives for the University of Tennessee and Tennessee Valley Authority. The call to a huge nuclear power conglomerate in Chicago could be made after 10:00, to a colleague in Sedona an hour after that, and then after noon I could reach the Los Angeles offices of the lobbyists for the electric power industry. Tokyo Power Company would come last, after 8:00 tonight. No problem.

As I dialed the Director of Federal Relations for the University of Tennessee, Daddy came in carrying a cardboard tray with a Styrofoam cup of coffee and a McDonald's bag. He set his breakfast on the counter and I told him about the ladies waiting in Room 3. He nodded, fished his sausage biscuit out of the bag, and began to unwrap it.

Then he looked at me with his head tilted. "What's that sound?" he said.

"I don't hear anything," I said, trying to stay focused on the opening pleasantries of my phone conversation.

He laid his biscuit down next to his cup of coffee and walked down the hall toward the back. I heard him pause at the doorway of Room 3 and say, "Good morn—" Then he shouted, "What the hell's going on in here?"

"Gotta go," I said, hanging up on the Director while she was talking. Then I bolted for the back.

Things were not the way I'd left them. The surgical table's motor, normally a low-pitched, almost inaudible hum, had changed to an angry whine. The head of the table was tilted as high as it would go, over five feet in the air, and the foot was down, almost touching the floor. Miss Viola had slid into a little wad at the lower end. Herma and Helma were frantically struggling to keep her from falling onto the floor, but she was oblivious. She smiled serenely as Herma tugged on her arms and Helma hoisted her ankles.

I couldn't understand why this was happening. It sounded like someone was standing on a cat's tail. I looked down reflexively and noticed that Herma had somehow come to be standing on the floor pedal that raised the head end of the table. She clearly didn't realize what she was doing, nor could she hear the table motor running.

Daddy shouted a one-word accusation, "Carolyn!" and leapt forward to snatch up Miss Viola. As she slipped off the end of the table, her dress peeled up over her head. He tried to set her on her feet, but she was so dizzy she couldn't stand by herself. He told Herma to get her foot off the control pedal, but she couldn't hear well enough to understand what he was saying.

He made a series of shuffling hops sideways, crushing Viola tightly against his side, and startled Herma by lifting her bodily off the pedal with his other arm. He held one lady under each arm while he stomped on the "Head Down" control.

All of this confusion and manhandling sent the sisters into a tizzy. And Daddy was incensed that anyone would dare touch the controls of his table, much less put such a terrible strain on it.

"What'd you do that for?" Daddy shouted at Herma in a voice so thunderous that she finally heard him.

"Do what? I didn't do anything. Your table there is broken."

"It better not be!" he said.

When the table was level again, he set Miss Viola back down in the center and flipped her dress down over her legs. She seemed neither startled nor embarrassed. In fact, she seemed to have missed the whole ordeal.

Under the circumstances Daddy decided to go ahead and tend to Miss Viola's medical problems before normal office hours. He patiently listened to the health concerns of all three ladies and wrote prescriptions all round.

As the ladies drove away, Daddy went back to his sausage biscuit. He stared at me while he chewed and then said, "Don't ever do that again."

"Don't do what?" I said. "Don't leave any old ladies alone with any of your stuff?"

"Just don't do it again," he snapped and took his biscuit into the back to eat it in peace.

We were both under a lot of stress.

A few minutes later, Alma, Daddy's nurse, confided that during her entire twelve years with the doctor she'd never heard him shout like that before.

"Well, just stick with me," I said. "I've been with him for forty years and I've been hearing it the whole time."

Daddy was fantastic at handling medical emergencies. He was unbelievably cool under pressure if, say, someone had cut off their arm or leg with a chain saw. But he simply wasn't equipped to handle the kind of emergencies that seemed to crop up whenever I was around. He could cope beautifully with every kind of chaos, except the kind I created. And right now he was stuck. He couldn't work with me, and he couldn't work without me.

I felt for him. It was a good thing I was only going to be subbing in this job for two days. If I stayed a week, he'd end up sharing a room with Momma in the cardiac ward.

TWO

I sat ignominiously on what now seemed like a dunce stool as my mind wandered all the way back to yesterday when I'd been a successful, competent adult. Daddy had called me out of a televised Senate hearing to tell me Momma was in the emergency room with a possible heart attack. I'd stuffed a jumble of clothes into a duffle in Washington, climbed into my car, and raced 500 miles home to East Tennessee.

During the drive I'd struggled to take in the shocking news. Momma had always seemed impervious to the blows of fate that sent other people reeling. I couldn't recall the last time she'd been sick. She'd been a cancer survivor for more than forty years and hadn't missed a day of work in decades. But as the miles passed, I kept coming back to the fact that she was seventy-two years old now, even though she didn't look or act anywhere near her age. Her hardworking, no-excuses personality had never allowed room for any of the infirmities commonly associated with getting old.

I'd torn through the Shenandoah Valley along I-81, blasting past Civil War battlefields and historic houses, numb to the beauty of the Blue Ridge

Mountains. It was mid-October and the fall glory of the largest hardwood forest on earth should have been a rare treat, but I wasn't in any condition to enjoy it.

Momma was trailing wires and tubes in all directions and hooked up to a dizzying array of electronic boxes that beeped and chirped a medical Muzak and blinked with all sorts of numerical and graphic readouts. I scanned them until I found one that seemed to indicate her heart was still beating. The beat was erratic enough that it seemed unlikely she was being continuously paced, or "jumped off," by a computer. So it seemed her heart was still working, at least for now. That had to be a good sign.

Such a massive display of brute technological force was oddly comforting. Surely no one could die in this modern Frankenstein lab. If anything stopped working, they'd just plug in another machine.

I was scared to see Momma like this. It wasn't like her at all. To tamp down my panic I tried to think of the ICU as a sort of spa. A really, really expensive spa. For unconscious people.

An impressive platoon of professionals were doing all sorts of tests, trying to determine whether or not she'd had a heart attack. She'd had an "episode," a "cardiac event," the previous afternoon while out walking. A retroactive diagnosis seemed pointless to me, but I guess it gave everybody something to organize themselves around. Daddy was out at the nurses' station getting the latest news.

Daddy'd told me that Momma was blaming the whole thing on the gentle walking program she'd recently undertaken. Her theory was that a couple of weeks of light exercise had hurt her more than fifty years of chain-smoking. She made a good case. She'd never done anything remotely healthy for seventy years. Despite the knowledge you might expect a medical professional to have about such things, she'd smoked like a chimney, was completely sedentary, and existed entirely on a diet of iced tea, hot chocolate, orange juice, and Goldfish crackers.

I stood by her side watching her breathe until it became clear there was nothing I could do. Then I turned to leave. Without even opening her eyes, Momma startled me by grabbing my sleeve with the speed of a martial arts expert.

She said in an uncharacteristically weak voice, "Somebody's got to help your father."

I'd spent the whole drive preparing myself for bad news—but I hadn't seen *this* coming.

Daddy was a solo family practitioner. He had a full-time nurse, but Momma was his receptionist, bookkeeper, backup nurse, lab technician, and jack-of-all-trades sidekick. They'd worked together in his small rural office for my whole life.

For someone who was officially certified to be at death's door, she gripped my wrist with surprising strength. "You've got to fill in for me for a couple of days," she said. "Just till the week's out. I'll be back on Monday."

I did some quick calculations. It was Wednesday. That meant she wanted me to work her job on Thursday and Friday. *Two whole days.*

I was trapped. A possum in the headlights. I wanted to be a good daughter and lessen my parents' worries. I loved my parents very much. It was just too bad that what they needed right now was not an expensively dressed nuclear expert or a fierce lawyer. I had those two areas of expertise down. It was just that, to their disappointment, I'd turned out to be squeamish and high-strung—characteristics that did not make for a reliable health care assistant.

Although I wasn't bothered by any medical problems, such as exposure to contagion, and could happily sit in a small room and swap stories with people who had flu, TB, or even black plague, I was terrified of being exposed to other people's surgeries. I dreaded the on-the-job injuries like the crushings and maulings that Daddy attended to for the zinc mines, the slashes and gorings from the sausage factory, and the spatter burns from the rendering plant, not to mention the miscellaneous farming and hunting atrocities that popped up out of nowhere with alarming frequency.

The triage process may sound straightforward, but it can get devilishly tricky. Once, when filling in after school while Momma worked on the books,

I'd registered a clean and especially fair-skinned young man who worked at the sausage plant. He didn't specify what he needed—he just gave his name—and because he had very little blood on him, I skipped asking him if he was bleeding. I let him take a seat and wait his turn. He sat perfectly still until Daddy happened to see him out in the waiting room and yelled, "Carolyn, what the hell are you thinking about? *Look* at that man's color, he's white as a sheet! Can't you see he's about to *faint!*"

The man turned toward Daddy and said, "I got stabbed in the leg."

It turned out he wasn't naturally that pale. He was quietly bleeding to death inside his rubber waders. How tidy, and sneaky, of him. He got sewed up pronto and fully recovered. I, on the other hand, was permanently traumatized by the certain knowledge that I would've let a twenty-year-old man bleed to death less than six feet away from me while I filed my nails. Previously I'd overreacted only to visible injuries, but now I had a paranoid fear that the people who looked fine were the ones who might be in the worst shape.

Even the phone wasn't safe. Once Daddy had walked up to the counter in time to hear me making fun of a woman caller, whose histrionic gasping and croaking I assumed was some sort of joke. I was only about thirteen then and going through an especially unsympathetic phase. Daddy, who was prescient about illness, grabbed the phone out of my hand in time to hear the woman gasping. Even though she never said an articulate word, he recognized her voice in time to rush over to her house and save her life. She'd been having a heart attack and had crawled to the phone to call for help. I still hadn't gotten over that one either.

What Momma and Daddy needed was a person who could calmly register nice people with hard jobs who routinely came in covered in hog or chicken blood, someone who could face apparent carnage with a sincere smile and casually inquire if any of the blood was human.

Only because I could see no viable alternative, I said, "Don't worry. I'll take care of everything," and tried not to sound like I was whining.

I didn't allow myself to speculate about the likelihood of Momma actually being back at work bright and early on Monday morning. And I told myself I could handle this little snag in my life plan. How tough could it be? I had seven years of higher education and another dozen of high-profile, high-pressure jobs, including the one I'd just left: Senate Counsel for nuclear issues.

I told myself I could do Momma's job with one hand tied behind my back (if I used the other hand to cover my eyes). And my father didn't need a nurse, what he needed was a receptionist. That I could handle. All I had to do for two days was answer the phone, register people, pull charts, and await whatever came down the road, be it a case of the sniffles or a shotgun blast to the head. Then I'd have the weekend to catch up on my real job.

"You just rest and get well," I said, patting Momma's hand as I pried it loose from my sleeve. But she didn't seem to have heard me.

Daddy's office was about a ten-minute drive from home in a small, old-fashioned shopping center. The row of buildings contained a flower shop, hardware store, dentist's office, and a beauty shop. A hundred feet farther down the highway was a matching strip of stores containing an auto parts store, a grocery, a tanning parlor, and another beauty shop. The shopping centers stood alongside one of the main highways through East Tennessee, east of Knoxville. For the last couple of decades, however, most of the long distance traffic had been siphoned off by the nearby interstate.

I'd been raised in this understated storefront. In the earliest days I'd stand on a small rolling stool in the corner of the room and watch Daddy sew people up while I ate a giant Tootsie Roll; or, if it was a bad cut, two giant Tootsie Rolls. I was eleven when I finally grew tall enough to see over the top of the examining table without standing on the stool. I started assisting Daddy afternoons and weekends by using a small pair of sterile scissors to cut the threads after he tied each stitch. Even then I usually kept a Tootsie Roll in my left hand throughout the procedures.

But that all changed when I was fifteen. Daddy was

stitching up a gash in the sole of the foot of a high school classmate who'd stepped on a broken bottle in a creek one Saturday afternoon. As Daddy worked he pointed out anatomical highlights of the interior of G. W. Nance's foot: the layers of fascia, the various muscles, nerves, tendons, and blood vessels. I stared in intense concentration. Then I noticed the bright light shining on the cut was going dim. That was strange.

"Let go of the light, dammit!" Daddy said.

I looked around to see who could be such a jackass as to be messing with the surgical lamp during an operation and realized with some confusion that it was me. I had hold of the handle on the side of the light and was swaying from it precariously, suddenly feeling very faint. I slid down the wall, forcing myself to let go of the light as I dropped below the level of the table.

Daddy warned, "Don't you touch those scissors on anything. Here! Just give them to me!" I carefully held the scissors away from myself and handed them up to him an instant before my head flopped over onto the floor. That was the end of my career as a surgical assistant.

Being the only local doctor wasn't just Daddy's job, it was a lifestyle. Not just for him, but for Momma and me too. Daddy treated everybody in the community, whether or not they could pay, and he didn't make appointments. Not a single one in nearly forty years. This meant that in addition to a normal family practice, he took care of the poor plus all the patients who were misfits of one kind or another: the intellectually challenged, the mentally ill, destitute and stray humans of every kind, and, from time to time, their pets and livestock.

Daddy hadn't gotten rich, but he'd gotten a lot of interesting stuff from the people who couldn't afford to pay with money. Sometimes he got things to eat, like handmade whole hog sausage or a sack of blackberries, but usually it wasn't such a stereotypical token. Over the years he'd been given a twig wrapped in newspaper that grew into a magnificent climbing yellow rose, a half stick of dynamite, a rusty Confederate sword found in the woods, Indian arrowheads turned up by a plow, a handful of bungee cords scavenged from alongside the interstate, and even the back half of a 1934 Chevrolet pickup truck that he was told would "make a good trailer to haul things in." Sometimes the gift was a burden in itself, but Daddy always accepted it gracefully anyway—a tiny blue jay that had fallen out of its nest, a cardboard box containing four deodorized baby skunks, an orphaned raccoon in a boot.

The most unusual thing he ever got was the body of a red fox that a patient had seen get hit by a car. Daddy had the beautiful corpse stuffed and displayed it for decades until Momma could no longer vacuum the dust out of its thick fur.

When Daddy and I drove back from the hospital and

turned the corner to go up our long driveway, we were greeted enthusiastically by the bugling of the donkeys our neighbors raised to rent out to Dollywood. A half-dozen speckled guinea hens saw us coming and whirled into the driveway in their characteristic suicidal greeting.

Our split-level brick house sat amid 100 acres of steep hills and valleys. In the southeast corner of the farm was a tiny ancient log barn that perched atop stacks of hand-chiseled rocks that provided a comfortable home for a roly-poly groundhog. Along the western edge of the property there was a wooden shed where we stored hay for the cows. The biggest barn stood near the house.

We immediately separated to get the animals fed before dark. At the moment there were four dogs, at least a dozen cats, a couple of dozen birds, and about thirty cows. I fed the dogs and cats because I knew what they ate and I didn't need a tractor to take their food to them. I filled the four stainless steel bowls, placed each one in a separate corner, then stood in the center of the room and acted as referee.

Next I headed out to the big red barn. I shoved hard against one of the huge doors with my shoulder, using all my weight to slide it along on its ancient rollers, then opened it wide. Inside a barn is a whole universe, with its own time zone and climate and ecosystem, a shadowy world of swirling dust illuminated in tiger stripes by light shining through the cracks between the boards. Old leather tack, lengths of chain, rope, and baling twine dangled from nails and rafters and draped over stall railings. Generations of pocketknives lay lost in the layers of detritus on the floor.

The barn was crammed with eight-foot-high stacks of hay that would feed the cows during the approaching winter. Two cats lounged calmly atop the hay, studying me, secure in knowing that they were out of reach. I moved just inside the doorway and let my eyes adjust to the dimness, shifting my weight from one foot to the other, unconsciously imitating the cows who stood alongside the manger patiently watching me. I fumbled for the light switch. It was comforting to move around under the familiar, weak, blue-green light of the ancient fluorescent bulb. I walked into the first stall where the cat food was stored in an old deep freeze. A small herd of cats squeezed out from between bales of hay and walked confidently along the top of the stall railings to reach their food without ever touching the barn floor.

I sat on a low stack of hay under the flickering, buzzing light and watched them eat. Daddy's best friend, Fletcher, suddenly appeared in the doorway.

"Hey Fletcher," I said. "What're you doing here?"

"Oh, I just thought I'd see if y'all needed anything. I figured what with everything, you two might need some help."

Fletcher was the nicest, most thoughtful man. He

was always helping us do whatever needed doing. He helped Daddy repair the tractors and other farm machinery. He'd helped me and Momma hold my beloved seventeen-year-old cat atop the clothes dryer while Daddy treated its injured leg. He'd even said, "Here, let me do that," and taken the rooster weather vane out of my hands and installed it atop a rustic hermit cabin I'd built for contemplation when he realized the clattering of the aluminum ladder was caused by my trembling legs.

He stood beside me and watched the cats for a few moments. "You gonna take some time off?"

"Yeah," I said, "The Senator's a good guy. He said I could take as much time as I needed." I looked up at Fletcher's weather-beaten face. "Momma and Daddy want to keep the office open like usual."

"How're they gonna manage that with her in the hospital?"

"Me," I said. "She made me promise to cover for her till Monday."

"Oh," Fletcher said. "That's good. When he's not open, there's not much people around here can do for a doctor."

"I know," I said. "I don't think sudden retirement would be too good for them, either. Not right now anyway. But they're both over seventy. It's got to come sometime."

"I know what you mean," Fletcher said, hands tucked into his pockets. "Well, I better go see if he needs help with the cows."

I got up and went with him to the door. We stood together and watched the last minutes of the sunset. The whole world was lit by a horizontal, gold wash. I looked at Fletcher, and he was gilded by the light from his worn baseball cap to his scuffed work boots. I was momentarily flustered, wondering if maybe this was the way angels looked, but I couldn't say that. "Fletcher," I said, "you look just like the FTD man."

As he walked away I turned to the north. The light from the west was being overtaken by gray clouds rolling in fast from the east. I could see and smell rain coming. I decided to wait for it.

The wind picked up in gusts and dust and leaves whipped by. It took about ten minutes for the rain to reach the barn. First it was a fine, blowing mist, then a downpour. The din of the deluge beating against the tin roof was a powerful tranquilizer. I flipped the light off and sat down in the darkness, surrounded by the sweet smell of the new hay and cow manure, and the rain.

THREE

Okay, so the first morning hadn't started off as well as I'd hoped. I tried to shake off the misstep. Things were bound to improve. The next few hours were considerably quieter, but not much less stressful. I followed Daddy up and down the hall asking him questions, trying to figure out how to handle an assortment of incomprehensible paperwork.

"What's a 'Spasm of the Sphincter of Oddi'?" I asked.

"What?" Daddy replied.

"A 'Spasm of the Sphincter of Oddi'? It's here in the Medicare codebook. What the hell is it? It sounds awful."

"It doesn't matter what it is, because nobody here's got it. How about Mrs. Holloway's ankle? Did you find the number for that?"

"Maybe. Was it fractured?"

"No."

"Is it a 'pain,' a 'strain,' or a 'sprain'?"

"A sprain."

"Okay, then I got it. But where's the Sphincter of Oddi?" But Daddy had already ducked into another examining room.

There are surely better examples of government

programs that started out as good ideas and ended up in a hopeless muddle, but I'd never personally encountered one as spectacular as the Medicare coding system. When I was a teenager I'd been able to fill out insurance forms easily with commonly used English words, but now that I was over forty and the government had allowed its legions of mathematicians, accountants, and computer experts to interfere, the mysteries of the new "streamlined" system were beyond my ability to penetrate. The most basic medical problems were the least likely to be found anywhere in the codebook. Instead there were comprehensive lists of the most lurid and preposterous conditions imaginable. I'd really like to know how often Medicare receives claims for the treatment of "Abderhalden-Kaufmann-Lignac Syndrome." And what the heck was "Double Whammy"?

I was aware of things like "Problem, Spoiled Child," "Quarrelsomeness," "Spring Fever," and "Clumsiness," but was amazed that Medicare considered them insurable medical conditions. They'd even assigned a code number to "Decapitation, Legal Execution (by guillotine)." What sort of Medicare claim would be reimbursable in connection with being guillotined?

It could have been funny, but I knew better than to laugh, because if I didn't find the right code we wouldn't get paid and would instead get a nasty letter threatening fines of tens of thousands of dollars and decades in the federal penitentiary for a twenty-cent mistake. I flipped endlessly back and forth through the coding manual, a book as thick as a major metropolitan phone directory, filled with tiny print and even tinier alphanumeric codes. Most of what Daddy saw seemed to be some kind of *-itis*. He saw people with three-syllable *-itises:* arthritis, bronchitis, bursitis, cystitis, gastritis, neuritis, otitis, rhinitis. Others had four-syllable conditions: cellulitis, dermatitis, labyrinthitis, laryngitis, pharyngitis, prostatitis, sinusitis, and tendinitis. But for all the fancy names and numbers, what we were really talking about were mostly sore throats, creaky joints, stomachaches, and runny noses.

So why couldn't I find any of that?

At about 11:00 I heard the front door bounce against the wall and looked up to see one of Harley Hawkins' huge silent teenage sons carrying him in. It was either Ronnie or Donnie. I wasn't sure which, because they were identical twins. I could usually tell them apart if they were talking because Ronnie's voice was a tad softer than Donnie's. But this one wasn't talking, he was simply standing there with his father's limp body in his arms. It was a flashback to similar scenes that had recurred regularly throughout my life. I'd seen Daddy carry Harley into the office the same way many times. Harley's face was all bloody, but that was typical too.

"Come on back," I said. "Hang on a second and I'll get the door for you."

I ran around the end of the counter and opened the door into the back and Ronnie or Donnie walked through, carrying a 200-pound load with no discernible strain.

"Where do you want me to put him?" he asked.

"Is he cut anywhere besides his head?"

Ronnie or Donnie shook his head no.

"Do you think we need to x-ray anything?" I asked.

Donnie—at least I was beginning to think it was Donnie—shook his head again.

"Okay, take him on back to Room 3 and put him on the table."

Harley Hawkins was a certified wild man. I guess it was a good thing because he had the scariest and most dangerous job I'd ever heard of. He worked for a company that specialized in sealing underground leaks. Not like in the basement of a house in the spring, but leaks two miles down at the end of some tunnel in an African mine where thousands of gallons a minute were thundering in because somebody had accidentally drilled into an underground river.

Harley would wade around in the raging torrent until he figured out some way to plug it—like a professional little Dutch boy from hell. He traveled all over the world doing this. Red Adair got famous for doing less because putting out oil fires was flashy and easy to photograph. Harley's work was so terrifying that no one was willing to go with him to take pictures. He worked mostly in the dark, because the electricity had to be shut off when there was an underground flood. He went into each job with 135 pounds of equipment on his back and, I suppose, an optimistic hope that there would always be a breathing space between the top of the water and the ceiling.

Between jobs, though, Harley had a tough time coping with everyday life. Whenever he was off, Harley drank and drank. Even sober he had to be one of the most reckless people alive, but alcohol transformed him into a lunatic. He never got hurt on the job, but when he was drunk he got hurt more than anyone I'd ever known. Besides liquor Harley had three great passions in life: his wife Avon, driving, and handguns. It was a volatile combination.

Harley loved Daddy, so he always insisted he be brought to him whenever he needed to be sewed up or x-rayed—which could be more than once a week if he was between jobs. His x-ray file was so enormous it was kept in four volumes: head, upper extremities, torso, and lower extremities. One year Harley's doctor bill was larger than that of Daddy's biggest industrial account, a zinc mining company with hundreds of employees. He had the body of a Greek god, but his skin looked like a crazy quilt that Daddy had been laboring over for years. Each scar held a memory—at least for Daddy. Harley probably couldn't remember much about it.

Daddy stuck his head out of Room 1 to glance at Harley as he was carried by, but then ducked back inside to finish what he was doing. He said over his shoulder, "Alma, draw up some Xylocaine." That was a shot to numb the area that needed to be sutured. Not that Harley needed much numbing. It was amazing what the man had saved in anesthetic.

In a couple of minutes Daddy came into Room 3. "What'd he get into this time?" he asked as he pulled on his surgical gloves. "You're Donnie, aren't you?"

"Yeah," Donnie said, smiling slightly at being correctly identified. "Aunt Arlene, Momma's sister, had to go in the hospital for a couple of days for some kind of female surgery. Momma went to stay with her. Before she left she poured out all his stashes and she took the car keys with her, cause you know how he likes to drive."

Daddy nodded.

"She forgot about the riding lawn mower though. He found some liquor somewhere and went for a ride down the shoulder of the four-lane. Momma's brother C.A. lives about a mile down the highway, and when Daddy went by, he decided Uncle C.A.'s yard needed mowing, so he turned off and mowed it.

"When he called us to come get Daddy, Uncle C.A. said he'd told his boy Samuel the yard needed mowing. Well, when C.A. got home and saw the yard, he went crazy. Daddy didn't get as much grass

38

as he did flowers. C.A. said he almost whipped Samuel over it. 'That yard looks like it was mowed by a damn drunk!' he said. 'It was,' Samuel said.

"Then Samuel took him around back and showed him where Daddy was laying in the yard passed out. He'd wrecked the lawn mower against the birdbath. That's how he cut his head."

Harley never spoke or even opened his eyes while Daddy sewed up his head, but when Donnie lifted him off the table to carry him back to the car, he mumbled, "Thanks, Doc."

Michael Mayshark was next after Harley. He'd come in to get the doses adjusted on his heart medicines. His health was precarious and juggling his pills was a delicate process that he talked out with Daddy fairly often.

Michael and I watched Harley get hauled out. Michael smiled impishly and said, "Harley needs to learn to get high on life." Then he slapped the counter top and laughed his big joyous laugh.

Michael suffered from congestive heart failure and it was taking a whopping amount of medicine to keep him alive. He was clearly in a lot worse shape than when I'd last seen him, but you'd never know it from his mood.

It was amazing to see the differences in the two men's approach to life. Harley had a death wish. He'd been graced with an extraordinary physique, and he abused his body and sought release from the world. Michael, who'd been born with a bad heart and several other major physical handicaps, struggled heroically to stay alive day by day.

If there was one thing I'd learned growing up in a doctor's office, it was that people's mood was rarely dependent on their external circumstances. Its origin was almost always internal.

Michael had been born with a rare health problem called Holt-Oram syndrome or "heart-hand" syndrome, which meant that he had deformities of both his heart and his hands. He hadn't been expected to live long with his heart defect, so his hand and arm deformities hadn't been a focus of attention during his childhood. On the left side he didn't have a thumb but had a partially working hand that was attached to a forearm that was noticeably too short. On the right side his forearm was especially short and he didn't have much of a hand at all.

Despite his physical problems, Michael was the happily married father of three smart, healthy children, a successful businessman, and a wildly popular guy. He was brilliant too, with some savant capabilities. He could remember license plate numbers. All of them, everybody's he'd ever seen in his life. He was a veritable Department of Motor Vehicles. The police could have radioed him to check for stolen cars. He was the same way with telephone numbers.

As he'd gotten older, his heart problem became

even more precarious. He was forced to manage his diet like a long-term, precise chemistry experiment —which was what it was. It was an experiment in trying to stay alive. He had to keep track of every ounce of fluid he drank and every bite of food he ate. He had to know the content of every morsel he took into his body and attempt to calculate, in advance, its effect on his fragile system.

Michael had an enormous heart. While that sounded like a good thing, it wasn't. His heart filled up the whole center of his chest x-ray, leaving considerably less room for his lungs and everything else in his chest. In addition to being too big, his heart had malformed chambers and leaking valves. It was getting bigger and bigger because its pumping was getting less and less effective. The muscle kept growing to try to take up the slack. It was a losing proposition.

But so it had been since the day he was born, and he was sixty now. He lived by the grace of God and a valiant nature second to none in this world. Michael didn't just think positive. He lived in a continuous state of joy, like each breath was a special treat.

He teased me about the Mercedes I'd tried to park as inconspicuously as possible at the extreme edge of the parking lot. I'd known he would notice it. We were both car nuts. He ran a large used auto parts business called Redneck Parts. He pointed out the window toward my car. "Better watch out," he said smiling. "That car will part out for three times what you think it's worth!"

"I'll keep an eye on it," I said.

After Michael left we checked with the hospital again and found Momma was resting easy. I decided to try to return some more phone calls while Daddy went home for lunch. I listened to my voice mail again in Washington and the robotic female voice warned, "You have twenty . . . six . . . messages."

I dialed the Hart Senate Office Building, or Hart SOB as it was abbreviated, to check in with my dear friend and coworker Jacob Goldman. Just as the phone started ringing on his end I saw Wanda Slover drive up. She'd been my babysitter and had never stopped treating me like a kid.

Elizabeth, secretary to both Jacob and me, answered. "Hey, Elizabeth," I said, praying Wanda was heading for the hardware store. "It's Carolyn."

"Carolyn. How's your mother doing? We've all been thinking about you."

"They don't really know yet what her condition is. So I'm gonna need to stay down here for a few more days."

"Well, don't worry. You're not missing anything here. The Senate's in recess and the boss is in Nashville. And Jacob's over at the Library of Congress. He'll be upset that he missed your call. He's really been worried about you."

I missed Jacob desperately. He and I had rarely

42

been separated for more than a few days at a time during the last ten years, functioning as two halves of a single brain. We made an odd couple. He was dark where I was fair and he had an intimidating ethnic nose to contrast with my small snubbed one. He was always perfectly turned out without a speck of lint or wrinkle anywhere, while I generally scored quite a bit lower on the scale of sartorial splendor.

Although the romantic part of our relationship was long over, having run a distant second in Jacob's mind to our crackerjack professional partnership, we'd been best friends for nearly a decade. It felt strange to have to endure any difficulty without his steady presence close at hand. But this time we were stuck 500 miles apart.

I said, "Well, if you need me for anything, just call."

"Oh, that obnoxious associate producer from CBS keeps calling," Elizabeth said. "She wants a quote from the Senator and she's getting mean. What do you want me to tell her?"

Wanda burst through the door and called out in her loud voice, "Is Doc in?"

I shook my head at Wanda and said into the phone, "Tell her I'm out of the country for a few days and will call her when I get back."

"Well where is he?" Wanda demanded.

I swiveled on my stool, turning my back to Wanda, and tried to concentrate on my telephone conversation.

Elizabeth was asking, "What about the dinner at the French ambassador's residence? Jacob wants to know if you're going. If not, he's got a long line of hopeful replacement candidates, some of whom are willing to pay."

"I forgot about that," I sighed. "Tell Jacob to go ahead and give my invitation to somebody else, but you're killing me with this kind of thing. I had breakfast at Hardee's drive-thru this morning and I'll be lucky to get *anything* for lunch."

At that moment my wishing Wanda would go away—or at least wait patiently—was abruptly interrupted. "Carolyn Jourdan, where the hell's your pa?" she asked irritably, leaning across the counter. "Does he know you're out here playing on the phone? I gotta get some help! My ass is on fire."

"Where are you?" Elizabeth asked, laughing.

"Please don't make me tell you," I said, swiveling back around to give Wanda a hard stare and point my finger at her in warning. "Anything else?"

"What?" Wanda asked in confusion. "Yeah. I got hemorrhoids. And they're killing me!"

Elizabeth burst out laughing again but diplomatically restrained herself. "Nothing you need to deal with right now," she said.

"I'll check with you again tomorrow," I said. "Okay?"

"No problem," Elizabeth said, giggling, and hung up.

Clearly, handling my business affairs by phone from Daddy's office wasn't going to work.

FOUR

Later that afternoon as I sat contemplating my dismal predicament and weighing it against Momma's worse one, the phone rang yet again. In fact, it never stopped ringing.

"Dr. Jourdan's office," I said listlessly.

"Joel's sick," said a woman in a clipped, demanding tone. "We're leaving the house now and when we get there you'll need to take him straight back to see the doctor without making him wait."

"Who's Joel?" I asked.

"Huh?"

"What's Joel's last name?" I asked.

"He's been coming there for years!"

"Well I've only been coming here for half a day so you'll have to help me out. What's his full name?"

She said something that sounded like "Joel Lick Wire."

"Joel what?" I asked.

"Lick Wire."

"Can you spell that for me?"

"L . . . e . . . q . . . u . . . i . . . r . . . e."

"Oh, okay," I said, belatedly recognizing the name of a boy I'd gone to grammar school and high school with. He'd been really popular, a baseball star, and had never known I was alive. I hoped we could keep it that way.

"Is Joel having chest pain?"

"No."

"Is he bleeding?"

"No."

"Has he got something in his eye?"

"Why are you asking me all these crazy questions?"

"Because if he's having chest pain you shouldn't be bringing him here at all. You should be taking him to the emergency room in Knoxville. And if he's not bleeding or got something in his eye, when he gets here he's going to have to wait his turn like everybody else. If he's been coming here for years he already knows that, though. No appointments and no call-ahead reservations."

"Joel can't wait—he's sick!"

"So's everybody else who comes in here. If he's so sick he can't wait, you should take him on to the hospital."

"Well he doesn't wanna go to the hospital. He wants to see Dr. Jourdan."

"Then he'll just have to wait like everybody else. Don't rush to get down here either, cause there's about six people ahead of him right now and I've got no way to know who's already on the way and will be getting here before you do."

She slammed the phone down.

I had about twenty minutes of peace presiding

over a moderate size crowd of hackers and sniffers before the door burst open and a spectacular looking woman rushed in. Her jeans and denim shirt were fringed and rhinestone studded and had the stupendously tight tailoring of something worn by Jane Russell in a 1950s western. She was loaded up with so much silver jewelry she tinkled and clinked when she moved. She had on a silver studded belt with a buckle so large there was no way she could sit down without causing abdominal damage.

She wore too much lip gloss, long pink nails squared off on the ends, and a cloud of perfume so strong I could have tracked her myself through miles of wilderness.

She said, "Joel's here. Get a room ready. I'm bringing him in."

"All the examining rooms are full right now," I said. "And there are people here who've been waiting. I'll put his name down and call you when his turn comes."

"He can't wait."

People in the waiting room shot discreet glances my way. This office had a pecking order that had to be observed. Nobody wanted to put their case of sniffles in front of a dying man's last gasping breaths, but they wouldn't sit still for any unwarranted line-jumping either.

"We already went through this on the phone," I said. "He'll just have to sit and wait his turn like everybody else."

Miss Rodeo stared at me. She gestured around the waiting room. "Joel can't sit in *here* . . . with *these* people. He'll *catch* something.

"And he might *vomit*," she added.

"Okay. I'll come and get you when it's his turn."

She clinked and clomped out, carefully using just two fingers to open the door to leave. Before getting in her convertible Trans Am, she fished around in her pocketbook for an antiseptic towelette and scrubbed her hands. A lumpy mound of fuzzy cloth I took to be Joel was barely visible in the reclined front passenger seat. Soft laughter broke out in the waiting room.

Something familiar about her nagged at me, but I couldn't get hold of it. I sat and stared idly at the car until I realized who she was: Cheryl Piatt. We'd been in the same grade, sort of. She'd been a cheerleader, and I'd been the geek with the crossed eyes. She'd never been mean to me, but I'd steered a wide berth around her anyway in morbid dread of what a single cutting remark from the class beauty could do to me.

About forty-five minutes later, I knocked on the window to signal Joel's turn. After a great deal of fussing, a man in his forties emerged wearing a terry cloth bathrobe that gaped to reveal wrinkled cotton pajamas. It gave him the look of a flasher or some other sort of pervert—enhanced considerably by his pink fuzzy house slippers. I was astounded. Never in my life had I seen anyone come in wearing pajamas.

48

People who were *dying* got dressed before coming in. I was so surprised I blurted to Daddy who was now standing behind me at the counter, "Daddy, there's a guy coming in here in his pajamas!"

He didn't even look up from writing a prescription. "That would be Joel."

"It is! How'd you know?"

"Because Joel is the only person who ever comes in wearing pajamas."

"Look at him!" I continued. He appeared to have just gotten out of bed and come in without brushing his teeth or anything. He shuffled his absurd house shoes across the asphalt, through the door, across the waiting room, and down the hall. Cheryl walked alongside him holding his hand and forearm, supporting him like an invalid.

As they passed by my desk she swung a cosmetics bag the size of a microwave oven onto the counter and said, "I brought his medicine so you can see what all he's taking and write new prescriptions for the ones that's running out."

Daddy unzipped the bag. "My, my, Joel, what've we got here?" he said. Joel didn't answer. He continued shuffling as if it took all his concentration just to move.

Daddy removed the scuffed amber plastic bottles one at a time, lining them up on the counter with the labels toward me. He said, "Make me a list of all this mess so I can see what he's doing to himself."

"Joel," he said, "you got a whole drugstore in here."

I started making my list. It took a lot of wrist work swiveling the bottles back and forth to read labels that wrapped clear around the containers. When I finished the inventory, it was a jumble. I needed to recopy it and group the pills by category before it would make any sense. Joel was taking twenty-three different drugs.

When Daddy came back to the counter after listening to Joel for more than thirty minutes straight, he sighed and rolled his eyes. He said in a soft voice, "Most hypochondriacs I've seen are women, but if you ever get one that's a man, they're way worse than any of the women."

The inventory of the pill bag was lying on the counter. Daddy picked up the list and started reading it to himself. He began to lose his poker face after a moment. "Joel, are you taking *all* of these?" he called out over his shoulder.

"That's my prescription medicine," Joel said. "I got another bag for over-the-counter. You wanna see it?"

"No . . . no," Daddy said. He walked back to the doorway of Room 1. "When you feel bad have you ever considered just taking an aspirin and laying on the couch, watching soap operas like everybody else does?"

"No," Joel answered.

"Well, you should," Daddy said and then went to

his private office to dictate notes for Joel's chart. As Joel started out of the examining room, Alma signaled a thumbs-up, which I took to be a signal to charge him more than I would a normal patient. I added $11 to his bill for the extra long office call, the pajamas, the pink fuzzy house shoes, and because Cheryl was still as pretty as ever. That seemed reasonable.

I looked at Alma and mouthed, "Forty-two?" She bugged her eyes and made the thumbs-up again. I said, "Fifty-three?" She shrugged. As they shuffled by I said, "That'll be fifty-three dollars."

At 5:00 I saw an elegant antique white BMW convertible pull up in front of the office. A tall man got out and looked around like he was checking for witnesses before coming in to rob us. As he walked toward our door, I was relieved to see that it was Matthew Wyatt DeHaven III. I'd grown up with him. Although I hadn't seen him in years, he was easy to recognize. He was six foot four and handsome, with dark curly hair and large light blue eyes.

"Hey Matthew!" I said, smiling.

"Hey Carolyn," he said. "What're you doing here? I thought you was in Washington."

"I was. Momma's not feeling too good, though, so I came down to cover for her for a couple of days. You're not sick are you?"

"No. I need to ask Doc for a favor."

"What?"

"I got a goat that's hurt and I was wondering if he'd take an x-ray of its leg for me. I don't trust the people at the vet hospital over at UT. They charge too much and they don't know half of what Doc does."

I knew Daddy would be glad to hear he was still staying ahead of the vet hospital. It was a sincere compliment. Animals were very important in a poor farming area, and particular ones could be especially prized for breeding stock or treasured as pets. It wasn't unusual for people to bring one into the house when it got sick. Once we'd kept a newborn calf in our garage for a couple of weeks. It had worn one of Momma's sweatshirts to stay warm.

"I'll ask him," I said. "Good thing it's the end of the day. No way would anybody let a goat jump the line and it'd probably chew the dash out of your car before its turn came."

"I kept that in mind," he grinned. "I'll pay you too. Same as if it was me getting the x-ray."

"I'd be afraid to charge you for this Matthew. It's probably illegal to be x-raying a goat on a machine for people. The Nuclear Regulatory Commission might come down on us. Send me and Daddy to jail."

Then I realized I'd just given away $24 worth of work for free, and on my first day. Momma always said Daddy and I didn't have the sense to run a business. She believed if Daddy and I were left unsupervised, we'd bankrupt the office in a matter of weeks. I decided not tell her about this little freebie. Something told me Daddy wouldn't be bringing it up either. And Momma would never find out because goats didn't have charts.

"When'd you start keeping goats?" I asked.

"Dad and his brothers retired a few years ago. They closed the dairy. I decided to use the pastures and barns for raising rare and endangered animals. It's just a hobby, but it gives me and Dad something to fiddle with. I still got my regular job at the mines."

"How cool! I'll tell Daddy you're here. Go ahead. Get the goat."

Daddy was more than willing to x-ray a goat. It was one of the reasons he liked practicing in a rural area. He was almost as interested in animal medicine as he was in people medicine. He'd cared for animals since he'd been a small boy forever carrying some injured critter around in a box.

The goat was a beauty. It was small and delicate with long luxurious cream-colored hair and long slender tan curly horns. It was docile too.

"That little rascal is a lot easier to handle than a cow," I said.

Matthew nodded. "You better believe it. Makes things a lot easier on me. I was always the one who had to milk the kickers, because my arms were the longest."

I could tell from his voice that he missed his cows. His family had been dairymen for four generations that I knew of. People like that were natural herdsmen and were miserable without animals.

He comforted the goat while Daddy positioned it and set up to x-ray one of its front legs. Matthew said, "These things are nothing but trouble. They can find a way to escape from anything ever designed by man, they got no brains, and they get hurt easy."

Daddy went away to develop the x-ray and then brought it back to show Matthew. "The leg's not broken. I guess just keep her up in a stall for a while and see how she does."

"Okay. I sure appreciate this, Doc. I won't forget it. I owe you one."

I watched as Matthew carried the goat out to his car and laid it in the small backseat. The goat seemed to enjoy the attention. It stayed put while Matthew drove off.

"Well, that's over," I said to Daddy as I locked the office door, ending my first hideous day as the world's most reluctant and inept receptionist.

We went to our respective cars and I followed his green SUV home where we would feed the animals before going on to the hospital to see Momma.

He'd made this same trip countless times over the last forty years, but always with Momma before. I wondered what was going through his mind now. Whatever it was, I knew he'd never talk to me or anybody else about it. He was utterly self-contained. Momma was the same way.

I'd always tried to match their style but had only spotty success. They were both stoic in nature, but I'd always been more a seething-cauldron-of-wildly-conflicting-emotions type. It was as if I was the vehicle for their suppressed emotions. All my life I'd been engaged in a mighty struggle not to ask any of the obvious questions like "Why do you two work so hard?" and "Didn't either of you ever want to live in a fancy house, drive a Ferrari, or even sleep all night long without having to get up and go to the office or hospital?"

As I wound along the narrow roads, I thought about the ironic detour my life had taken. I had never wanted to leave home to begin with but hadn't been able to get a job in the mountains as anything but a cook or waitress. I'd made the terminal mistake of not studying either teaching or nursing and had instead gotten degrees in biomedical engineering and law from the University of Tennessee. Finally, in despair, I'd left and gotten one job after another, culminating in my current life as a Senate attorney.

I'd been spoiled during the past fifteen years. I'd grown accustomed to being surrounded and supported by an entourage, having my bags carried, and riding in limos and private jets. And I'd strayed far, far away from the traditional Appalachian diet of pork accompanied by things fried in pork grease.

I missed being a VIP, but I had a more pressing concern that I hardly dared to contemplate—the possibility that I might encounter one of the more toxic locals who would recognize me and expect me to resume my status as the area's most hopeless nerd.

Lord, it had been bad before, growing up where everyone could note the not totally successful operations to straighten my crossed eyes, the full braces I wore for ten years, which did indeed straighten my crooked teeth, and marvel at the hideous green leather orthopedic shoes I was forced to don every day to straighten my right foot. And on top of it all, despite being two years younger than some of my classmates, I was still the tallest person in the room. It had been awful.

Now, even after ditching the braces and shoes and giving the boys time to grow, my misfitness was light-years beyond where it had been before. I prayed I'd be able to slip away before being noticed. But just as I sent up the prayer I spied the marquee on the church near our house. It said,

CULTURE MAKES THE WORLD A BETTER PLACE
. . . TO GO TO HELL FROM.

It was already too late. I'd been spotted by the Baptists.

FIVE

Fletcher was out in the barn cutting the twine off bales of hay and tossing them into the manger when I went to feed the cats.

"How'd it go today?" he asked.

"Not so good," I said. "I didn't actually kill anybody, but I shook up Daddy and the Hankins sisters pretty bad."

He sat down on a short stack of hay and looked at me. "You're doing a good thing helping him out. You know that don't you?"

"Shows how desperate he is, doesn't it?"

Fletcher grinned. "I remember when he first came out here," he said. "There wasn't a doctor for miles."

I fumbled around in the old broken freezer we used to store feed, and dug out a couple of pounds of Little Friskies.

"Your Daddy picked this place when he heard about that fellow getting electrocuted over at Mascot, the one the old doctor operated on with a pocketknife."

"Yeah," I said. I'd heard the story many times. It was in the days before CPR. The doctor had opened a man's chest with a borrowed pocketknife and restarted his heart with his bare hand.

"You know, that's a great story," I said, "but I've never believed the last part of it—that a guy who was illiterate before he got electrocuted suddenly could read after they restarted his heart. How could that be true?"

Fletcher smiled. "There's a lot of strange things in this world, Carolyn. Things I can't understand." He sat fiddling with his green pocketknife, opening and closing the blades. "Your daddy's smart," he said. "He could've done anything, could've been any kind of doctor and got rich, but he came out here instead cause he wanted to help people." He closed his knife. "You might be like that too," he said.

"I don't know," I said. "Being a receptionist isn't exactly my dream job. I'm just staying for a couple of days till Momma gets going again. You know she thinks Daddy and I'd run the place into the ground by ourselves anyway."

"Well," he said as he rose, "I know you'll do whatever's right."

He stood inside the dark barn with his back to the blinding glare of the sunset. I squinted toward his black silhouette, outlined in brilliant yellow beams, but couldn't make out his features.

That evening Daddy and I went to visit Momma and were relieved to learn that she'd been moved to a less critical area of the ICU. Her condition had been downgraded from very dicey to merely critical. Her new room had walls made of restful blue curtains instead of glass. There was still quite a bit of equipment at the head of the bed, but each patient was positioned directly under a large skylight, giving them a direct view of blue sky or stars. I asked Daddy, "What's the story with the skylights? So God can keep a close eye on the sickest ones, or vice versa?"

"They've found that heavily medicated, really sick people get disoriented in the hospital," Daddy said. "They benefit from being able to see outside. That way they can keep track of up and down and day and night. It helps them get well faster."

That seemed like a good idea. I felt pretty disoriented myself. It was easier to find your way around inside the J. Edgar Hoover Building which had been designed to be tricky and misleading by some of the most paranoid people in the world. We walked down the aisle, peeking into curtained cubicles, looking for Momma. I heard her before I saw her. She was talking up a storm. This, however, turned out not to be as good a sign as I had imagined, because she was alone. She lay in her hospital bed, babbling an intense monologue, eyes open, nobody home.

I had a moment of panic, fearing she'd suffered brain damage or had a stroke that we hadn't been told about. A stroke wouldn't be unusual for a person with a heart problem, but then I realized I'd never heard of a stroke that made a person speak in tongues. This was weird. The first time I'd seen her, she'd looked like she was in a coma, but she'd been sharp as a tack. Now her eyes were open and she was talking and gesturing, but she was loopy. Daddy and I stood on either side of her bed and looked down at her. She gestured to emphasize some incomprehensible point and I noticed something a little strange about her wrist where it poked out of the edge of the blankets. I summoned the same calm, gentle, encouraging voice Daddy always affected when inside the hospital. "Why do they tie people up in ICU?"

He looked at me, incredulous. "They don't *tie people up* in the ICU!"

"What's this on Momma's wrist?" Maybe it was some new kind of medical device I didn't understand.

Daddy took two fingers and flipped the sheet and blanket down to her waist with an impressive expert snap and stared in amazement at the straps that had Momma's wrists bound firmly, one to each side rail.

He stuck his head out into the central aisle and looked for a nurse. He went to the closest one and demanded in something less than a whisper, "Why is my *wife* tied to the bed?"

The implication of his question was that, while it might be okay for the nurses to tie *some* people to their beds, it was definitely against the rules to tie up doctors' wives. I couldn't see either Daddy or the nurse, but I could hear their conversation perfectly through the flimsy curtains.

The nurse said in a diffident voice, "The previous shift restrained her because one of them spotted her down at the end of the hall, heading for the emergency exit that opens out onto the roof. She'd torn off her monitor leads and oxygen tubes and was using her IV pole like a walker. She said she was going outside for a smoke and was, I believe, rather insistent."

Momma was a very determined person, to say the least. She'd been more than two days without a cigarette. That was probably pretty rough after fifty years of chain-smoking, even if she'd been unconscious most of that time. Daddy didn't say anything. He returned to Momma's bedside considerably chastened.

We stood beside the bed, trying to be attentive. It was soon apparent however that, despite the intensity and forcefulness of her speech, Momma wasn't really saying words. She was talking gibberish. Total nonsense.

I was no novice about downers. Both Momma and Daddy had doctorates in pharmacy. Our dinner table conversation had been on topics like the difference among various types of tranquilizers, sedatives, and antianxiety drugs, stuff like soporifics and somniferics versus hypnotics.

"She's doped out of her mind," I offered.

"Heart patients do better if they can relax a little bit," Daddy said. "It's standard to give them something to help them feel relaxed."

Relaxed? In my opinion, Momma seemed more in the way of being *stoned* than *relaxed*. I felt sure her escape attempt had earned her a substantial increase in the level of her relaxation chemicals. But there were probably limits to the amount of knockdown they could administer to someone with an iffy heart condition, and when the maximum allowable dose hadn't worked on Momma, they'd taken the additional precaution of hog-tying her.

We stood at the bedside for a couple more minutes, trying to communicate with her, but because we weren't able to discern any signs that she knew we were there, we soon switched to talking softly to each other. Eventually we just left.

This was not the sort of thing Daddy had pictured for a member of his own family. He had certain ideas about how hospital visits were supposed to go. When I was three years old, he comforted me by buying me a Mickey Mouse watch and holding it to my ear and letting me hear it tick as I lay in bed with heavily bandaged eyes after my first operation. Then when I was thirteen he'd saved me from having to eat Jell-O by slipping in pizza after my second surgery.

I tried to console him as we navigated the labyrinth of the hospital to return to the parking lot. "There wasn't anything we could say or do that she would have known about," I said. "She's out of it. We'll try again when she comes out from under all the dope."

Daddy was so distracted that he didn't answer. It

seemed to take a really long time to find our way back to the car. Once we dead-ended at the laundry and I noticed that we passed the same heart catheterization lab two or three times, but I decided not to mention it. I'd picked up some diplomatic skills and a little discretion in Washington.

The next morning Miss Hiawatha Hancock arrived. Miss Hiawatha had the most joie de vivre of anyone I'd ever known. Wherever she went, it was like the carnival had just come to town. She was barely five feet tall, round, and eighty-two years old.

As far as I know, she never stopped talking for more than a few moments at a time. At least I'd never seen her be quiet for longer than that. She was a whirlwind of words. They came out in a continuous blast, a torrent, like water spewing from a fireplug. She covered an astonishing array of topics from the most mundane to the most intimate, all in the course of one great run-on sentence. You could hear her coming before she got to you and you could hear her voice gradually fade out as she rode away, driven by one of the neighbors who took her wherever she needed to go.

She had special outfits for every conceivable holiday, but she wore them according to her own schedule. She had an extensive selection of costume jewelry and was never seen without an outlandish pair of earrings and at least a dozen rings. Year round, even in the middle of summer, she wore brightly colored knitted hats, usually with a Russian style border of simulated curly sheep skin.

Unless you were used to her, her makeup was startling, even frightening: bright red rouge in golf ball sized circles on the center of her cheeks, a generous amount of eye shadow in the general area of the eyes, lipstick that strayed pretty far outside the line of the lips, and dramatic, erratically positioned eyebrows drawn on with thick black pencil.

For years she'd been senile in an eccentric but charming way. But lately, in addition to her senility, she'd developed an obsessive-compulsive disorder that spurred her to collect trash. Not tacky knick-knacks. Garbage. She'd begun to keep piles of it inside her house, both bagged and strewn around. She was way more than even the most attentive family could deal with, so once a month a group of volunteers from her church would go over and, while one person diverted her attention with conversation, the others would dash around, scoop up as much trash as they could manage without her seeing them, throw it into the back of a pickup truck, and race away.

They'd learned the hard way that if they piled an afternoon's haul, maybe twenty large black plastic garbage bags, in the carport for someone else to take away later, she'd just wait until they left and bring it all back inside. She was especially fond of old Maalox bottles and had a huge collection of them which she displayed on every windowsill and tabletop. She admired their particular shade of blue.

I loved Miss Hiawatha. Everyone did. She was the object of more genuinely selfless charity than anyone I've ever known. People loved her so much they didn't want her to catch them doing things for her, because it might embarrass her, so they did all sorts of things in secrecy: decorating the porch with hanging baskets of flowers or quickly mowing her yard while she was being taken to the grocery store. The entire community colluded to take care of her.

She came in wearing her Valentine's Day outfit and greeted me as if we'd just seen each other the day before. In fact, I hadn't seen her in years. She was talking about her recent birthday dinner when she arrived. Her son Cade had taken her.

"Cade, he's an accountant. He took me to dinner at the Cracker Barrel for my birthday. I had the best time. Two of my neighbors had died and I didn't even know it. I wouldn't have found out if Cade hadn't taken me to the Cracker Barrel. The waitress told us. I think Cade used to date her. You know I think of my father all the time. He's been dead for sixty-five years now. He died when I was a child. I think of him all the time. I broke my hip, you know, and two husbands have died on me since then. Do you like these earrings?"

"Oh yes," I said. "I love them."

"Well, here, you take them." She pulled them off and held them out toward me.

I took them and put them on. They were flashy, with large simulated gemstones of red, yellow, blue, and green glass glued to a piece of painted cardboard.

She continued to talk at her rapid pace, looking out the window away from me most of the time, while I mentally inventoried the jewelry she was wearing: sixteen bracelets, twenty-two rings, four necklaces, and the pair of earrings which I now wore.

"Cade's getting fat. He used to raise chickens, but now he's an accountant. He took me out for my birthday. We went to the Cracker Barrel. I had the fried chicken. It was delicious. He took me driving the day before that too. I can't remember who gave me those earrings. Do you like them? You can keep them. I have lots of earrings. Cade used to have fighting roosters. He'd let you look at them. Do you remember? You were a little bitty thing then."

"I remember. Cade was really good to me," I said. "Those roosters were beautiful, weren't they? Does he still keep any?" But she'd moved on to another topic.

"My diarrhea's clearing up I think. I just think of my Daddy all the time. I saw him standing in the corner of my room yesterday. Do you believe me when I say that?"

"Of course," I said, meaning it.

"I saw him so clearly. He stands at the foot of my bed sometimes. My stomach's hurting me today. I think I should see the doctor about it, don't you?

Do you think Maalox would help? My neighbor says to take Pepto, but I just hate that pink color. I prefer the Maalox. I like the blue much better. You're looking lovely today. And those earrings go so well with that outfit. They go perfectly really."

She was right.

I'd lost the thread of her conversation, but in a second she came back around to Cade and the birthday dinner, so I could catch hold of it again. When it was her turn to see the doctor, I heard her tell Daddy that she'd had chest pains last night and thought it was indigestion.

When she came out of the room she tried to pay, but Daddy refused the money, saying he'd bill her insurance company. She didn't actually have any insurance, but she didn't know that. The neighbor who was chauffering her that day came forward and helped her into her coat. "Take me to Frankie's next," she said. "I've got to get my medicine."

"Frankie" was Franklin DeCoville, the local pharmacist. I talked to Frank several times a day, either calling in prescriptions or relaying questions and answers between him and Daddy. Frank was another Hiawatha fan, so when she left I called his small independent drugstore and said, "Frank, one of your cousins is heading your way. They should be there in about five minutes."

"Who is it this time?" he asked.

"I don't want to spoil the surprise, but let me just say, 'Get out your Maalox.' "

"Oh God, lock the doors, it's Miss Hiawatha!" he said in mock despair. "She ain't *my* cousin. She's one of my *wife's* people." He let out a heart-felt sigh.

I had two hours of relative quiet until Adron came in. Adron Breedlove was a tall slender man in his midseventies. He'd once been a freckled redhead, but over the years his luxurious hair had turned snow white and a lifetime of farming had caught up with his fair complexion. He had an assortment of small skin cancers on his cheeks, nose, and the tops of both ears where they stuck out beyond his billed cap.

Adron was, to use the local euphemism, "not smart." So even on a good day you couldn't have a normal conversation with him. He was extremely sweet and polite and had a handsome, fine-boned face, but he was so slow on the uptake that trying to communicate with him was maddening.

Daddy said, "Adron, I've told you time and again, you need to have those places taken off your head. They're cancer."

"Oh, I ain't worried," he answered.

"Well I'm telling you, you *should* be worried. *I'm* worried."

"Don't worry, Doc. You and the good Lord'll take care of me. I know that."

"I'm trying to take care of you Adron, but you won't let me! I'm telling you, you need to go to the

68

plastic surgeon and get those places taken off, or I don't know what's going to happen to you."

Then, to everyone's surprise, Adron said, "Well, okay, I reckon I will."

Victory at last. Daddy told me to handle the details and went off to see the next patient. Adron had no money, so I had to cook something up through public assistance. It took at least a dozen phone calls, but I eventually worked a deal out with the State of Tennessee. Adron would go to a family practice gatekeeper in Lake City (about an hour's drive north) and get a referral to a plastic surgeon in Oak Ridge (an hour's drive west).

Adron couldn't drive and he lived in the back of beyond, so someone had to be found to take him to his appointments. "Adron," I called out toward the waiting room, "I need somebody to take you out to Lake City to see a doctor who can give you the code number to get the state to pay the plastic surgeon for you. Who should I ask?"

"What?"

I started over. "Who can I get to drive you to Lake City?"

"Where's Lake City?"

"It's about a hour north."

"I don't live out there."

"I know you don't, but the state wants you to go out there to see a doctor who can send you on to the plastic surgeon."

"Why?"

I decided to try a different tack. "Adron, who drove you here today?"

"Pup."

"Pup who?"

"I don't know. He lives up there. At the bottom of the big hill."

I prayed for patience. "Where is Pup now?"

"He's out there," he said pointing through the picture window to a man who looked to be in his twenties, sitting in a car made up of panels of several different colors.

"Will he take you somewhere if I ask him to?"

"I don't know."

He went out front to talk to Pup. I watched them through the window. Adron bent down to talk to Pup, who turned to look at him with a dull expression. He shouted, "Hey Pup!" into the rolled up driver's side window.

Pup shouted back through the glass, "What?"

They were both so loud I could hear them plainly at my desk. Adron shouted, "Can ye take me somewhere?"

"Where?" Pup screamed through the glass.

"I don't know!" Adron said.

I went outside and signaled for Pup to roll his window down. He cranked it down about two inches and put his lips up to the crack.

Adron put his mouth down toward the opening and Pup removed his lips and tilted his ear up as they prepared to go another round.

I half shouted, "Pup, would you mind getting out of the car?"

"Okay!" he shouted back. He shoved hard against the driver's door and there was an ominous squealing of the hinges. Then he shouted straight into my face, "What do ye want?"

He was so loud he made my ears ring, and I was so startled I couldn't remember what I'd meant to say. "I . . . I need somebody to take Adron to the doctor in Lake City."

"I thought the doc was around here somewhere," he said looking around in confusion. "I was supposed to bring him to the doc. Is there a doc around here?"

"There's a doctor's office right here, Pup. You brought Adron right to where the doctor's at. But now Adron needs to go to a different doctor in Lake City. Can you take Adron there?"

"Unn unn," he said shaking his head back and forth slowly. "I can't drive in a city. I get too nervous. I don't know where that city's at neither. I'd get lost."

I stood beside the car and thought for a second. I didn't believe I was going to be able to work with Pup. I was going to need someone who could read a map.

"Adron, is there anybody else that can drive you somewhere?"

The three of us stood in the parking lot while Adron thought. Just when I was about to ask the question again, he said, "Them people's got a car that lives down the road."

"Who's that?" I asked.

"I don't know their name."

I waited while he continued to think.

Then he said, "Tom can drive."

"How do I get ahold of Tom?" I asked.

"He don't have no phone."

"You know anybody else that's got a car?"

"They's lotsa people that has them cars," he said gesturing with one hand toward the cars streaming up and down the highway.

"Adron, do you have any family I can call?"

"My son works at the electric company in Knoxville."

"He does?" I said. "How can I get ahold of him?"

"I don't know. He's at the electric company. He works over there."

I went back inside and made several calls to the Knoxville Utilities Board. I learned that Adron's son did indeed work there, but couldn't be reached by phone until he returned from a repair job.

In despair I called the gatekeeper doctor's office in Lake City and tried to explain the problem to an uninterested nurse, to see if they could suggest a way to handle the referral by mail or get a waiver or something. No dice. We'd treated Adron for free for thirty-nine years, but they wouldn't do it for five minutes. I sat swiveling on my stool in frustration.

Adron came back in, sat down, and said, "I got another son."

"How can I call him?"

"He don't have no phone neither."

This was a situation where all the energy, intelligence, and business skills in the world were pretty much wasted. I was pulling at my hair in frustration when Daddy walked up to write a prescription on the counter behind me. He said, "What's the problem?"

I told him. "His brother was worse, if you can believe that," he said. "He's dead now. He was in the hospital for several days before he died, and every time I'd go in his room he'd be laying in bed waving his arms, talking to himself. He thought he was still at work. He'd get an imaginary nail out of his apron, hold it up to something, and hammer it in. He 'worked' right up until he died." Then he leaned over and whispered, "Adron has a daughter who's smart. Mary. She's as sharp as a tack and she can handle all this."

I swiveled around to face the waiting room, leaned out over the reception desk, and called out, "Adron, do you know Mary's phone number?"

"No. But it's in my pocketbook."

I waited for him to fish his billfold out of his overalls, but he just sat there.

"Adron?"

"Yeah?"

"Would you see if you can find that phone number for me?"

"Okay." He started rummaging around in his pockets. The rummaging went on and on. Suddenly I realized that Mary had been a patient, so we'd have a chart on her that would have her phone number in it. Ha! I found it and dialed her up while Adron continued to rummage.

"Hello?" a female voice said.

"This is Carolyn at Dr. Jourdan's office. I've got a problem here," I said.

Mary took down all the information, told me not to worry, said she'd arrange transportation for her father to and from the various offices, and thanked me for my help. Right before she hung up she said, "Sorry for all the trouble, Carolyn, but when you're dealing with this family, you've gotta learn to sort of . . . *coast* . . . if you get my meaning."

I got it. I was going to have to downshift from the fast-lane pace that was a prerequisite for survival in Washington. Here, I just needed to coast.

Six

Friday afternoon the waiting room was full of people who were groaning. They moved in slow motion clutching the smalls of their backs with one hand and breathing through gritted teeth, hissing as if in agony, vividly enacting the symptoms of back pain. It was a safe bet that not a single one of them would be able to step up even the two or three inches it took to get onto the scale to be weighed because of the pain. The terrible, terrible pain.

It was an act that had repeated itself every Friday afternoon for as long as I could remember. It was one of the ways time was measured in the office: a week went from Monday morning's hangovers needing a note from the doctor saying they were missing work because of the flu, to Friday afternoon's drug addicts facing the prospect of living through an entire weekend without the aid of narcotics. I remembered how, as a child, a year was measured by the progression from allergies and pulled muscles in the spring, to poison ivy and accidents in the summer, and finally to colds, flu, and pneumonia in the winter.

On Friday afternoons there was a constantly changing cast of characters. Drug addicts new to the area had to learn for themselves that the back pain act wasn't going to work in this particular office. When they registered, I tried to head them off by telling them Dr. Jourdan didn't prescribe narcotics. Drug addicts weren't hard to pick out: the timing, the age, the look in their eye, the slur in their speech, the instant belligerence at any perceived reluctance to dispense what they wanted.

If they concealed the reason for their visit, or they lied to me convincingly, Daddy would recognize them with that sixth sense of his. He'd warn them again at the counter that he'd be happy to see them but wouldn't dispense any pain medicine, particularly hydrocodone or any of the *cets,* such as Lorcet, Percocet, or Darvocet. They'd usually leave then with an abbreviated burst of insults, but sometimes it got ugly. I dreaded it. I felt sorry for the addicts, but not sorry enough to help them get what they wanted.

At 3:30 I answered the phone and barely had time to say "Dr. Jourdan's office" before a woman began talking in a frantic voice.

"Carolyn! I can't find her anywhere! I've looked and looked and I can't find her!"

"Bennie?" Bennie was Momma's best friend. She worked in the Women's Pavilion of the hospital.

"Yessss, it's *me.* I'm telling you, she's not any-where to be found!"

"Momma? You can't find Momma?"

"Not anywhere. And all her stuff has been taken out of her room. I've been places I had no business going. They'd fire me if they found out! I went to ICU, Cardiac Care, and Coronary Observation, and she's not in any of them. I even went to the recovery room and she wasn't there either."

I felt sick. Not Momma. Not invincible, indestructible Momma. Oh God. Oh God. Bennie rattled on with more details and I think I just let go of the phone after a few moments.

I called out, "Dr. Jourdan!" Then I lurched off the stool and rushed down the hall, looking in each room as I went by to find Daddy. He was in Room 3 sewing up Arvil Hackworth's cut thumb. I stuck my head in. "Bennie can't find Momma. She's looked everywhere: her room, ICU, CCU, COU, recovery. Her stuff's been removed from her room. Bennie says Dr. Goldman has been trying to reach you for hours. They've been paging us all over the hospital!"

"What?"

I started repeating the whole story in a very fast, probably incoherent, babble.

"Stop. Stop," he said.

I stopped and stood wringing my hands.

"What are you saying? Dr. Goldman can't have been trying to reach me for hours, because I've been here every minute since 7:00 this morning. Has he tried to call here?"

"Not that I know of," I said weakly. I thought I was going to faint.

Daddy calmly continued to sew with his back to me. Then he said, "So, what are you saying? That Dr. Goldman has lost your mother, or that the hospital has lost her, or is it just Bennie that has lost her?"

"I don't know. Everybody I guess."

"I bet Bennie is the only one who has lost her. I *know* Bennie. I refuse to get sucked in to another one of her wild scenarios."

"You don't think they took her to the basement do you?" I couldn't make myself say "morgue."

"Why would they do that?"

"If she, you know, was . . ." I couldn't make myself say "dead" either.

"What?" he said turning toward me with his bloody gloves held waist high.

Daddy said in exasperation, "The morgue's not in the basement. Where are you getting all this? Did Bennie tell you that?"

"No, I just figured that was where the morgue was . . . in the basement. It seemed like it would be there."

"Well, it's not. As I seem to recall from our last visit, that's where the laundry is." Then he thought better of himself and said, "Good grief, Carolyn. Just because Bennie can't find your mother doesn't mean she's *dead*. You know how Bennie is."

That helped some. I did know how Bennie was.

"Your mother's probably hiding somewhere smoking."

That did sound far more likely. I said, "Will you call Dr. Goldman and see what's going on?"

"Now?" he said, gesturing with his gloves. He held a threaded needle in one hand and a clamp with a sterile gauze swab in the other.

"Yes."

"No. I'll call him when I get finished sewing up Mr. Hackworth here."

Mr. Hackworth said, "Oh no, Doc, don't you worry about me. You go see about your wife. I ain't in no hurry."

But Daddy didn't leave the room. I waited in the hall a moment and then went back to the reception desk. The telephone handset was dangling by the cord and I picked it up and said, "Bennie?"

"Hey. I'm still here. Did he call Goldman?"

"No. He doesn't think Momma's dead. He thinks she's off smoking somewhere."

Bennie didn't have a quick response to that. I guess it sounded pretty likely to her too. "Well, I'll make a few calls and let you know if I find out anything."

"Okay."

I spent a horrible ten minutes, throughout which I stared into space without moving a muscle. Then, when he'd finished with Arvil's thumb, Daddy went into his office and called Dr. Goldman. When I walked in, he was just hanging up the phone. He said, "Your mother's fine, but she's going to have to have some more tests."

I nearly swooned with relief. Thank God.

"She'd just been moved to a temporary room in a backup COU used for overflow," Daddy said. Okay, so he'd been right.

"She's going to have a heart catheterization. It's a bigger test than the others, so they want to give her the weekend to further stabilize. They'll do it Monday."

Damn. I was back to feeling faint again. So much for her being back at work on Monday. Well, that hadn't been a very realistic plan anyway. I didn't dare ask for a revised schedule, though. I was afraid of what it might be.

Daddy sighed, "Dr. Goldman wants to talk to 'the family' at the hospital. We can go when we get through today."

I could tell he was miserable at being on the outside of the medical system for once. I wasn't loving it either.

Lord a mercy. I went into the x-ray room, closed the door, lay down on the hard table, and curled onto my side in the fetal position. Being a receptionist was tough. I needed to rest.

It was demeaning to have to hide in a barn to conduct my affairs, but I didn't want to worry Daddy about my missing work in Washington, and since this was the most private location I could think of,

I jogged through the barnyard with my cell phone, determined to return a couple of calls before close of business for the week. At least in the barn nobody would be able to humiliate me within earshot of people who thought I was a smart, competent, professional adult.

I ducked inside, slid the massive doors closed, and sat on a bale of hay with my phone and a list of calls I needed to make. As I dialed Phil Cranowitz in the San Francisco office of People Against Nuclear Power, the cats, who had begun to recognize me as a food source, came out. The big orange striped, fight ravaged tomcat walked straight to me and began to rub against my legs, and then he jumped onto my lap. I sat and petted the dusty creature as I spoke, but Thomas wasn't looking for affection. He wanted dinner and complained in a coarse *yeowl*. I gave in instantly to his blackmail and carried him over to the old freezer to get the cat food.

Phil didn't seem to have heard him. He said, "You've got to shut these plants down. Now."

As soon as I opened the freezer, cats began to appear from everywhere. I quickly poured out a huge bowl of food to keep them quiet. "Sure, Phil," I said, "then where are you gonna get the electricity to run all the blow dryers in LA?"

My presence in the barn had not gone unnoticed by the cows either. They'd ambled over to see what was going on. When they saw the cats scoring some chow, they became interested in getting a little sweet feed for themselves. They waited what they thought was a reasonable amount of time, then became noticeably restless.

"It'll be a wake-up call to all the people who've been ignoring where all this energy waste is leading us."

"Phil, what's wasted energy to one person is an essential component of a civilized life to another. I don't use a blow dryer either, but I'm pretty attached to hot water. The people of California voted to go with nuclear power and now they're stuck with it."

The cows were shuffling their feet, swishing their tails, and making low murmuring sounds. I tried to make eye contact to signal them to be quiet, but it didn't work. A clear moo rang out. I made for the sweet feed.

"What was that?"

"What?"

A bag of sweet feed weighs fifty pounds, and before it can be dispensed the end tape must be torn off, like opening a huge bag of dog food. That's normally no big deal, but I'd neglected to bring a knife with me. In desperation I hacked and sawed at the heavy two-layered bag with the raw edges of a lid from a can of cat food.

"That noise, Carolyn. It sounded like . . . an animal. Where are you calling from?"

"I didn't hear anything," I said, frantically walking with the bag, spilling its contents into one of the wooden mangers that lined each side of the barn. If I didn't move at warp speed the mooing would become more insistent and louder. And in between the moos the cows would be wheezing like donkeys as they drew in the next breath to moo with. But of course, hindered as I was by cradling the phone between my shoulder and ear, I wasn't working fast enough so one of them tilted her huge nostrils toward me and plaintively mooed.

"There it is again. It's a *cow*. I *know* it is."

I suppose it would have been too easy if the cows had all been on the same side of the barn, but no, they were on both sides, so I had to make a fifty-foot dash up one side and then down the other, with the bag of feed. "You must be getting some interference on your line or something," I panted, "cause there sure as hell ain't no cows where I'm at."

There was a long silence, then Phil said in a slow, considering tone of voice, "Gosh, Carolyn, no offense, I mean I realize your ethnic heritage is southern highland, Appalachian, but just then you sounded almost like Elly May Clampett."

I was too humiliated to respond.

"I've never seen this side of you before. It's sort of cute. Strange, but cute." Then Phil continued, now in a more obviously censorious tone, "I'd be careful who I talked to like that though. Other people might not understand."

* * *

I called my best friend to commiserate.

Jacob was a brilliant and cultured Princeton- and Stanford-trained astrophysicist-turned-lawyer. Our extraordinary closeness was a constant source of surprise to others because what we had in common was not obvious. He was an NPR, foreign film, classical music sort of guy. I was a *People* magazine, romantic comedy, Tina Turner type. We also originated from opposite ends of the political spectrum. What we had in common was far more important though: we shared a moral code. In a town like Washington, where if you wanted a friend you were advised to buy a dog, we'd sensed in each other a shared commitment to honesty and integrity, no matter what the cost. So instead of fighting about our superficial differences, we'd combined forces and used them as a powerful business asset.

After answering his kind inquiries about Momma's health and my emotional state, I said, "Tell the truth, what am I missing?"

He thought for a moment and then said, "Well, let's see, it looks like you'll be missing a great dinner at Jean-Louis de Brissac's Washington chateau, but nothing else important. Oh, this is so great you won't believe it: Senator Warner came up to me after the hearing today and asked me where I buy my ties! He liked the one with the purple and black stripes."

"Of course I believe it. What else can you say

about a former husband of Elizabeth Taylor except that the man has great taste?"

"True," Jacob said.

We were both quiet for a moment thinking about the surreal quality of being up close to celebrities. Then I flashed back to my current circumstances and said, "Jacob, I'm finding it way more stressful to be a flunky than I'd imagined. You wouldn't believe how hard it is to be a receptionist. I had no idea. And I'm beginning to hallucinate about good food."

"Where would you like to eat?" he said.

"Somewhere without a speaker in the back."

"How about Le Dome Capitol? They've just finished the renovations."

"Sounds fabulous. Do they have sausage biscuits?"

"Afraid not. I'll take you there as soon as you get back."

I couldn't wait.

On this, my third visit to the hospital, Momma was both lucid and open-eyed. Like they say, third time's a charm. When Daddy and I came into her new solid-walled room, Momma's cardiologist, Dr. Goldman, was sitting on the edge of her bed in a starched white lab coat with his stethescope stuffed into the breast pocket. Dr. Goldman was only forty-one, a year younger than me. After a few minutes of somber doctor chitchat, it began to dawn on him that Daddy and I weren't going to be sitting in the family lounge while he performed her procedure on Monday morning. This upset him. When he realized, come Monday morning, the office would open as usual and that Daddy and I would be at work during Momma's heart catheterization, he looked at us like he'd stumbled onto some strange cult.

I wasn't sure whether he thought we were mistreating Momma, or him. Momma had already made herself perfectly clear. Daddy and I had been given our marching orders. She didn't want us sitting anywhere except Daddy's office. But Dr. Goldman wanted us at the hospital. He was so startled he made the mistake of attempting to revisit Momma's decision with her. Daddy and I sat in the corner of the room and watched.

Dr. Goldman said, "But surely your family will be here for you!"

Momma, lying there looking pale and tinged slightly green by the fluorescent lights, snapped back, "Aren't you going to be doing the procedure in an operating room?"

"Of course I am!"

"Then the family can't 'be there' anyway, can they?"

"No, but . . . I've never heard of the family not coming."

"Why should they? Aren't you going to put me to sleep?" she asked.

"Of course I am."

"Then I won't know if anyone's there or not, will I?"

"Well, no, but this is not a risk-free procedure. We don't expect any problems. We expect everything to go smoothly, but—"

"I know. You could break off some plaque or knock a clot loose and I'd die. Or you could tear a hole in a blood vessel and I'd bleed to death. Tell me, if I start to die on the operating table, can my family come in and try to save me—or even say good-bye? No. Because you wouldn't let them in and I'd be unconscious anyway, so what difference does it make?"

There was a long, stunned silence. Poor guy. He hadn't understood who he was dealing with. Daddy's patients hadn't nicknamed her "Sarge" for nothing.

"Well I don't like it. How will I tell your husband what we find?"

"You can call him. Here, I'll give you the number at his office."

"He'll be at work?"

"Certainly. You want to get paid don't you?"

All in all the family made a pretty bad impression on Dr. Goldman. He wasn't used to this kind of treatment. He didn't understand a family like ours, and I don't think he understood the sort of practice Daddy had either. For forty years, twenty-four hours a day, seven days a week, Momma and Daddy ran a homemade, low paid 911 service for a large rural community. There was no such thing as a day off, ever.

Dr. Goldman's patients lived in town and made appointments to see their doctors. They had insurance and cars that would run and telephones. If he didn't show up for work there were a dozen ladies in his office who would call his patients and cancel their appointments. If push came to shove, there were at least ten other heart doctors in his group who could cover for him. Daddy didn't have any of that. He didn't want any of it. But it still put us on the defensive. Daddy and I looked at each other and made a wordless pact to try not to do anything else to upset Dr. Goldman. We wanted him in top form for the operation, and he was clearly a high-strung guy.

At 7:00 Monday morning I was back manning the reception desk. On the way in that morning I'd tripped on the two-inch asphalt curb in front of the office door and been struck by the contrast between the homely little threshold of Daddy's office and the glorious sweep of white marble stairs outside the Capitol, between his worn linoleum floor and the splendid handmade floor tiles at the Senate. Momma had patched holes in Daddy's floor with seconds from the Vinyl Barn, while the government had contrived at stupendous effort and expense to reopen a defunct china factory in England in order to reproduce exact matches for the 200-year-old floor tiles.

Alma was already inside.

"What're you doing here this early?" I asked.

"Oh, I do some home health care nursing on the side and I got an old fellow over the mountain there," she pointed east, "who needs his insulin shot and medicine at breakfast time. He's a early riser, so I have to get up at about 5:00."

"I can't believe you get up at that hour for anybody," I said.

"Well, he's ninety-eight and hardly eating anything, so I hate to make him wait his breakfast for me."

"Ninety-eight?"

"Yeah. He's real sweet. He can't hardly get around, so his family's penned his chickens right at the back door of the house, so he can feed them without having to go outside. He says his life wouldn't be worth living if he couldn't keep a few chickens. He stands in the kitchen door and throws them their corn and scratch while I check his blood sugar."

"You must see all sorts of stuff if you're going into houses over on the mountain," I said. "Daddy's told me about people over in Owl Hole Gap sleeping on straw pallets on dirt floors and stuff like that."

"I see more than I want to," she said. "Last week I was driving around in a subdivision over in Blaine trying to find a new patient's house, but I got lost, so

I pulled into a big circle driveway and went up to one a them mansions and knocked on the front door to ask directions. It was 12:30 in the afternoon and a man come to the door stark naked. He asked could he help me, calm and cool as you please. So I thought, What the hell, and asked him for directions. He gave me good directions too."

I was amazed at her composure, but I supposed it was an essential quality for both a nurse and a single mom.

"When I finally got to the woman's house I was supposed to be at, she's a diabetic, her blood sugar was 350. She swore up and down that she hadn't had nothing sweet to eat. Hell, I knew she was lying. She weighs at least 300 pounds and she's lost the feeling in her feet.

"Well I took a little look around the bedroom and what a surprise. I found a family size pack of M&M's and a bag of Chips Ahoy under the bed and a box of chocolate covered doughnuts hid behind the toilet paper in the cabinet underneath the bathroom sink. So, I confiscated them. And buddy, she went wild."

In that moment I realized that there existed at least one job that was worse than my temp receptionist job.

I realized I was getting off light. Very light.

I hauled out the coding manual and bravely began to fill out the topmost paper in a stack of Medicare forms.

When Daddy arrived he did a startled double take at me and blurted out, "What have you got on?"

"Scrubs," I answered, smiling.

"*Black* scrubs? *BLACK* scrubs?" Apparently this was not a good surprise.

"I got a catalog from Alma. I ordered them Friday night and had them FedExed. I think they're cool."

"They're *awful*. They look like something a morgue attendant would wear. If you had to get the damn things, why couldn't you get a regular color?"

"Because those colors wouldn't go good with my other clothes." I was wearing a $200 black cashmere turtleneck and a $600 pair of Joan & David boots under my new $29 scrubs. Daddy would have been way more upset if he'd known how much the sweater and boots had cost.

He turned and went back to his office with his biscuit and coffee, like he needed to protect his digestion from such a sight. He'd always shunned "doctor clothes" as pretentious. He'd never wear either scrubs or a white lab coat. He wouldn't even wear his stethoscope draped around his neck as he walked around inside the office because that was what TV doctors did. He thought it looked silly.

I thought I looked pretty good though, giving the medical receptionist look a sophisticated twist. And it was just $30 for a whole outfit! You couldn't buy lunch for that in Washington. And the fabric repelled body fluids like Teflon. What a deal. I'd ordered two pairs of black pants, a black top, and another top with sharks on it.

I couldn't wait till Daddy got to see the one with the sharks. He loved *Shark Week* on the Discovery Channel.

There must have been something going around because that whole morning I was surrounded by a cacophony of hacking that had a nightmarish resemblance to an orchestra tuning up.

I'd never really thought about how many different kinds of coughs there were. Coughs could be either dry or wet, wheezing or whooping, and solo or accompanied by sniffling, sneezing, or snorting. Currently in the center of the waiting room sat a real pièce de résistance, Estole Chesney, with his hocking, racking, all out, bent over, gagging heave. Estole was the Typhoid Mary of the community. Both Daddy and Alma warned me to use evasive maneuvers when dealing with him because they were sure he gave them whatever he had every time he came in.

On my right a lady was attempting to register, but every time she tried to tell me her name, the effort set off a fit of coughing. She tried to cover her mouth with a small wadded-up tissue but was too weak to do an effective job of it. On my left, the man who was paying his bill was not so considerate. He barked a spray of germs and spittle directly onto my face from an astonishingly loud and explosive cough that displayed his tonsils and the entire length of his tongue.

I needed a helmet. Patients seemed oblivious to the fact that they were spewing germs all over everyone they came into contact with. I was amazed. In Japan sick people wore a simple little mask out of courtesy for everyone else. Why couldn't we do that? Instead, here, it was the opposite. Sick people went around huffing and puffing and whining and complaining all over everyone they knew, oblivious to the results of the contact.

As soon as I got the chance I searched the cabinets for protection. I tried on a surgical mask, but when I looked at myself in the bathroom mirror I realized that a receptionist in a mask would probably scare people when they tried to register. The only other thing I could find was a spray can of DisCide. I "dissed" the air around me every few minutes. The label on the can said DisCide would kill everything from AIDS to flu to herpes, but it smelled suspiciously like Lemon Pledge. Each time a coughing person got near me I'd try to hold my breath until they walked away, then saturate the air with lemon fumes before taking a breath. I clutched the can protectively.

"Gosh, you look just like your momma sitting there," a man's voice said.

I looked up to see Ulysses Hamilton, a slender, elegant black man, who worked as a courier for the pathology lab in Knoxville where we sent speci-mens to be analyzed. He came by several times a week, whether we had anything for him to pick up or not.

Ulysses' comment highlighted an important issue. Although I strongly resembled my mother, I had an entirely independent existence proceeding at full speed elsewhere, even in my absence. And I in-tended to catch up with it soon. "Well, don't get used to the sight of me on this stool," I snapped, "because it's temporary."

I was immediately embarrassed to have been rude and tried to think of something more upbeat to add before he left. "I don't suppose working here is a *totally* worthless experience. There's certainly no other place quite like it!"

Ulysses flashed his bright smile at me and said, "Boy, that's the truth! You never know what'll turn up next, do you?"

He was so right.

SEVEN

Jim Garrison, a neighbor, drove up in a huge candy apple red pickup truck with dual back wheels. The driver's seat was at least four feet off the ground, the back fenders were nine feet wide, the whole thing was gleaming with wax and Armour All. But why not? He and his brother owned one of the biggest car dealerships in Knoxville.

Jim was a lean man, dressed from head to toe in mismatched camouflage: oak leaf shirt, desert brown pants, jungle green jacket and hat. He was supposed to meet his brother in half an hour to go bird hunting. He had his dogs in their cages loaded in the truck bed. He had a cold that was getting worse instead of better, though, and a few minutes to spare, so he'd decided to swing by the doctor's office on his way.

Daddy had just bought a new SUV from Jim a month or so before. He kept a four-wheel drive so he could get up the steep mountain roads to make house calls in bad weather. I could hear them talking about the SUV and hunting. Then Daddy came out of the examining room to write prescriptions. He looked at Jim's chart for any drug allergies and then called back over his shoulder as he did dozens of times a day, "Are you allergic to any medicines?"

"Nope," Jim answered.

"Alma, give Jim forty milligrams of Depo-Medrol IM."

"IM" meant intramuscular, which could mean the arm but usually went in the butt. Depo-Medrol was a long-acting steroid that reduced inflammation. Then Daddy wrote out prescriptions for an anti-biotic, a decongestant, and a pill for sinus irritation.

Jim picked up the sheaf of blue prescription papers and left. There weren't any other patients just then, so we sat around in the quiet, looking out the window.

"Damn!" Daddy said all of a sudden. "I forgot to tell Jim about my windshield wipers not working."

"What?" I said.

"On the SUV. They work fine whenever the sun's out, but if it rains, they won't come on. Oh well, I'll say something next time he comes in."

We only had to wait about half an hour. I heard the whoosh of the front door and the clomp of heavy boots as someone came in moving fast. I looked up to see Jim. "I think I'm having a reaction to my medicine," he said.

His whole face was red, extremely red, like a bad sunburn. I jumped off my stool and waved for him to come on into the back. I called out, "Mr. Garrison's having a drug reaction."

Both Daddy and Alma came down the hall pronto. Jim was standing in the middle of the lab area flailing his arms, tugging at his shirt. "Paul, I think I'm allergic to something you give me. I'm itching. And I feel funny."

It was obvious he was miserable and frightened. Daddy took him into Room 1 again and had him stretch out on the examining table. Alma helped him take off his coat and then pulled his outer shirt off over his head, exposing a short-sleeved undershirt. Then she took his pulse and looked at Daddy with her eyes wide. With an unreadable expression Daddy took Jim's wrist between his fingers and thumb.

Jim's face was cherry red and he was sweating through his T-shirt even though it was cool in the room. Daddy untied Jim's hunting boots and pulled them both off. Then he peeled off both socks. There were fist-sized splotches of purplish red across the arch of each foot that looked like bruises.

"What'd you take?" Daddy asked calmly.

"I took one of each of them you wrote me. I can't remember the names."

Daddy would have dictated what prescriptions he'd written for Jim shortly after he finished examining him, but there hadn't been time for the list to be transcribed into Jim's chart.

"Where are the bottles?" he asked.

"Out in the truck."

"Carolyn, will you go out and get his medicine so we can see what he's gotten hold of."

"Okay," I said and took off like a shot. I was glad

to be part of the team. This was my first medical emergency as an adult health professional. I was shaking all over.

The bag of pills was lying in the middle of the bench seat. There were four computer-generated labels stuck to the outside of the bag indicating the contents, dosages, everything. Four bottles of pills were inside. Good.

Back in Room 1 Daddy was telling Alma to make up an injection of Benadryl and epinephrine: an antihistamine and adrenaline. Jim had gotten so uncomfortable that Alma had brought in the small clamp fan she kept by her desk. It was set up to blow across Jim's face and chest and another fan was running near his feet to try to cool him as he lay on the examining table. The flushing from the drug allergy was making him hot and that was making the rash itch worse. His face and the arches of his feet were still red, but his thrashing around had subsided.

I knew people could die very quickly from antibiotic allergies, but I didn't know how to judge how bad things were. I kept looking at Daddy and Alma and Jim to try to judge the seriousness of the situation. Daddy wouldn't let go of Jim's wrist. That was not a good sign. I'd never seen him latch onto someone like that and not let go. He was monitoring the man's pulse discreetly but continuously.

He began to explain to Jim in a soft, comforting tone, "This isn't any fun, I know. You're having an allergic reaction to your medicine, that old antibiotic Cefaclor. Having a little anaphylaxis."

He said the word "anaphylaxis" in a singsong way like it was a lady's name to take the sting out of it. But I knew then to be scared. He was talking about anaphylactic shock. Sweet Lord!

This was all too much. I was just a temp receptionist. My whole job was to say hi, sign people in, stamp the day in their charts, and answer the phone. Death scenes weren't part of the deal. It was supposed to be boring and degrading, not horrifying. But here a family friend who wasn't even fifty years old was about to die. While I was looking him in the eye. Not a single patient had ever died in the office. Not *one* in forty years. Why now? Why Jim? If someone had to die, why couldn't it be a stranger? Or someone obnoxious or ancient?

I paced around outside the open door of the room so I could hear if they needed me to do anything. I found myself wringing my hands, thinking, *Somebody's gotta do something about this*. Then my brain kicked in and I realized "somebody" was Daddy, the only person within ten miles who knew what to do. My God. What a hideous responsibility. And he didn't even have any blinking or beeping expensive equipment to back him up. Then the phone started to ring and I hurried off to answer it. The phone, at least, was something I could handle.

A woman's voice said, "This is Dr. Goldman's office calling for Dr. Jourdan."

Momma's doctor was calling *now?* Hell, why not the President of the United States?

What a choice: Jim or Momma, friend or family, an emergency up close or one across town. Who took precedence? What would Miss Manners say? I was stumped for a couple of seconds, then I said as if it was the most normal thing in the world, "I'm sorry, but the doctor's busy right now. Can I take a message?"

"No," the nurse said as though I was some sort of super dunce. Then she repeated herself slowly, placing great emphasis on the names. "This is *Dr. Goldman's* office calling for *Dr. Jourdan.*"

She wasn't going to like it, but there was no way I was going back there to tell Daddy he had a phone call. No matter *who* it was, no matter what it was about. Even Momma. My voice shook as I said, "Dr. Jourdan isn't available to take a call right now. I'll have to take a message."

She hung up.

I sat for a moment wondering if I'd done the right thing, then went back to stand outside Room 1. Now I was scared for both Jim and Momma. And for me. Should I have interrupted Jim's brush with death to tell Daddy? Didn't he have enough on him right now? I wondered if something had gone wrong at the hospital. The nurse would have said something if that was the case, wouldn't she? She didn't sound worried, just bossy. Like "I'm a heart specialist's nurse and you're just a country doctor's receptionist." It was mean of her to hang up without telling me anything.

After another few minutes Jim's pulse had slowed to almost normal and his blood pressure was good. I thought maybe his face was a little less red. Still Daddy had not let go of his wrist. He was holding onto him, calming him and comforting him, willing him to get better.

Jim had calmed down enough to start worrying about his dogs. It was cold and they were stuck out front in their traveling kennels. "Can somebody call Gary to come get the dogs and take them back home?" he asked Daddy.

"That's no problem," Daddy said. "Carolyn, will you call Gary to get the dogs?"

"Sure," I said, happy to have something else to do.

I made the call and paced around for about ten minutes until Gary arrived, also dressed in mismatched camouflage.

When I walked him back to Room 1, telling him Jim was having an allergic reaction to a single antibiotic pill, Daddy was asking, "Have you ever had a reaction to any medicine before?"

"Well, a couple a times when my throat would get scratchy I took a pill or two out of some my wife had left over," Jim said. "I think maybe once or twice when I took them I felt a little itching and didn't take no more."

"Do you know what they were?"

"No. They's whatever you give her last time."

Daddy looked up at me and I said, "I'll get her chart."

Sure enough, it was another cephalosporin group antibiotic. Jim had developed an allergy to cephalosporin after taking a few of his wife's left-over pills. Then he'd taken another one today, and that had turned out to be one too many.

"Well, we know what you're allergic to now. That's a whole group of antibiotics you can't take now," Daddy said. Then he added, "The shot we gave you should settle things down. Now we'll just wait till you get to feeling better."

Jim cooled down enough for the little fan to be turned off, but then he started to shake. He was trembling uncontrollably, all over—arms, legs, torso, head—like he had severe chills.

"This looks sort of scary," Daddy said to Gary, "but it's completely normal for anyone who's just been given a shot of adrenaline."

I was confused by the new problem. "How do you know when the reaction's over?" I said stupidly.

Daddy shot me a private look that would kill and said gently and vaguely for Jim and Gary's benefit, "Just wait and watch."

The phone rang again.

"*This* is Dr. Goldman's *nurse*." Her voice was very forceful and authoritative. "Dr. Goldman needs to speak with the doctor."

I wasn't some little receptionist they could push

around. I was a freaking Senate Counsel. And I was getting irritated. I said, "I *know* he does. And I'm telling you," I said turning my back to the waiting room so I wouldn't be overheard, "he can't come to the phone right now."

"But this is about *Mrs. Jourdan!*"

"I'm sorry," I said, "but the doctor *can't* come to the phone, will you *please* leave a message?"

"We're calling about the doctor's *wife!*" the nurse said.

"I know who it is!" I snapped back. "She's *my* mother!"

There was a long silence on the other end of the phone. Maybe Dr. Goldman had already been talking to his staff about our working during Momma's operation. Maybe he'd made comments to his nurse about how very odd we were.

This time she begged, "Will you just tell Dr. Jourdan that Dr. Goldman wants to talk to him?"

"No . . . I won't," I said. How could I explain? Was I supposed to say, "No, he can't come to the phone to talk about his wife who might be dying because he's got a guy right here in his own office who might also be dying"? I didn't want to have to get into the details.

I said, "I'm telling you he's busy—*real* busy. He's with a patient, and I'm not going in there right now to ask him if he wants to take a damn phone call! Why can't you just give me the message? I'm a relative too."

The nurse slammed her receiver down and I did the same. I left the desk and again went to stand in the hall and wring my hands, listening to Dad and Jim. What the hell was going on with Momma? How had I gotten into this mess? I was just supposed to be the receptionist. Just for two days! This was already the third day and people were maybe dying left and right and they all wanted to talk at the same time and I couldn't do anything about anything. I wanted my life back. I wanted to be in charge, in a world I could understand and control—a world where I was smart and successful and everyone knew it.

We all watched Jim and waited. Over the course of five or ten minutes the redness in his face faded, the blotches on his feet disappeared, and his tremors subsided. Whew. Everybody relaxed. And then it all started again. Jim's face turned fiery red, he began to sweat heavily, the blotches came back, and his pulse skyrocketed.

Now we were all truly afraid. Daddy had a second shot of Benadryl and adrenaline standing by for just such an event and gave it to Jim now.

Gary stood at the end of the examining table behind Jim's head. Every so often Jim would roll his eyes back so he could see his brother. I wished he would stop doing it. Seeing his eyes roll back in his head like that was unnerving. Every time I thought he was fainting or dying. Gary awkwardly patted the sides of his brother's head and said in a comforting but worried voice, "This is scary, isn't it buddy?" Jim just nodded in agreement. He couldn't speak because he was gritting his teeth.

I had to grit my teeth too. I wanted to go back to Washington. This was not the job for me. I didn't have the guts for it. I wanted to help people, but I wanted them to be strangers, and I wanted to do it from a vast impersonal distance. To hell with trying to save a dying friend from less than an arm's length away.

I was glad I wasn't responsible, glad I didn't have to make decisions about what to do and then stare into someone's eyes while waiting to see if my bright ideas panned out. Or not. Jim would die right there in front of us all if Daddy guessed wrong.

What if he picked the wrong medicine, or not enough of it, or too much, or made any kind of mistake, or had gone to lunch, or taken the day off? This was why he had stopped taking vacations years ago. A patient died every time he left town, so he got afraid to leave. He thought maybe if he stayed he could keep everyone alive.

While everyone waited, Daddy explained to Jim that there were three depths he could give the injections. "The deeper the injection," he said, "the faster the medicine gets into the body." He'd had Alma give the first injection deep into an arm muscle because he didn't know how serious the attack was going to be. He'd given the second injection shallow in the skin of the arm. So it would take effect more slowly.

What he didn't tell Jim was that he had a very long needle he could use, and in fact had used on two previous occasions, to inject adrenaline directly into the heart. I prayed he wasn't going to have to get the big needle out of the special glass case where all the last ditch remedies resided. When I was a child I'd stood on tiptoe a hundred times to look into that glass-covered stainless steel box at "the longest needle." It was the scariest thing in the office. I could look through the glass, but was forbidden to touch the box. It had an almost religious taboo for me even now as an adult.

The phone rang again.

This time it was Dr. Goldman himself. He said impatiently, "This is Dr. Goldman, Mrs. Jourdan's cardiologist. I need to speak to Dr. Jourdan about his wife."

I tried to stay calm, but my voice was quavering when I said, "Dr. Goldman, this is the doctor's daughter, Carolyn." I swiveled on my stool again so as to face away from the waiting room so the patients couldn't hear me. I whispered rapidly, holding my hand over my mouth and the receiver. "I don't mean to be rude sir, but the doctor is working."

"What? I can't hear you," he snapped.

I slid off the stool and crouched with the phone beneath the level of the reception counter. "The doctor's with a man who's in anaphylactic shock right now. He may be, you know, *dying*. So Daddy can't come to the phone."

There was absolute silence from Dr. Goldman. I could hear him thinking, *My God, not only do they not care about the wife and mother, but they're killing another one right now in their office.*

I stumbled on, "I'll have him get right back to you, when he, the man, does something, either stabilizes or, you know what I mean." Again, silence from Dr. Goldman.

My mind was gone now. It took all the concentration I had to not sob openly into the phone. Dr. Goldman was still silent. "Can you, ah, tell me," I finally said, "you know, I'm not the doctor, but could you tell me if my momma is still alive?"

"Of course she's *alive!*" he shouted. "She's doing *fine.*" His tone seemed to imply that he didn't kill people who came to him for help like we did.

Dr. Goldman said, a lot more kindly this time, "Have Dr. Jourdan call me when things settle down there and I'll tell him what we found."

I sat in the floor still clutching the phone in a death grip, listening to the dial tone, wiping off my face with one hand.

The crisis in Room 1 had been going on for more than thirty minutes now, so I decided I'd better explain to the people in the waiting room what was happening. I leaned across my counter and told them the doctor was having to stay with a man who was *very* sick, but we hoped to get to them soon.

I glanced down at the registration sheet to see how backed up we were and found one name I couldn't account for. Mrs. Dill. She wasn't out front. Where was she? Room 3? Oh no! We'd forgotten the lady in Room 3. We'd taken her back there and left her with a thermometer in her mouth for thirty minutes. I dashed back down the hall, and sure enough, there she was, sitting on the examining table smiling. She'd laid the thermometer down beside her. I started apologizing and she interrupted me. "Honey, I can hear that feller down the hall. Don't worry about me. You just get him fixed up first. I don't mind the wait."

Daddy walked out of Room 1 into the hallway. "You should go on to the hospital once we get you stabilized from this second injection," he said to Jim. "You'll have thirty minutes or so to get there before this all starts again, if it's going to start again."

Gary had me dial his son to come get Jim's dogs and his truck. Then we called Jim's wife to meet them at the hospital. He tried to pay for the two shots, but Daddy said, "There won't be any charge for that."

"I guess we won't be getting the windshield wipers fixed for a while," I said as I watched him being driven away.

Daddy looked up at the ceiling, his arms drooping at his sides. "Why is it always people like *that*

that these things happen to? Why isn't it ever the ones nobody can stand, or the crazy ones? It's always the *last* person in the *world* you would want it to happen to!"

I said, "I was wondering the same thing."

Then what he'd said hit me. Oh God! This sort of thing had happened before. Did this stuff happen a lot?

"How often does this kind of thing happen?" I asked, trying to sound casual.

"Maybe once a year," Daddy said. "For maybe an hour a year something scary will happen. Then the rest of the time it's just looking down sore throats."

An hour a year. I'd be long gone before the next one.

I gave him about fifteen seconds to catch his breath, then I told him about Dr. Goldman's call. He was mortified. In forty years he'd never failed to come to the phone for another doctor and now this, and it was about his own wife. He said I'd done the right thing, but I could tell he was as miserable, humiliated, and conflicted about it as I'd been.

He went back to his private office and tried to return Dr. Goldman's call, but it was too late. Dr. Goldman was gone and his answering service didn't know anything. We'd just have to wait to find out how Momma had done.

Daddy walked slowly down the hall toward Room

3 to see poor Mrs. Dill. Then he had to see the other eight patients who'd backed up in the waiting room while he was working on Jim.

Finally, we learned that Momma was fine. The heart catheterization revealed that she had only a partial blockage of a single vessel. Dr. Goldman had gone ahead and put in a stent, some sort of high-tech culvert for blood vessels, and said Momma had experienced no problems at all. Thus, her heart was fixed and was not only good as new, but was better than it had been in years. She was now Bionic Momma. I was nearly overcome with relief. My mother was alive and kicking and expected to stay that way for years to come. And, as a bonus, it appeared that Jim would stay alive too. The day was really looking up.

EIGHT

Tuesday morning was remarkably unremarkable, but I accumulated a pile of paperwork, so I stayed in the office during the lunch break. I'd asked Daddy to bring me a Diet Coke and a burgerless cheeseburger from the McDonald's drive-thru. I ate sitting on Momma's stool, staring out over the heads of the people in the waiting room, through the picture window, toward the parking lot, and then to the highway beyond. While I contemplated all the people free to drive up and down the highway at will, someone suddenly stood bolt upright. It was Ralphine Furrow, a young woman in her twenties. Without saying anything she headed for the restroom at high speed holding one hand over her mouth. She jerked at the knob, but the door wouldn't budge. Someone else was already inside. Ralphine rattled the knob, left hand still covering her mouth, and a haughty female voice said from inside, "It'll be *just* a *minute.*"

Ralphine turned to look at me with her eyes bulging. I started to ask what was wrong, but I barely got out the "Wha—" when yellow liquid spewed out from between her fingers. Oh. That was what was wrong.

Because I'd grown up around this sort of thing, it didn't strike me the way it would other people. I observed it with a kind of surprised detachment. During the few seconds it took me to locate a basin to hand her, she wandered off down the hall, vomiting as she went. I called out too late, "There's no bathroom back there. This is the only one!"

But Ralphine still didn't stop, so Alma, who'd heard the retching, called out in her most authoritative voice, "Stop! Stay right where you are. Don't you *dare* move." Ralphine stopped and then looked around herself in a daze.

In the ensuing silence, the belated flush of the toilet was painfully obvious. The lady who'd been in the bathroom couldn't have missed or mistaken the noises. She opened the door and peered out warily. But she wasn't going to be able to leave the room she was in. Neither was anybody else. Heads were poking out of every room up and down the hall, but nobody could go anywhere because the hall floor was awash. Daddy, Alma, Ralphine, a couple of patients, and the lady in the bathroom were all trapped where they were.

Then it occurred to me. Nobody could move but *me*. I could take off right now and no one could follow me and drag me back. But in a tragic irony, a situation had finally presented itself wherein I was needed and, unbelievably, I actually knew what to do.

I grabbed a roll of paper towels and went toward

the closest edge of the mess. I bent to swab, but Alma called out, "Wait!"

"Wait?" I said. "Don't worry," I laughed, "we've finally found a job I'm perfectly qualified for."

"Well, . . . actually you're not," Alma said. "OSHA has regulations on cleaning up biohazardous materials, and you've got to be trained and certified," she said.

"You're joking," I said. "OSHA has regulations on how to clean up barf?"

"Yes. No. You can't use those paper towels."

Daddy said, "Forget it. Go ahead. Let them fine me. It can't be that much."

"A couple thousand dollars," Alma said. "Carolyn, there's a biohazard spill kit up there in the cabinet. It's in the corner in a sealed white plastic tub."

I retrieved the kit and held it up so Alma could see it. It was sealed with an impressive array of warning stickers.

"Break the seals," Alma said, "and look inside for the stuff that soaks up biohazard liquids."

I broke the seals and opened the large plastic container. It held a pair of clear plastic gloves and a vial the size of my little finger containing flakes of some sort. "Is this what you mean?" I asked, holding up the tiny glass vial.

"I don't know. It's a new regulation and we haven't ever had to open a spill kit before," Alma said. "What else is in there?"

"Nothing," I said rotating the tub so she could see it was empty.

"What did we pay for that?" Daddy asked.

"A hundred and fifty dollars," Alma said. "Well, throw the stuff in the vial onto the spill."

I tossed the teaspoon of tan flakes, which looked suspiciously like fish food, into the middle of the closest puddle. We stared at the flakes as they slowly sank, disappearing with no visible effect. I had to laugh. "Our government at work! Wow! That stuff made all the difference. What do you want me to do now?"

Daddy said tiredly, "Get the mop."

It took a mop and three rolls of paper towels to clean up the mess. When Ralphine had gone I realized I'd finally risen to a medical challenge. I felt competent for the first time since I'd arrived.

The feeling didn't last long. About 1:30, Alma came to my momentarily clean desk carrying a huge armload of paper. She dropped the stack in front of me and said, "Mail."

"What am I supposed to do with all this?"

"Open it."

It must've been a week's worth. We had *JAMA: The Journal of the American Medical Association*, with yet another painting on the cover of an especially slow and painful death selected by someone with clinical depression. *JAMA* had access to an apparently unlimited collection of art by and for the suicidal. I tossed the magazine aside. Same thing for *Cutis*, with a life-size, full-color photo of a hideous skin condition on its cover. Then there were half a dozen glossy financial magazines specially targeting physicians.

As I opened one after another envelope containing cleverly disguised junk mail, I was experiencing such a precipitous loss of status that at any minute I expected to get a nosebleed. I hadn't realized it was possible for a person, especially *me,* to be treated so differently based simply on the job they held.

My whole life I'd been treated like Miss Smarty Special Person. I'd assumed it was because whenever anyone looked at me, that's what they saw. It was now becoming apparent that I'd been treated well because I'd been standing next to well-known, smart, powerful men: a federal judge, a congressman, a senator. I was quickly discovering that when I wore a $29 outfit and sat on a wooden stool answering the phone, my genius was no longer obvious to passersby.

I was also learning that one of the very lowest positions in the societal pecking order was allotted to the person who answered the phone in a doctor's office. And the job was not only thankless; it was hard too. Everybody you talked to was either sick and cranky or at their wit's end trying to take care of someone else who was sick and cranky. Of course, they might also be crazy, senile, angry, or obnoxious. Every time the phone rang it was a new challenge to try to follow the train of a frustrated, confused, or panicked conversation.

Freda Bolinger called, obviously in distress, and asked if the doctor would please call her in some nerve pills.

"What's the problem?" I asked in a bored tone.

Freda said she was about to leave for the hospital and was going to have to decide whether or not to pull the plug on her father.

"Oh goodness!" I said. "I'm sorry!" I knew my father would always give tranquilizers to patients who had immediate family members in extremis. "Don't worry, we'll call you something in."

"Thank you. I really need it."

"What happened?" I asked.

"Well, you know he's had five bypasses and has only two-thirds of a lung anyway and emphysema. *Now* he's got pneumonia. They don't think he's gonna make it."

"That's awful. I'm so sorry. How long has he been in a coma?"

"He's not in a coma."

"Oh, well. Unconscious then."

"He's not unconscious. I was just talking to him."

I said, "Is he *asking* you to do it?" What an awful situation to be in. I felt bad for her.

"No," she said, "he's not asking."

This was baffling. "Is he just rambling, talking out of his head?"

"Oh, no, his mind is fine."

I said, "Well, why would you be pulling the plug on him then? I don't understand."

"He always said if he ever got real sick, he wanted us to just let him go. That he wouldn't want to live like that."

"Is he *still* saying that?"

"No, but he used to say it *all* the time. I bet he's told me that a hundred times."

I perceived an overlooked distinction between the phrase "let him go" and "make him go." I was confused and shocked and frightened out of my mind for Freda's father, but I pulled myself together and attempted to inject reason into the situation as diplomatically as possible. I was, after all, a medical professional.

"Freda, you know, I don't think they'll let you do it that way. If he's still talking, I think the hospital and the doctors, you know, ask *him* what he wants. And then they have to go with what *he* says. They won't ask *you* unless they can't ask *him*. You know what I mean? At least I'm pretty sure that's the way it works. But hold on a minute and I'll ask the doctor." Good Lord. Murder was about to be committed.

I put Freda on hold and went to the back to interrupt my father, who was seeing another patient. I told him in a horrified whisper about the conversation. "What does she mean 'pull the plug' anyway?" I said. "The man's not on a respirator! Is she gonna have somebody hold a pillow over his

117

face or what? We've got to *do* something! *What do* we *do?*"

Daddy didn't like to be interrupted when he was examining a patient. He asked in a tired voice, enunciating each word carefully, "What . . . does . . . she . . . want?"

"Oh," I said, "she's asking for some nerve pills."

Daddy gave me his head-tilted-eyebrows-raised look and said, "Carolyn, wouldn't you agree that *this* is a *perfect* example of somebody who would *clearly benefit* from the use of a tranquilizer?"

"Oh *yeah! Good point.*" I'd lost sight of the simpler and more treatable medical condition. No telling how many lives had been saved by the judicious administration of strong tranquilizers to healthy bystanders. I raced back to the phone. "Freda," I said, "I'll call in those nerve pills for you right now." And then, I thought, I'd like to call in some for myself.

NINE

I was living *The Commedia*. I needed to change some of Dante's nomenclature, though. Upper Hell could still contain the incontinent but some of the rings would have to be renamed for the hypochondriacs, the accident prone, and people with coughs and runny noses. Nether Hell could still be for the violent, but I'd rename some of the rings for vomiting, diarrhea, and reserve the special lake in the middle for rectal and foot-related ailments.

I couldn't wait to get out of the office and go home—to somewhere safe and quiet and predictable. But then, shortly before it was time to quit for the day, Daddy came to my counter and said in an offhand way, "Carolyn, call over to the mines and ask Matt DeHaven what's the easiest way to get enough dynamite to blow three stumps."

So much for safety and quiet.

At age nineteen Daddy had been trained by the Marines to be a demolitions man in the Korean War. And then, like so many other Appalachian mountain men, he'd transferred his new skills to civilian life by turning farming into a paramilitary exercise.

"Which stumps?" I asked, so I'd have an idea of

the size of the explosion he was planning.

"The oak ones near the log barn."

Of course it would be those. They were huge. The oak trees had shaded a log barn for more than 150 years. They'd finally been killed by lightning, and the tall stumps stood charred and rotting in the hayfield. He'd been mowing around them forever.

Blowing stumps out of the ground with dynamite was standard procedure locally if the stumps were too large to pull out with a tractor. Daddy had done it several times, each time encountering some little technical snafu that resulted in a near-death experience. Now he was using Matthew's guilt over getting a free goat x-ray as leverage to extort some dynamite so he could do it again.

I dialed the mine. "Hey Darla, it's Carolyn at Dr. Jourdan's office, can I speak to Matthew DeHaven?"

"Hey Carolyn. Matt's not scheduled to be at work right now. He won't be in until tomorrow morning."

Damn. The miners worked rotating shifts, so it was hard to tell where they might be at any given time.

"Do you want to leave a message?" she asked. "I can try to leave it where he'll see it. But he's a foreman, so he stays underground most of the time."

I knew better than to leave a message asking for dynamite or to make Matthew have to talk about it from the telephone in the main office. The miners had their own ways of getting the stuff and I didn't want to draw attention to what might not be a strictly legal transaction. "No," I said, "that's okay." I thanked her and hung up.

I looked up his home phone number and dialed it. I let it ring a few times, but there was no answer. How frustrating.

I told Daddy about my lack of progress.

"Well, I'll go on home and get everything fed if you'll run by his house and see if you can find him," he said.

I nodded and grabbed my car keys.

Matthew's family farm was about five miles from the office. It was a local showplace: an enormous old white farmhouse and several huge barns sitting in the center of hundreds of acres of rolling vivid green fields surrounded with pristine white board fences.

From the road, before I reached the house, I spotted a tractor moving about in a hayfield. I pulled onto the shoulder and looked closer until I made out Matthew on the tractor. He was mowing in great concentric squares. At the moment he was heading away from me. I got out of the car and stood at the edge of the field and watched him mow. When he turned a corner and began to make a pass parallel to the road, he saw me and waved. I climbed over the fence with the ease of long legs and forty years of practice. I estimated his speed and set off walking along a diagonal that would intercept him after he turned the next corner and began to mow toward the road.

When I got within a few feet of him, he stepped on the clutch to stop the tractor from rolling, but the noise of the engine and the mower was so loud I'd have had to shout at the top of my lungs to be heard. He reached down with his right hand and before I had time to think about it, I'd reached up and he'd pulled me up to sit atop the wide rounded fender close beside him. He immediately let the clutch out and continued to mow. I laughed to find myself riding with him the same way we'd both ridden with our fathers. For farm kids a lot of quality time is spent riding on a tractor with Daddy.

The tractor was moving only five miles an hour or so. Matthew seemed perfectly at ease and we both remained silent for a couple of minutes, hypnotized by the noise and vibration and bright sun. It was relaxing to roll through the field watching the grasshoppers spring out of the way. I marveled at the patience it would take to mow such a huge field. Then I suddenly came back to myself and said, "Daddy wanted me to ask you for some dynamite."

Matthew shot me a mild questioning look.

"He wants to blow some stumps in the hayfield."

He nodded. "How big?"

"*Real* big. Three oak trees, couple of hundred years old."

He nodded again.

"Just tell me when you've got it," I said, "and I'll come pick it up."

He smiled at me and shook his head.

I felt patronized and disappointed that he would turn out to be one of *those* kind of guys. "I'm not scared of dynamite!" I snapped.

He kept his face forward. "I'm sure you're not," he said.

This might have been East Tennessee, but I'd been living in Washington for a long time. I wasn't going to let anybody, even Matthew Wyatt DeHaven III, exclude me from anything just because I happened to be female. Even though I positively dreaded having to stand around while Daddy handled powerful explosives fifty years after his brief training course, I lied and said, "Daddy knows how to use dynamite. And he always lets me help him with stuff. We can handle it."

Matthew turned to face me at point blank range. "I'm sure you can, and I could probably sew myself up if I had to. But, Carolyn, I make my *living* shooting dynamite. Y'all stick to doctoring, and let me do this. Okay?"

I had to admit that what he said made sense. Well, I was willing to admit it to myself. I wouldn't have admitted it to him even if he'd held a gun to my head.

Then he said, "Give me a few days and I'll be over."

His mowing had brought us to an edge of the

field near an especially fancy-looking paddock. "Come look," he said, cutting the engine.

A huge area was surrounded by a high-tensile wire fence that was more than seven feet tall. That was very expensive fencing, so it had to be protecting something special. I looked around to see what that might be. All I saw was a group of small, cute, spotted goats. Matthew opened the gate and I went toward them.

I put out my hand to pet the closest one and it began to move away from me slowly. I followed it as it walked away, its gait becoming oddly stiff-legged. Just before I got within touching distance, the goat fell over on its side. I was horrified. Then the two goats nearest to us did the same thing. I turned and gaped at Matthew in open-mouthed shock.

He burst out laughing, "Don't worry, they're fainting goats. You've heard of them, haven't you?"

I jerked my head in a quick nod. I'd heard of them, but never seen one of them do their famous trick. They were a rare indigenous breed, Tennessee fainting goats. I quickly recovered from my embarrassment and wondered why in the hell anybody would want an animal that swooned when you got near it. "Why do they do that?" I asked.

"I don't know. It had to be some sort of spontaneous defect that occurred in the breeding line, but since it was so useful, they breed for it instead of away from it."

"Useful?"

"People put them in the field with valuable stock. As protection."

"What kind of protection is an animal that faints?"

"The coyote or wolf, or whatever it is, eats the goats until he's full. That way he leaves the expensive animals alone."

"Oh." How pitiful. I couldn't help but be moved by these pretty little creatures whose sole purpose in life was to be economical predator-fodder. As we walked through the pasture we left a trail strewn with little goats lying on their sides. None of them had gotten back up yet, either. How long did they stay like that? Maybe Matthew was lying and they were dead.

When Matthew saw my expression, he said, "Don't worry. They're fine. Really. They're pets. I'll never sell them and Lloyd won't let anything get near them."

"Who's Lloyd?"

Matthew nodded toward a tree fifty yards away. I saw the tree, but couldn't see anything else. Matthew whistled and a white blob moved. A white dog stood up. The dog was huge and it had the bushiest fur I'd ever seen.

"Lloyd lives out here with the animals and keeps predators away."

"He looks big."

"A hundred and twenty-five pounds. Great Pyrenees get attached to animals way more than they do to people. Lloyd loves all these little rascals," he swept his arm around, indicating the whole field. "Even on the coldest nights I can't get him to come in the house. He won't leave this field. It's his job and he takes it serious. He's smart too. He stays down, off to the side of the animals where you wouldn't notice him, and holds real still. He won't stand up until it's time to move with the herds. Unless something comes into the field, that is. It's funny to watch when somebody tries to come near the animals. He lets them get right up on him before he stands up. Then it's *way* too late to get away. He can be pretty scary."

"Is he mean?"

"Not really, but he's very protective. He'll kill any animal that intrudes into his field, and unfortunately that includes a house pet. And he'll hold a man down. But he won't bother anything that stays outside the fence. And he'll never hurt any of the animals he watches over. Some of the babies sleep next to him." He pointed up a small hill to the edge of the woods and said, "I got a herd of fallow deer in here too. They're real shy. Hard to see."

I looked and at first didn't see anything. Then I saw movement and realized there was a lovely group of tiny deer with big antlers. They looked like miniature reindeer.

Then I felt something pluck at the back of my pants and wheeled around.

Matthew was laughing again. "Don't be scared.

That's Phillip. He won't hurt you. He's just real curious."

I jerked in surprise when I found myself looking nearly point blank into the eyes of some sort of prehistoric creature with a small head, pointed beak, and a huge pair of unblinking brown eyes that were *at the same level as mine*. The creature's eyelashes were at least two inches long. I had a nervous moment before I realized what I was looking at.

"An ostrich?" I asked.

"Emu. They make better pets."

Phillip's long, hairy, serpentlike neck was a bit disconcerting, but he seemed gentle and friendly. I reached to stroke his feathered back.

Matthew said quickly, "Don't do that!"

But it was too late. Phillip's legs buckled and he flopped to ground, flat as a pancake, the instant I touched him. I shrieked.

"It's okay! It's okay. Don't worry," Matthew said through his laughter. "You didn't hurt him. It's a reflex. They all do that if you touch them on the back. It's a protective instinct. Their mommas use it to make them hide when anything dangerous comes near."

I looked up at him in confusion.

"The mommas hide the babies by touching them on the back and making them squat down on the ground. Then she runs off with a big show so the predator chases her and doesn't see the baby."

Phillip stood up quickly, apparently none the worse for wear, and continued to peer into my face at close range. He didn't seem to be holding a grudge either. What a sweet animal.

So the dingo, or whatever, ate the momma emu? Everything around here was a little too close to a slavering mouth in the food chain for my peace of mind. And all any of them had to rely on was a possumlike tactic. That was no defense at all. It was horrific. In my overflowing compassion for Phillip's situation, without thinking, I reached to pat him again.

Big mistake.

I stared, appalled, at his deflated body, collapsed at my feet for a second time in less than a minute and felt my face go red. Tears started to leak out of my eyes. All this dropping over was getting to be too much, and it was too close to what I pictured had happened to Momma. I needed it to stop.

Matthew stopped laughing when he saw my face and, misunderstanding the cause of my upset, said, "Oh Carolyn, don't cry. He's fine. You should see him run. Emus can't fly, but they don't need to. They're unbelievably fast. Nothing can catch them."

Phillip got up again and still didn't seem pissed off. I put my hands in my pockets this time to prevent any further incidents.

"Want to see the sheep? I raise three endangered breeds. I keep a white mule and some donkeys in the field to watch over them."

Good Lord, he had attack mules and donkeys? At the idea that there was yet more of this survival of the fittest to be experienced firsthand, I almost fell to the ground myself, but I tried to be polite and said, "Oh, no thanks, maybe later. I better get on home."

Daddy's office suddenly seemed like a peaceful and safe hidey-hole. I sure as hell wasn't going to touch anything else around here. The whole place was an incomprehensible jumble of predators and victims.

Matthew nodded. "Well, you can meet Forrest on the way out."

"Forrest?"

"Forrest Gump."

"What?"

"He's a water buffalo. He was in the movie *Forrest Gump*."

"What?"

"You know the scene where Forrest is talking about how in Vietnam they took long walks every day?"

"Yeah?"

"Well, there's a water buffalo in that scene. The soldiers walk right past him, along the edge of a rice paddy."

"Yeah?"

"I bought him. That's him." He pointed to a monstrously big brown animal that looked like a cross between a Brahma bull, a short-haired buffalo, and something African with unusually shaped horns. "I named him Forrest."

The man had bought a water buffalo because it was in the movie *Forrest Gump*. That was my favorite movie. I'd started crying during the opening credits and just kept on the whole way through. I'd been the different kid in my school—the one with the orthopedic shoes and the crossed eyes. I identified with Forrest and the way he was tormented by people for things he couldn't do anything about.

I thought to myself, *Run, Forrest. Run!*

But Forrest the water buffalo didn't look like he would run from anybody. He was huge and had gigantic swept-back horns. I noticed there was an especially stout fence around him. He was looking at us as we walked past.

Matthew said, embarrassed, "Sometimes I can't understand why I bought him. I guess everybody's crazy at least once in their life for just long enough to raise their hand at a rare animal auction. He wasn't that expensive, but it cost a fortune to get him here."

"From Vietnam or Hollywood?"

"He was in Iowa when I bought him."

I wondered how he'd gotten to Iowa. Had he been born and raised in Iowa and flown to Asia for his big scene? Then flown back to Iowa? Or had he been born and raised in Asia and brought to America after the film was shot? Either way, *why?*

"He's pretty mean," Matthew said. "You can't get into the field with him."

Hunh, I thought, star mentality. The buffalo had been in a movie. Okay, so the movie had won a carload of Oscars, but the buffalo had been in only *one scene,* and he'd already gotten an attitude.

TEN

I'd been at the office for a full week and Jacob called to mark the occasion. "How are you?" he asked.

"Fine," I lied.

"I will assume that was a falsehood bravely told for the sake of preserving civility," he said.

"You would be correct in that assumption," I said. "What's new?"

"Hmm, let's see. Oh, sorry you missed a fantastic event at the French ambassador's," he said. "I've never seen anything like it. He seemed to be trying to reproduce the effect of eighteenth-century French court life—and for the most part he pulled it off. But, hey, the guy's a nobleman, so maybe that's just the way he lives. The dinner was served at this long, long table in a gilded and mirrored dining room lit by about half a million candles and there was a separate waiter who stood behind each chair throughout the entire meal."

"You're kidding. Liveried footmen? Did they wear white gloves and powdered wigs?"

"Gloves, yes, wigs, no. But mine did help me into my chair and then, to my surprise, he unfolded and placed my napkin in my lap. I thought males over the age of five could be trusted to do that job for themselves, but apparently not in France. He remained *very* close throughout the meal, prepared, I believe, to step in at a moment's notice to correct any mistakes in my table manners."

"Did you make any?" I asked.

"I'm pleased to report that his intervention was not required."

"Thank goodness. Well, you *are* a very civilized, very urbane guy."

"I like to think so," he said. "That's all the news here. The Senate's still out, so not much is happening in the office."

"Well, the big news from White Oak is that Daddy and I've reached a standoff about meals. I won't cook meat and he won't eat vegetables, so it's been fast food for both of us."

"Sorry. That's rough. Oh, guess what? I just realized we're going to have a fascinating question of separation of powers come up in the next hearing."

"Please tell me you've not got your head stuck in *The Federalist Papers* again."

"Federalism is my passion," Jacob said.

"Jacob, believe me, this I know," I said, lamenting the ways of Washington. "What could possibly be more stimulating than wrangling over questions of Original Intent of the Founding Fathers?"

Jacob was a true scholar. Both of his parents were college professors. Nothing in life made him happier than pawing through a cavern filled with the dusty papers of someone like James Madison for a few months and then writing an article with a couple of hundred footnotes for some arcane journal.

On the Bicentennial of the Constitution he'd taken me on a date where we, along with a million other people, spent all night inching up the steps of the National Archive to see what Jacob had breathlessly described as "a once-in-a-lifetime event: the *entire* U.S. Constitution on display." For his thirtieth birthday present, he'd made me go with him to an obscure warehouse leased by the National Archive and listen to an assortment of Nixon tapes.

"By the way, when are you coming back?" he asked.

"I'm not sure. I think I'll need to stay at least another week or so and finish out the month's bookkeeping. Is that a problem?"

"Not for me," he said.

"I miss you, Jacob."

"I miss you too, Carolyn."

"I miss *everything*."

"It'll be okay, Carolyn."

"When?"

Jacob diplomatically refrained from speculating.

"People around here vomit."

"Unnnhh."

"And they bleed and have rectal—"

"Thank you. I believe I have a picture."

"I'm a really *bad* receptionist."

"But you are a very fine attorney."

"Yeah, but—" I couldn't go on.

After an awkward pause, Jacob said, "Carolyn, I had the oddest dream about you last night."

"What was it?"

"We'd driven out into the country and, as I was driving along, you saw this very unusual looking animal standing in a field near the road. You made me stop so you could look at it. There was a big yellow sign on the fence that identified the animal as a 'Soft-Shelled Yak.' The sign said, 'Do Not Pet the Yak,' but you couldn't stand it. You just had to pet it. I begged you not to, but you climbed the fence and walked over to the yak and patted it on the head. It instantly fell over on its side. It dropped *dead* the instant you touched it. I guess that's what the 'soft-shelled' warning meant. Isn't that a nutty dream?"

I considered defending myself by suggesting that maybe the yak had just fainted, like Matthew's goats, but decided not to go there. "Yeah, nutty," I said.

After the first week, I intentionally blanked my mind with respect to time, otherwise I was pretty sure I was at risk for spontaneous human combustion. I didn't want to think of myself as a prisoner making scratch marks on the wall either, even mentally, so I spaced out.

We'd brought Momma home, but she wasn't the

same Momma I'd known. She was a wraith now, subdued and unsure of herself. She was also confused some of the time. We hoped it was temporary. Expectations were adjusted all round. I'd have to stay a bit longer.

"Dr. Jourdan's office," I said.

No one spoke, but I could hear a sound that was a mixture of whimpering and choking. Something rustled against the receiver and then a female voice shouted, "Shut up, I'm talking on the phone!"

"Is this Jourdan's office?" the woman said.

"Yes it is," I said.

"This is Opal Slimp. He's acting antsy and bothering me. He wants to come over there, but I don't think he needs to."

"Who's 'he'?" I asked.

"My idiot cousin, who else?"

"What's his *name?*" I asked.

"Adron."

"Adron Breedlove?" I asked.

She shouted into the phone again, "Adron, shut up!"

The horrible wheezing was clearly audible in the background. "Is that Adron making that funny sound?" I asked.

"What?"

"That awful sound in the background. I can hear it. Is that Adron having trouble?"

"He's such a pest. He won't leave me alone."

"It sounds like he's smothering. You'd better call

an ambulance right away and take him on to the hospital in Knoxville. He sounds really bad. He needs to get some help."

"What I *want*," she said, "is for the Doc to call him in some nerve pills, so he'll quit bothering me. He don't need to go to no hospital."

God, what a monster, I thought. Instead, I said, "I think you're wrong there. He's *bothering* you because he can't breathe. Nerve pills aren't what he needs right now. He needs somebody to help him out. Do you want me to call the ambulance for you?"

She slammed the phone down. I went and told Daddy what had happened. He shook his head. "Adron's been a heavy smoker all his life. It's catching up with him. Call over there in a little while and make sure she's sent him down to the hospital."

Thirty minutes later a car swerved into the parking lot. A huge woman got out of the driver's side in a singularly unflattering flowered housedress. Adron lurched out of the passenger side and scrambled toward the front door, looking back at the woman like she was the devil.

I called out to Daddy, "Adron's here."

Adron didn't seem to be able to get air into his lungs. I'd never heard anyone having such a struggle simply to breathe. He was making a great effort to inhale and inflating his chest, but you could tell that not much air was going in, just squeaks and rattles. His face was blue gray, his lips purple, and his eyes were wide with panic. He threw his arms around Daddy and hid his face in Daddy's chest.

Daddy held him. "It's okay Adron. We'll get you fixed up in just a minute. It's okay." He looked toward Alma and said, "Set up the oxygen." He pulled away from Adron slightly and said, "Adron, let's go in here and get you some air. Okay?"

Adron nodded and Daddy led him into Room 1. Just as Adron disappeared through one doorway, the huffing, puffing, hydra came in through the other. "Where the hell did he get to?" she said.

"Who are you?" I said, trying to imitate my mother's most authoritative tone.

She ignored me and started toward the examining rooms.

"You stop right there," I said. "I don't know who you are, but you go sit your ass down in the waiting room right this instant or leave. Or I can *help* you leave, whichever you want." I came around from behind the counter, letting my rage show.

She said, "Who the hell do you think you are?"

"The doctor's daughter," I said.

If she didn't turn around immediately I'd snatch up Alma's wooden stool and have a go at her with that. No way was I going to let this woman bully a retarded elderly bachelor who'd come to us for sanctuary. I was a purebred redneck, a thirteenth generation American, with untold riffraff simmering in my bloodstream. She was outclassed.

She turned toward the waiting room, where she stopped and looked at me over her shoulder. I remained standing in the hall, praying she'd be stupid enough to start back toward me. But she went outside instead and got into her car.

Cotton Barnard, who'd been sitting in the waiting room, said, "Wow, Carolyn. You was the image of your mother when you was telling that woman off. I didn't think anybody could get as tough as old Sarge, but you sure can. It was like watching the WWF."

I smiled and swung the stool at him in mock warning and then resumed my post behind the reception desk.

Adron was having a rough time. He got some sort of shot, a blast or two from an inhaler, and was breathing oxygen through a mask. The whistling noise was gone, but his lips were still working like a fish thrown up on the riverbank. Poor Adron, degraded and humiliated at every turn. He had a life like Quasimodo.

After about thirty minutes, Daddy came and asked me who was driving Adron. I pointed to the car.

"Who's that?" he asked warily.

"His cousin, and a worse specimen of humanity you would never want to meet."

"She looks pretty big," he said.

"And mean as hell too."

"Well, go get her," he said with resignation. "I've got to talk to her about Adron."

I went outside and told Ms. Slimp the doctor wanted to talk to her. She heaved herself out of the car and into the office.

"Ms. Slimp," Daddy said, "Adron needs to go on down to the hospital now. He's stable for a few minutes, but I don't have the equipment to handle him if he gets into another really bad broncho-spasm. He needs a breathing treatment. If you'll just take him straight on right now, you can get him there a lot quicker and cheaper than an ambulance. Which hospital do y'all use?"

"He don't need to go to no hospital," she said.

"He most certainly does," Daddy corrected. "He almost died just now."

"Give him some nerve pills so he'll leave me alone."

"You'd be nervous too if you couldn't breathe."

"He's driving me crazy complaining."

Something snapped in Daddy and he shouted, "The man's just about dead right now! Can't you see that? He can't breathe. Of course he's trying to get your attention. He needs help."

That seemed to subdue her. Daddy walked Adron out to the car, carefully rolling the oxygen tank alongside him. Then he tucked Adron into the backseat and set the tank in beside him. He told Adron half a dozen times not to remove the mask from over his nose and mouth. The situation was pitiful. Adron's eyes were large over the top of the oxygen mask. He looked at Daddy in trusting, pleading, adoration in between shooting fearful glances toward his cousin, his malevolent lifeline.

Adron searched through his pockets and produced a pollen mask. He held it up to show Daddy. Daddy said, "No, Adron, you don't need to wear that one right now. Just wear this new one till you get to the hospital, okay?"

And, as an added safety measure that wouldn't have occurred to me, Daddy reached into Adron's shirt pocket and removed an open pack of Camel cigarettes. "No smoking on the way to town. That would be dangerous while you're using this oxygen tank. Do you understand?"

Adron nodded, looking at the tank warily.

"Promise me," Daddy said, "you won't smoke on the way, okay?"

Adron nodded again, but I wondered if he really understood the danger.

Ms. Slimp drove off, with Adron in the backseat. Daddy and I stood in the parking lot and watched them disappear.

"Wow," I said. "I never would have thought about Adron trying to smoke on the way. That would've been a disaster."

Then we both started to giggle.

"Can you picture it?" I said. "The car would look like something out of Buck Rogers, tearing down the highway with flames coming out the back."

Daddy said, "Ms. Slimp never got such good mileage." Then he added, shaking his head, "His eye is on the sparrow, and I know He watches me."

ELEVEN

Momma was still spending most of her time sleeping or trying to figure out how to open medicine bottles and load the new pillbox I'd gotten her at Wal-Mart. It was a green plastic contraption that had twenty-eight separate compartments—seven columns for the days of the week and four rows for pill breaks throughout the day. She broke a fingernail trying to get one of the lids open, then complained about the fingernail more than she had about her heart.

I contemplated relative health hazards. In Washington I frequently had to endure headaches from camera lights, clip earrings, and a tight French twist. And I'd even gotten a stress fracture in my foot from standing too long on marble floors in high heels. But a lot of local men had *truly* dangerous jobs.

Wednesday morning a man walked up to the reception desk and laid an overstuffed manila envelope on the counter. He looked at me with sad brown eyes, but didn't say anything. Then he hesitantly pushed the envelope toward me. I picked it up and looked at it. It was from the personnel department of the local zinc mine.

Daddy had been the doctor for the zinc mines

for nearly forty years. So I took an educated guess. "Do you need a physical?"

He nodded.

Then I saw a note clipped to the top of the papers that bore one scribbled word: "Disability." Oh, it was a disability physical. That was a little surprising, though. The man looked healthy and younger than me. The papers were for a man named Billy Fitzgerald. I asked, "Are you Billy?" He nodded again.

I filled out his name, social security number, and birth date at the top of each of a half-dozen forms, along with other general information, and then he was ready to see the doctor. He seemed nervous and a bit depressed. I flipped through his paperwork. I scanned letters from an internist, a psychologist, and a psychiatrist saying Billy was permanently and totally disabled due to the trauma of witnessing an accident in the mine. His diagnosis was a "fixed delusional state caused by post traumatic stress syndrome." The prognosis was that he would never recover.

How awful. I wondered what he'd seen that had done that to him.

Daddy did the physical back in Room 3. When he finished, he came out and told me I'd need to pull the chart of one of the Sanders brothers and mark it "Deceased." He thought it was Frankie, but he wasn't sure. *Oh no,* I thought. I knew both of the Sanders brothers.

It was customary for each of the miners to be saddled by his coworkers with some outlandish nickname, the name he was known by underground. Often the miners knew each other only by these nicknames. Billy had referred to the dead man as Possum, a nickname Daddy didn't recognize. It wasn't unusual for Daddy not to know a nickname, because many of them were profane and sometimes even a man's own family wouldn't know it. But it was *very* unusual for Daddy not to know when someone had been killed. In fact, it was unheard of.

The mine personnel office was often the only place where the nicknames and real names could be matched up. I dialed them to see which chart I needed to pull.

"Hey Darla. This is Carolyn at Dr. Jourdan's office. We've got Billy Fitzgerald over here for his disability physical, and he told us about one of the Sanders brothers getting killed. That's awful. We didn't know anything about it. Who was it?"

"Did he just tell you that? Today? That Possum had been killed?" Darla asked.

"Yeah. We hadn't heard anything about it. What happened?" I knew from past experience it could have been one of several causes: a fall, electrocution, explosion, cave-in, or heavy equipment accident.

"Well, *no one* died. I can't believe he's still saying that."

"I don't understand. I thought he was here because

he was with Possum when he got killed, and he feels guilty or something and can't get over it."

"Goodness gracious! We had to go round and round with his internist, then his psychologist, and then finally with the psychiatrist. And now you too."

Daddy was standing at the counter, waiting to hear which man had died. He was making faces at me for not telling him quicker. I covered the mouthpiece and said, "Nobody died." But that just made things worse so now Daddy was asking what was going on at the same time Darla was explaining. There was a conversation going on in the background on Darla's end too.

Darla said, "Hang on a minute, Carolyn. Matt DeHaven's standing right here. He was there when it happened. I'm gonna send him down to explain. Okay? He'll be there in about five minutes."

"Okay," I said.

In a few minutes Matthew pulled up in front of the office. Matthew's nickname was Rambo, King of the G.I. Joes. I refused to speculate about how he'd gotten that one.

"Hey Doc. Hey Carolyn," he said. He leaned toward Daddy and me and whispered, "Where's Billy?"

"He's in a room in the back with the door shut," Daddy said. "He can't hear you."

"This is the craziest, awfulest story," Matthew said, shaking his head. "Billy and Possum, Frankie's called Possum, were raised together and came to work in the mines together. They worked as a team for years. Billy ran the drill and Possum did the blasting and cleanup."

I'd been into the mines and knew the routine. Billy would drill a couple of dozen holes about an inch in diameter, six to ten feet deep. When he finished drilling he'd move off a safe distance and start a new set of holes while Possum shoved dynamite in and set timed charges. He'd always drill in the same diamond shaped pattern, taking care not to redrill an old hole, because sometimes they contained unexploded dynamite. If he did that, the drill would set the dynamite off and kill him. While Billy was drilling the next set of holes, Possum would blow his section of the rock face to pieces and then load the bits of rock into a cart.

Matthew said, "Billy'd moved down the rock face and was drilling a new set of holes when a section of roof where they'd been working broke loose and fell. When Billy heard the popping he ran back to see what'd happened and found Possum buried under the rock shower. He'd been wearing his helmet but his face had got smacked against a corner of the waste rock cart and it'd knocked out an eye. Billy dug him out and ran with him to the hoist and the hoistman called an ambulance.

"It was pitiful. Billy wouldn't let go of him till the ambulance got there. Then one of the medics said Possum probably wouldn't make it to the hospital and Billy just went to pieces."

"That would be awful," I said. "Seeing your best friend get killed."

"But he didn't get killed! Possum didn't die. He was hurt terrible and it took nearly a year before he got well enough to come back to work, but he's back now. He's there today, in fact. But Billy just won't accept it. Nothing anybody says or does makes any difference. His psychiatrist even set up a meeting between the two of them at his office so Billy could see Possum was okay, but when Possum came in the room Billy went crazy. He thought Possum was a ghost or something. It's been over a year now and everybody has given up trying to reason with him."

Daddy said, "Well Matthew, I'll have to agree that he's disabled. But that's the strangest one I've ever heard."

"Yeah," Matthew said. "It's a tragedy." Then, after a moment of somber contemplation, he said, "I'll be over after work to blow those stumps for you, Doc. See you later."

Daddy sent me back to tell Billy he could go. As he left I watched his careful gait and slumped shoulders and tried to imagine what it would be like to live locked inside a nightmare. Then I wondered what kind of demon a man would have to be carrying that would punish him like that.

Daddy and I were out in the barnyard hammering loose boards back tight against the fence posts when Matthew drove up the long driveway. He got out of his truck holding an innocuous looking brown paper bag that I suspected contained enough dynamite to kill all three of us and at least half the cows on the farm.

"Hey Matt!" Daddy called out, waving to him.

"Hey Doc. Hey Carolyn," Matthew answered and flashed a smile. "If you'll show me those stumps, I'll shoot them for you."

"You don't have to do that, Matt," Daddy said. "I'm grateful for you getting the dynamite, but I'll do the blasting. It's okay. I've done it before."

I decided for a second time not to fill Matthew in on the details of Daddy's previous experiences with dynamite.

"Doc, I'd be in real trouble if anybody knew I brung this out of the mine, but I'd get in *worse* trouble if I let anybody else mess with it."

Daddy was visibly disappointed not to be in the lead, but still happy to be able to watch. Explosions were about as exciting as things got on White Oak Road. They had an obvious appeal to a man who bought expensive Russian military surplus night vision goggles so he could observe the ramblings of possums and skunks after dark and who had concocted a device as senseless as a "spud gun" (a precariously rigged combination of a four-foot length of PVC pipe, a sparking device, and a can of hairspray) designed for the sole purpose of hurling raw potatoes.

I really couldn't criticize him much, because it was fun to be able to watch the night creatures stirring, and the recoilless nature of the spud gun did enable me to appreciate what it was like to shoot a bazooka or a shoulder-mounted rocket launcher. Or so I was told.

Daddy and Matthew got into the front of our old blue pickup truck. I sat on the tailgate as we bounced through the hayfield to within a few feet of the stumps. Matthew rummaged around in the bag and produced two sticks wrapped in brown paper. He fished a pocketknife out of his jeans and cut each of the sticks in two, then punctured one end of each stick. He shoved little red caps into the holes he'd made. The caps trailed twenty or thirty feet of cord. Daddy told me to move the truck and I did, backing it up, but stopping close enough so Matthew would be able to stand behind it when he set off the blast.

Matthew scraped out niches in various places under the trees and set the dynamite. He backed up to the length of the electrical cord and took an ordinary looking fist-sized battery out of a back pocket. He said over his shoulder, "Cover your ears."

I covered my whole head and about two seconds later a deafening blast began ricocheting around the hollow. The noise was so extraordinarily loud and in such a distinct burst that I could follow it as it moved through the air—round and round White Oak Hollow, up and down the walls of the valley.

When I finally peeked, the trees were in a new position, lying over on their sides with their huge roots twisting into the air. Dirt clods had been tossed out for a dozen yards. Daddy and Matthew were beaming at each other.

"Thanks, Matt," Daddy said. "Now it'll be easy to drag these off with the tractor."

I didn't thank Matthew as effusively as I wanted to, because I didn't want to embarrass Daddy by indicating what a stupendous treat it was to have a dynamiting episode that ended without a single injury to man or beast. It was the first nondescript explosion in Daddy's entire blasting career, which, so far, had lasted from age nineteen to age seventy-two. That was *one* in fifty-three years.

The next morning, a shockingly emaciated Taylor Jackson came walking out of the examining room with a confused look on his face. I'd noticed in his chart that he'd been in several times recently, and each time he'd lost more weight. He'd always been a handsome man, over six feet tall, slender with a great shock of white hair and bright blue eyes. He came to my desk to pay his bill, and as our eyes met he said, "So what you're telling me is that I'm going all the way out on this'n."

I looked at him in confusion and thought to myself, *I haven't told you anything, Taylor.* Then I realized the significance of what he'd said. Daddy must have just told him he was dying. Surely he'd told him back in the privacy of the examining room and given him time to adjust to the news. Taylor must have walked out in a daze before it had sunk in.

I smiled into his blue eyes but I was frozen. I just couldn't think of anything appropriate to say.

"Just a minute, Mr. Jackson, let me get the doctor."

I went down the hall looking for Daddy.

"Dr. Jourdan," I called out.

Daddy was standing in his private office facing the only window in the room—a high, barred hole the size of four concrete blocks with several small cactus plants on the ledge. He was talking into a small black handheld tape recorder, dictating notes.

"He is bringing up very tenacious white sputum. No purulent or bloody sputum. He states he is now bringing it up both day and night. This is different from before. He now has spasms in the back around the belt line when he bends forward. He feels sure this is from a strain that he has had off and on this year. I, of course, wonder about metastatic lesions. He insists he cannot yet go to the pulmonary doctor for the test required for diagnosis. Apparently he is significantly financially stressed at this time."

I waited for him to finish recording his notes. "Mr. Jackson's out front, and I think he has some more questions to ask you," I said.

"Okay, I'll be up there in a second."

I went back to my desk. Taylor was sitting on the

hard wooden stool Alma kept in the lab area. He was clutching the two sputum sample bottles he'd been given for TB testing. The bones in his knuckles stood out and he sat hunched over in obvious distress.

"Maybe it's TB or something they can fix with medicine," I said.

He turned his head to look at me with a half smile. There was a wealth of meaning in the look. He didn't think he was going to get well, and he wanted to go with as little fuss as possible.

Now that I was paying attention to him I noticed how his shirt and slacks hung loosely on his thin frame. The skin covering his aristocratic cheekbones was gray green. I hoped it was the fluorescent lights and his shirt making him look that way.

Daddy came out and said, "Taylor, we can't be sure what you've got unless you agree to let the pulmonologist put an instrument down into your lungs and take a look. He can get a little piece of whatever it is while he's in there, and they can send it off to be analyzed so we'll be sure what we're dealing with here."

"No," Taylor said, shaking his head. "I don't want to go anywhere. I don't want all that. Let's just try this here," he said gesturing with the sputum bottles. "That'll be good enough."

We all stood around helplessly. Everyone stood in their normal place, but all eyes were on Taylor. I looked at Daddy and Alma to see what to do. We were all mimicking Taylor's stoop to varying degrees, head down, shoulders slumped.

Taylor looked up at Daddy and repeated the question he'd asked me, "So what you're saying is, I'm going all the way out on this'n?"

Taylor couldn't make himself use the *d* word. So Daddy did it for him. "Taylor, we're all dying."

"But some of us are headed downhill in a way faster gear," he shot back.

"I'm trying to get you in the slowest gear possible," Daddy said calmly, showing none of the frustration over not being able to run the normal tests needed to make a diagnosis. "Let's run this test for TB. That's something we can treat." Then he handed Taylor a double handful of samples of a powerful antibiotic. He gave him all we had—about $500 worth. Taylor would never have been able to afford them on his own. Maybe that would help. He stood up slowly and came over to my desk again.

Oh no. Now I was supposed to charge him? Charge a poor man for telling him he's dying?

I looked over at my father wild-eyed. He shook his head *no*. I said, "There's no charge for today, Taylor."

"Okay," he said without looking at me. "Thanks." Then he walked out.

The most shocking and profound moment of a man's life had just been played out in front of me, and there was nothing I could do but watch.

I looked at the clock. It was only 8:45 in the morning. God, this was a heartbreaking job. I wanted my real life back: a life where I didn't have to face tragedy suddenly, intimately, as a likely but unpredictable part of a normal workday.

Every day in this place was spent viewing the most personal and critical moments of other people's lives, but from an oddly disjointed perspective. It was like waiting at a railroad crossing at night and then watching a train suddenly flash by, the lighted compartments providing a succession of vignettes without enough context.

I was inadequate to the experience. It was inappropriate to have a superficial engagement in an event that was so important to Taylor, but I wasn't sure if I could cope with the alternative. I was afraid to let myself feel the full reality of it, because it would hurt. A lot. So I tried to hold everything at a safe distance. I was biding my time to get away from this level of reality altogether.

Winter

TWELVE

I had been at the office for nearly a month. I sat in the barn on a low stack of hay and thought about painful situations and tough choices. Life was looking a lot like a double bind. I wanted to get the hell out of Dodge, but couldn't leave yet. I watched the dust motes swirl in and out of the stripes of light. I felt hollow inside. How much was I supposed to care, to feel? What was I doing?

I stared across the open manger at the winter landscape. All the leaves were off the trees and bare branches scraped against the barn's tin roof making screeching sounds.

Fletcher appeared in the open doorway and asked, "What're you doing, Carolyn?"

"Oh, nothing. Hiding, I guess," I said, trying to smile.

Fletcher smiled at me in a kind way. "What're you hiding from?"

"My life."

He looked at me in confusion.

"Ever tried to figure out how much to charge somebody for telling them they're dying?"

Fletcher stood with his hands tucked into the front pockets of his jeans and thought about that.

He shook his head and said, "That's rough."

He turned and stared out the door. "Your Daddy and Momma have got more guts than anybody I ever seen. I guess that's what it takes to do that kind of work."

It was not lost on me that this was being said by a man who was the only one in his crew of specialized masons who had the wherewithal to slide on his back, propelling himself by kicking, through the long, dark, claustrophobic tunnels of the toxic waste incinerator at Oak Ridge so he could repair the fireproof lining.

He turned and smiled at me sympathetically. Then he ducked out of the barn.

I sat and wondered how much I really loved "the good people of the great State of Tennessee." Was that just something I liked to write in speeches for the Senator? Did I really care about any of them? The answer seemed to be "Yeah, but only from about 500 miles away." And even then I wanted to be able to dress up and eat well while I did it.

Then I wondered how much I really loved my parents. Did I love them enough to perform the task they'd asked of me? It frightened me how hard I had to think about that and still no answer came.

In Washington, I could seem like a big deal to an entire nation full of strangers. Here, I was a lowly friendly face to the sick people of a small rural community. I desperately wanted to see myself as somebody who mattered in this world. That's what I really wanted. Surely I was meant for more important things than working in a little country doctor's office. Wasn't I?

The phone was already ringing when I arrived at the office the next morning. I now realized that it had been ringing pretty much continuously for my whole life, all day, all night, all weekend. But Momma had answered it before. I'd never understood how relentless it could be.

I picked it up and said, "Dr. Jourdan's office."

A voice said, "My back's killing me. I need something for it."

It was yet another in an endless series of calls from the community's most charming drug addict. I said, "Hello, Langston."

"How come you always know it's me?"

"I guess I'm just a good guesser."

"I'm in terrible, terrible pain." He pronounced this with great dramatic effect as "turrible, turrible."

I said, "Have you tried aspirin?"

"It don't help."

"How about Aleve or Motrin or some of those kinds of things?"

"They don't help."

"Tylenol?"

"Don't work."

"How about a muscle relaxant?"

"They don't even touch it."

"They don't?"

"They don't *touch* the pain."

"Gosh, Langston. This sounds serious. You might really have torn something up this time. Have you thought about going to an orthopedist?"

"Don't need one. Dr. Jourdan's all I need. And my Darvocets."

"Langston, I'm scared you've got something bad wrong. You better come in and let him take a look at you."

"Don't have time. Gotta work. Can't you just call something in?"

"I'll ask him."

"Okay, bye."

Two days later the hospital called. "This is Dr. Jennings' office," a woman's voice said. "Dr. Jennings wanted to notify Dr. Jourdan that we lost Mr. Breedlove yesterday."

"Adron?" I asked. "Adron's died?"

"Oh no. I'm sorry. I shouldn't have put it that way. What I meant is, he's gone. *Missing*. We think he's run away. Anyway, we can't find him."

"Good God," I sputtered. "The man's retarded. He doesn't know how to tell anybody who he is or where he lives." I struggled to quell a rising panic. "He can't drive and his emphysema is so bad, he can't even walk very far. Where could he go?"

"We don't know, but he doesn't seem to be in the hospital anymore."

"Good grief. He could end up anywhere. He could get hurt."

"We're sorry."

"I don't understand how this happened. Adron's no problem to deal with. You'd think he'd enjoy getting away from his awful cousin."

"She's a real piece of work, isn't she," the nurse said.

"She reminds me of one of those wild hogs that runs loose in the Smokies that they're always warning you about."

The nurse laughed. Then she said in a whisper, "Adron took off because the orderlies scared him. Some fool decided to catheterize him. He didn't understand what they were doing and didn't like it. It took three men to get the catheter in."

"Well hell, Adron must have thought the place was full of perverts. No wonder he took off."

"Exactly, but you didn't hear it from me," she said.

I gave Daddy the message and the explanation. "Where do you think he'll go?" he said. "What'll he do?"

I shook my head and threw up my hands.

Everyone was massively relieved when Mary called a couple of hours later to let us know that Adron had turned up at home, apparently none the worse for wear. No one was sure how he got there. Daddy was right again. God's eye was on the sparrow . . . and Adron too.

The phone rang again.

"Dr. Jourdan's office."

"Did you call it in yet?"

"No, Langston."

"I need new orders on Mrs. Honeycutt," Alma said. "I think I should check on her more often. She's getting bed sores, and I can't make the family understand."

"What about her husband?" Daddy said. "Stewart's a really nice fellow, can't he turn her?"

"Mr. Honeycutt's gotten senile. He don't know what world he's in."

"That's too bad. He's an awfully nice man. I've known him for years."

"Well he ain't nice no more," Alma said. "Every time I go over there the old fool chases me around the room. He's always asking me if I wanna 'see something.' I tell him every time, 'Old man, if you show me *anything,* I'll take a skillet and bust you in the head with it so hard I'll knock you into next week.' Can you believe that? Right there in the same room with the woman he's been married to for more than fifty years."

"What about the daughter?" Daddy asked. "Isn't she around? Can't she help?"

"She's a dope addict," Alma said. "The only reason she comes around is to see if she can score any of her momma's pain medicine. She doesn't know

I count the pills whenever I come by and hide most of them from her. She keeps trying to get me fired. If I wasn't there, she'd take up all the dope in the house and leave her momma to lay there suffering."

Daddy was nonplussed. "What happens to people?" he asked. "Stewart, I guess, just got old. The man I knew would never have done anything like what you've described. He'd be mortified if he could see himself. He was a *good* man. And he loved his wife. They even used to dress alike, in matching outfits. Now she's laying there dying, and he's lost his mind, and their daughter's a drug addict." He looked at Alma. "You do whatever you think best," he said. "Draw up the orders and I'll sign them." Then he walked back toward his office. When he got halfway down the hall he stopped and spoke to Alma over his shoulder. He said in an odd voice, "You're doing a good job, you know. They'd thank you if they could."

Alma looked at me with a grim but determined expression.

I said, "But a hearty thanks may not be immediately forthcoming."

She said, "I ain't gonna hold my breath."

Then I walked down the hall to Daddy's private office.

He was standing with his back to me, looking out the small, high, barred window that made the room seem like a tiny prison. His shoulders were sagging. When he didn't turn around, I realized he must have been rattled by the news about the Honeycutt family. He had to watch the implosion of yet another family that had been close. For different reasons—illness, drug addiction, and senility—they'd lost each other at the very point when they needed each other the most.

I'd never seen a chink in his armor before. It brought me up short. I had no idea what to say or do, because I'd always taken my cues from him.

I stood in the doorway, a few feet behind him.

We were a family famous for being stoic in a community of the most stoic people in the country. It was a source of local pride that soldiers from the mountains of East Tennessee always won more medals in battle and took the highest casualties, both injured and killed, in *every* war. Courage, or at least poker faces, was our trademark. We *never* showed vulnerability, never asked for help, never showed any sign of strain. To anybody. Ever.

Finally I said, "If you promise not to go senile, I promise not to get hooked on drugs."

Then the phone rang and I went back to the reception desk to answer it. After a while, Daddy came out of the back looking composed and resumed seeing patients.

THIRTEEN

"Incoming," I warned.

"Who?" Daddy asked.

"Miss Hiawatha has just been driven into the parking lot."

Daddy mumbled, "Mercy, mercy," and reached for the Almond Joy he kept stashed behind the *Dorland's Medical Dictionary*. He ate it in four quick bites and then crossed to the lab and reached for the bottle of Tylenol we kept on top of the refrigerator. He took three.

"Ready?" I asked.

"No," he said shaking his head and staring at the floor. He remained standing beside the refrigerator where Miss Hiawatha wouldn't be able to see him when she registered.

As she walked through the front door she was talking a blue streak. ". . . and they threw them out of the heart ward cause they caught them having sex in the waiting room. Their Momma was there cause her heart had attacked her. They hadn't been married long."

"Hi, Miss Hiawatha," I said. "How're you doing?"

She came to my counter and said, "It's hurting in the place I call my skull, between my arm and my neck, near the fingers, cause of my leg, over on the other side. It hurts. Ye might wanna jab a needle in it."

"Okay," I answered, relieved that I wouldn't be the one who had to try to figure out what all that added up to. "It'll be just a minute."

She took a seat next to the preacher's wife who was her chauffeur today and continued, "I need to get my feet and ankles x-rayed. I took the flu, got diarrhea, and it went to my feet. It didn't help that I dropped a piece of wood on them either."

The preacher's wife, used to Miss Hiawatha's ramblings, nodded and took a knitting project out of her tote bag.

Then Miss Hiawatha said, "I told her it'd help her complexion if she'd get one of them yellow bug lights, they're cheaper than the pink ones, and they'll still make ye look good."

The preacher's wife nodded again.

Later, after Miss Hiawatha had been examined, she came out of the room, saying, "I told her to tell him, 'If I can't have your love I don't want your damn Vidalia onions!' "

"Miss Hiawatha, are you giving advice to the lovelorn?" I asked her.

Daddy said, "Miss Hiawatha's stomach and chest pains aren't going away, so I'd like you to make an appointment for her with the gastroenterologist."

I had to go to the back and close the door to make what would otherwise have been a routine call because I had to explain that Miss Hiawatha couldn't pay anything and that she wasn't exactly all there mentally. This was not the GI doctor's idea of a dream patient, but he agreed to see her since it was Daddy asking him. Then I gave the appointment information to the preacher's wife who said she'd make sure Miss Hiawatha got there.

Before Miss Hiawatha left she looked at me and said, "Carolyn, last night I dreamed angels were chasing me. To get away from them I jumped out of a cloud. I fell down and down and when I hit the ground it made me wake up. I found myself laying on the floor where I'd fallen out of bed. It really shook me up. I been waiting ever since to get here, since before sunup. I cleaned out the medicine cabinet while I was waiting. Took some of everything."

"How come you wanted to get away from the angels?" I asked.

"Cause it's not my time yet," she said. "When it's my time I'll know it and I'll go with them, but it ain't my time yet."

I was thinking how glad I was that it wasn't her time yet. "Ye don't wanna die in my family anyway," she said.

I looked at her in confusion.

"The eejits like to faint and fall all over the casket. Freda likes to fall right into it. Messes up the body. And they write *poems* to the dead. Awful poems. And then if ye die in the spring or summer so they got time they'll set the poem to music and have a song for the dead by Christmas. I been dreading Christmas since April cause I know they'll have some horrible song they'll wanna sing in remembrance of poor cousin Wallace. I'm sure he'd rather be forgot."

When the preacher's wife drove out of sight, I dialed up the drug store. "Frank, your sister's on her way over. Estimated time of arrival is three and one half minutes."

"Whoever she is, she's *not* my sister," he said, then he hung up.

My phone rang again in just a few seconds. "Dr. Jourdan's office," I said.

Frank's voice said, "Are you sending Miss Hiawatha over here again?"

"That's an affirmative," and before he could hang up again, I said, "Hey Frank."

"What!" he barked back.

"Miss Hiawatha told me the cure for warts her daddy taught her. You wanna hear it?"

"Hell no."

"Well here it is," I said. "I wrote it down so I wouldn't forget anything. 'To cure warts, you pick the wart until it bleeds. Then you rub a piece of corn in the blood and feed the piece of corn to a chicken. That'll cure the wart. You don't have to eat the chicken. Or you can rub fat meat on the wart and then throw the fat meat over your shoulder. Or you can tie a knot in a string for every wart you

it Glover was arguing with his wife Ble
they came through the front door of th
Kermit was limping, cradling one arm, and
n was right behind him.

dn't see what was wrong, but I could tell
e racket that it wasn't your basic case of
. Plus, it was Kermit, so there was a strong
od it wasn't anything normal. I opened the
ing door to the waiting room and took a

l Lord, Kermit. What happened?" I asked as
l him on into the back. Receptionist Rule
was that people who were bleeding got to
e line. And Kermit wasn't just bleeding; he
filthy and skinned up all over. His hair was
out in little tufts in all directions and what
d of his clothes looked like they'd been
a laundry in hell.
kon I need to see Doc," he said.
ean raised up on her tiptoes and shouted
rily from behind him, "Doc, I want you to
s tale he's telling and see if you believe it
er than I do!"
ted to help Kermit as he hobbled down the
t couldn't see anywhere to put my hands
uldn't hurt him. Kermit had been a Golden
boxer in his youth, and from his face, even
oday, you could tell he wasn't very good at
ng himself. But today he looked like he'd
un over by a train—again.

have and bury the string under a rock or an apple
tree or a peach tree.' "

Frank sighed, "You know what she's doing
now?"

"I couldn't even begin to guess," I said.

"Well, first of all she wanted me to fix her
vacuum cleaner. I went over to take a look at it
and it smelled like I don't know what—bad. She'd
vacuumed up the mess from where a pressure
cooker full of green beans had exploded all over
the kitchen! Lord! I just bought her a new one and
took the old one to the dump.

"And you know what else? Now we have to
staple her bags of pills closed with three staples, no
more and no less, and we have to initial each staple
three times or she won't take her medicine. She
won't take more than a few at a time either, so we
have to go through this at least once a week. When
I try to get her to take a month's supply she says,
'Frankie, I don't know how much longer I'm gonna
be around. I don't have money to throw away. I
don't even buy green bananas! I don't want to die
with a bunch of expensive medicine setting in the
cabinet that I don't need anymore. Waste of money.'

"And that's with me *giving* it to her!"

"Are you paying for her medicine out of your
own pocket?" I asked.

"Hell yes. She doesn't have any money!"

"We've been treating her for free for years too,"
I said, laughing. "No wonder everyone else is mak-

ing so much more money than we are. They make people *pay*."

I filed away this bit of information on Frank's business tactics. Maybe I could use it to provide some cover when Momma looked at the books for the weeks since her heart attack. She wouldn't say anything about Miss Hiawatha or Adron or any of the dozens of others who had been treated free for decades, but when she saw that all the chest x-rays to diagnose pneumonia had been done for free because I didn't know the right Medicare code, she'd be upset. Maybe I'd eventually be able to find out the right code for the x-rays, but no power on earth could prevent Daddy from periodically indulging in whimsical sprees like everybody-free-today-because-it's-Thursday or an all-diabetes-related-ailments-free day.

No, Momma was not going to be happy about that. She was the only one in the family with enough sense to keep us out of bankruptcy.

If left to himself, Daddy wouldn't charge anybody. He just didn't have the heart for it. I didn't either. It was a lot easier to have a Senate paycheck electronically deposited to your bank than to look sick and injured poor people in the face and ask them to give you $30. Especially when you knew you'd have to wait until walnut or ginseng season to be paid, since foraging was the only way they had to make any cash.

Momma had given me a singl[e]
how to do her job: charge people fo[r]
did. I was supposed to grill him ev[ery]
out of an examining room and the[n]
Alma to be sure I'd gotten everyt[hing]
dire warnings, I couldn't be relied [on]
that one simple thing. But neither c[ould]

I stared out the window at the hu[ge]
snow that fell, stuck for a moment,
to leave big wet spots. It was Dece[mber]
been at the office for *two month*[s]
recuperating, reading and playing
computer, but she was still too fra[il]
old job. Regardless of Momma's
Senator Hayworth couldn't forgive
delay. He'd already been a saint ab[out]
absence. Then out of habit, I shove[d]
away. I maintained myself in a so[rt]
animation, with a vague hope tha[t]
force would step in and resolve
didn't have the guts to do it on my [own]

The phone rang and I turned
window to answer it.

"Dr. Jourdan's office."

"Did you call it in yet?"

"Not yet, Langston."

As I hung up, I heard a commotio[n]
loud *baaa*ing was coming from t[he]

"Baaaa . . . You ain't gonna make
out of me! Baaa . . . baaa."

The first time was when I was a kid. He'd been standing in the middle of a track in the railroad yard where he worked, talking on a walkie-talkie, when an engine "boosted" some cars, nudged them so they would roll a short distance out of the way by themselves. He'd had his back to the cars as they came rolling slowly down the track and he didn't hear them coming. They hit him square in the back and knocked him flat.

Luckily he fell right into the center of the tracks. He lay there unconscious while fourteen cars rolled over him. He didn't lose any body parts, but he did have to take a TKO, early retirement. In the twenty or so years since his retirement, he had devoted his considerable strength, courage, energy, absentmindedness, and accident-proneness to farming.

Daddy came down the hall, took in the scene, and asked casually, "What'd you get into this time, Kermit?"

"I think I'm hurt, Doc."

"Sure looks like it. You been scuffling with Blendean?"

"Trying to stay out of arm's reach of her. Scuffling with the dang tractor's more like. I was gonna set some posts to fence off a couple of acres for my daughter's horses. I was digging the holes with the tractor."

Uh-oh. I knew exactly what he was using because we had one just like it: a hellishly dangerous contraption that stands five feet tall and looks like a giant screw. The tractor spins it at high speed to bore holes in the ground. It's supposed to be faster and easier than digging by hand, but the augers are famously hard to use and they're dangerous.

Kermit said, "The digger was going crooked, so I got off the tractor."

I suspected this translated to: I got off the tractor, left the auger spinning at about a million rpm, and went around the back to wrestle with it. You were supposed to turn the thing off before touching it, but farmers rarely did that because it took too much time.

"When I reached hold of the top of that thing, it latched onto the cuff of my glove."

Bingo.

"I tried to get aloose, but before I could get my hand out it had snatched up the sleeve of my shirt too! The last thing I remember is wrenching back as hard as I could and seeing the arm of my jacket going right on in with the rest of it. I figured it was gonna kill me . . . least take my arm off.

"It must've knocked me out. I don't know how long I was out. But when I come to myself I was still laying out there in the field. The tractor was still running, the damn digger was still going, and I felt like I was on fire all over. It had tooken me in one side and throwed me out on the other."

I hurt just thinking about it. I wouldn't have thought there was nearly enough room between the auger and the tractor for a man to pass through. That explained his cuts and bruises. It was a miracle he was still alive. I figured the story was over and started to turn away, but something held me up for just a beat. So what exactly didn't Blendean believe, and why was she so mad?

"I got up and went to dust myself off, and that's when I seen it," Kermit continued. "I swear I don't know how it happened!"

Kermit shot Blendean a cautious sideways glance and she looked back at him like she wanted to hit him over the head with a skillet.

"Well, at first I thought I had a lot of dust on me cause my clothes was all brown looking, but then I realized that wasn't it. I was smacking at my pants and shirt, and I was slapping right through to the skin! My clothes was gone! Every bit of them. That rascal had took my shirt and jacket and pants and everything and was a burying them! All I had left was a boot! And there I was standing in the middle of the pasture like a jaybird!"

This was even more embarrassing than it might have been because his field ran alongside a busy road.

"I tried to get my things back, but I couldn't even find some of them. I grabbed up what I could and started to the house, but I was hurting and it was pretty slow going. And then that dad-blame Donnie Stipes come down the road and saw me out there. He laid down on his horn and I could hear him all the way up in the field laughing his head off. It's more than a hundred yards up to the blame house! I didn't remember till I got up onto the front porch that we keep the front door locked. I started knocking and this here old woman, *my wife,* come and took a look at me through the window and wouldn't unlock the damn door. I had to go around the back and put this mess of rags back on before she'd even talk to me. She still won't let me in my own house till you tell her I ain't having some kind of fit."

Blendean was a strict Baptist.

She snapped, "The fool was running around the yard in his birthday suit! I ain't having no crazy nekkid old man in *my* house."

Kermit looked at Daddy and said, "I had a devil of a time getting her to bring me over here, Doc."

I'd have paid to hear that discussion. He couldn't have driven himself. He'd torn up his shoulder joint and pulled all sorts of stuff loose down his right side. All Daddy could do was try to get him comfortable and cleaned up a little before sending him down to the hospital in Knoxville. He also tried to patch things up between them by telling Blendean that if Kermit's clothes hadn't been torn off, he'd have been killed for sure. That helped some. But I don't think she believed Kermit couldn't have at least kept his shorts on if he'd really tried.

A few days after Christmas, on a cold, gray day, I sat alone in the basement "family room" watching a have and bury the string under a rock or an apple tree or a peach tree.' "

Frank sighed, "You know what she's doing now?"

"I couldn't even begin to guess," I said.

"Well, first of all she wanted me to fix her vacuum cleaner. I went over to take a look at it and it smelled like I don't know what—bad. She'd *vacuumed* up the mess from where a pressure cooker full of green beans had exploded all over the kitchen! Lord! I just bought her a new one and took the old one to the dump.

"And you know what else? Now we have to staple her bags of pills closed with three staples, no more and no less, and we have to initial each staple three times or she won't take her medicine. She won't take more than a few at a time either, so we have to go through this at least once a week. When I try to get her to take a month's supply she says, 'Frankie, I don't know how much longer I'm gonna be around. I don't have money to throw away. I don't even buy green bananas! I don't want to die with a bunch of expensive medicine setting in the cabinet that I don't need anymore. Waste of money.'

"And that's with me *giving* it to her!"

"Are you paying for her medicine out of your own pocket?" I asked.

"Hell yes. She doesn't have any money!"

"We've been treating her for free for years too," I said, laughing. "No wonder everyone else is making so much more money than we are. They make people *pay*."

I filed away this bit of information on Frank's business tactics. Maybe I could use it to provide some cover when Momma looked at the books for the weeks since her heart attack. She wouldn't say anything about Miss Hiawatha or Adron or any of the dozens of others who had been treated free for decades, but when she saw that all the chest x-rays to diagnose pneumonia had been done for free because I didn't know the right Medicare code, she'd be upset. Maybe I'd eventually be able to find out the right code for the x-rays, but no power on earth could prevent Daddy from periodically indulging in whimsical sprees like everybody-free-today-because-it's-Thursday or an all-diabetes-related-ailments-free day.

No, Momma was not going to be happy about that. She was the only one in the family with enough sense to keep us out of bankruptcy.

If left to himself, Daddy wouldn't charge anybody. He just didn't have the heart for it. I didn't either. It was a lot easier to have a Senate paycheck electronically deposited to your bank than to look sick and injured poor people in the face and ask them to give you $30. Especially when you knew you'd have to wait until walnut or ginseng season to be paid, since foraging was the only way they had to make any cash.

Momma had given me a single instruction on how to do her job: charge people for the work Daddy did. I was supposed to grill him every time he came out of an examining room and then follow up with Alma to be sure I'd gotten everything. Despite her dire warnings, I couldn't be relied upon to do even that one simple thing. But neither could Frank.

I stared out the window at the huge wet flakes of snow that fell, stuck for a moment, and then melted to leave big wet spots. It was December and I'd now been at the office for *two months*. Momma was recuperating, reading and playing solitaire on the computer, but she was still too frail to resume her old job. Regardless of Momma's health, however, Senator Hayworth couldn't forgive much more of a delay. He'd already been a saint about my extended absence. Then out of habit, I shoved those thoughts away. I maintained myself in a sort of suspended animation, with a vague hope that some outside force would step in and resolve my dilemma. I didn't have the guts to do it on my own.

The phone rang and I turned away from the window to answer it.

"Dr. Jourdan's office."

"Did you call it in yet?"

"Not yet, Langston."

As I hung up, I heard a commotion at the door. A loud *baaa*ing was coming from the parking lot. "Baaaa . . . You ain't gonna make no escape goat out of me! Baaa . . . baaa."

Kermit Glover was arguing with his wife Blendean as they came through the front door of the office. Kermit was limping, cradling one arm, and Blendean was right behind him.

I couldn't see what was wrong, but I could tell from the racket that it wasn't your basic case of sniffles. Plus, it was Kermit, so there was a strong likelihood it wasn't anything normal. I opened the connecting door to the waiting room and took a look.

"Good Lord, Kermit. What happened?" I asked as I waved him on into the back. Receptionist Rule No. 1 was that people who were bleeding got to jump the line. And Kermit wasn't just bleeding; he was also filthy and skinned up all over. His hair was sticking out in little tufts in all directions and what remained of his clothes looked like they'd been through a laundry in hell.

"I reckon I need to see Doc," he said.

Blendean raised up on her tiptoes and shouted out angrily from behind him, "Doc, I want you to hear this tale he's telling and see if you believe it any better than I do!"

I wanted to help Kermit as he hobbled down the hall, but couldn't see anywhere to put my hands that wouldn't hurt him. Kermit had been a Golden Gloves boxer in his youth, and from his face, even before today, you could tell he wasn't very good at protecting himself. But today he looked like he'd gotten run over by a train—again.

The first time was when I was a kid. He'd been standing in the middle of a track in the railroad yard where he worked, talking on a walkie-talkie, when an engine "boosted" some cars, nudged them so they would roll a short distance out of the way by themselves. He'd had his back to the cars as they came rolling slowly down the track and he didn't hear them coming. They hit him square in the back and knocked him flat.

Luckily he fell right into the center of the tracks. He lay there unconscious while fourteen cars rolled over him. He didn't lose any body parts, but he did have to take a TKO, early retirement. In the twenty or so years since his retirement, he had devoted his considerable strength, courage, energy, absentmindedness, and accident-proneness to farming.

Daddy came down the hall, took in the scene, and asked casually, "What'd you get into this time, Kermit?"

"I think I'm hurt, Doc."

"Sure looks like it. You been scuffling with Blendean?"

"Trying to stay out of arm's reach of her. Scuffling with the dang tractor's more like. I was gonna set some posts to fence off a couple of acres for my daughter's horses. I was digging the holes with the tractor."

Uh-oh. I knew exactly what he was using because we had one just like it: a hellishly dangerous con-

173

traption that stands five feet tall and looks like a giant screw. The tractor spins it at high speed to bore holes in the ground. It's supposed to be faster and easier than digging by hand, but the augers are famously hard to use and they're dangerous.

Kermit said, "The digger was going crooked, so I got off the tractor."

I suspected this translated to: I got off the tractor, left the auger spinning at about a million rpm, and went around the back to wrestle with it. You were supposed to turn the thing off before touching it, but farmers rarely did that because it took too much time.

"When I reached hold of the top of that thing, it latched onto the cuff of my glove."

Bingo.

"I tried to get aloose, but before I could get my hand out it had snatched up the sleeve of my shirt too! The last thing I remember is wrenching back as hard as I could and seeing the arm of my jacket going right on in with the rest of it. I figured it was gonna kill me . . . least take my arm off.

"It must've knocked me out. I don't know how long I was out. But when I come to myself I was still laying out there in the field. The tractor was still running, the damn digger was still going, and I felt like I was on fire all over. It had tooken me in one side and throwed me out on the other."

I hurt just thinking about it. I wouldn't have thought there was nearly enough room between the auger and the tractor for a man to pass through. That explained his cuts and bruises. It was a miracle he was still alive. I figured the story was over and started to turn away, but something held me up for just a beat. So what exactly didn't Blendean believe, and why was she so mad?

"I got up and went to dust myself off, and that's when I seen it," Kermit continued. "I swear I don't know how it happened!"

Kermit shot Blendean a cautious sideways glance and she looked back at him like she wanted to hit him over the head with a skillet.

"Well, at first I thought I had a lot of dust on me cause my clothes was all brown looking, but then I realized that wasn't it. I was smacking at my pants and shirt, and I was slapping right through to the skin! My clothes was gone! Every bit of them. That rascal had took my shirt and jacket and pants and everything and was a burying them! All I had left was a boot! And there I was standing in the middle of the pasture like a jaybird!"

This was even more embarrassing than it might have been because his field ran alongside a busy road.

"I tried to get my things back, but I couldn't even find some of them. I grabbed up what I could and started to the house, but I was hurting and it was pretty slow going. And then that dad-blame Donnie Stipes come down the road and saw me out there. He laid down on his horn and I could hear him all the way up in the field laughing his head off. It's more than a hundred yards up to the blame house! I didn't remember till I got up onto the front porch that we keep the front door locked. I started knocking and this here old woman, *my wife,* come and took a look at me through the window and wouldn't unlock the damn door. I had to go around the back and put this mess of rags back on before she'd even talk to me. She still won't let me in my own house till you tell her I ain't having some kind of fit."

Blendean was a strict Baptist.

She snapped, "The fool was running around the yard in his birthday suit! I ain't having no crazy nekkid old man in *my* house."

Kermit looked at Daddy and said, "I had a devil of a time getting her to bring me over here, Doc."

I'd have paid to hear that discussion. He couldn't have driven himself. He'd torn up his shoulder joint and pulled all sorts of stuff loose down his right side. All Daddy could do was try to get him comfortable and cleaned up a little before sending him down to the hospital in Knoxville. He also tried to patch things up between them by telling Blendean that if Kermit's clothes hadn't been torn off, he'd have been killed for sure. That helped some. But I don't think she believed Kermit couldn't have at least kept his shorts on if he'd really tried.

A few days after Christmas, on a cold, gray day, I sat alone in the basement "family room" watching a cold, gray movie. It was Franco Zeffirelli's *Brother Sun, Sister Moon*, about St. Francis of Assisi. I'd rented it so I could review all the best arguments for giving up my Mercedes, my condo in Washington, and my six figure income for a life of obscurity and poverty dedicated to the service of other obscure and impoverished people. Since that was what I seemed to be doing, I wanted to be sure I was doing it as artistically as possible.

The Zeffirelli film made dire poverty look appealing, romantic, and, above all, extremely cinematic. It was a good movie. I was starting to imagine being like St. Francis and giving away all my expensive clothes and devoting myself to service of the poor. So I tried putting it into a little prayer, "Okay, God. I've received your message to me through the harshly altered circumstances of my life. You're requiring a pretty big sacrifice of me, but I'll do it. I'll remain here and be a poor nobody. You've sent me a sign and I will obey. I'll stay at least a little bit longer in this awful job."

At the precise moment I completed my trial pact with God, I saw a flash of red out of the corner of my eye and heard a *thunk* against the sliding glass doors, less than a foot away from where I was sitting. An imprint of a bird arrested in midflight was on the glass, perfectly painted by the oil and dust on the bird's feathers. I looked down at the ground beneath the imprint and a gorgeous male cardinal was lying there dead. He'd flown into the glass door so hard, he'd killed himself.

Was *this* a sign from God? This beautiful little avian kamikaze?

I looked at the dead bird lying in the cold wet grass and then back at the television where an overjoyed St. Francis was walking around barefoot in the snow carrying large, heavy rocks. St. Francis looked a lot happier than either the bird or me.

It was going to take at least one more sign to clear this up.

But please, God, I thought, *don't kill any more animals just to talk to me. Okay? Just tell me straight out next time, will you?*

FOURTEEN

Over the weekend I took a secret trip to OfficeMax, determined to replace the antique office equipment with something less rustic. First went the ancient telephone. I got a new one with a NASA-like control panel, Rolodex with keyboard input, automatic dialers, built-in digital answering machine, and Caller ID—so I'd have a few seconds warning to brace myself for some of the more obnoxious patients. Into this I plugged a lightweight headset with an extra long cord so I could reach the files and copy machine while listening to patients' descriptions of their troubles. I installed a plain paper fax, so I wouldn't have to scissor a long scroll into separate pages every time someone sent us something.

I swapped out the old one-page-at-a-time copy machine, the kind with a lid that traveled at least a foot from side to side while making a single duplicate, for something more efficient and discreet. Then I brought in my new pride and joy—a tall swiveling architect's chair with a footrest and an ergonomic shock absorbent seat to replace Momma's plain wooden stool. This was more like it. Things were going to change around here, starting now.

Luckily I'd been able to do all this with my own money and didn't have to tell Momma. I had a massive savings account culled from hillbilly prudence encountering a lavish Washington paycheck. I hoped she wouldn't find out what I'd done for a long while because when she discovered it, she'd probably have another heart attack. Low overhead was the only thing that allowed Daddy to treat so many people for free. Low overhead meant no greed and no luxury either. Well, none of these obscene indulgences, like buying a pair of scissors instead of relying on discarded scalpels, would come out of their hide, and it would enable me to stay sane and even lend a little panache to the reception area.

Momma was still so heavily medicated and weak that I knew I had a while before I'd be discovered. She hadn't come back to the office yet, even for a visit, seemingly satisfied with the debriefings we provided over the dinner table at the end of every workday.

I put on my headset and answered the first call of the day, "Dr. Jourdan's office."

A familiar voice said, "Did you call it in yet?"

"Dammit, Langston!" I shouted, then clicked the headset off forcefully.

So much for modernization. At this moment, the only change I'd wrought was that I'd lost the satisfaction of being able to slam the phone down when I hung up on someone.

* * *

This time, despite the absence of the pj's and the bunny slippers, I recognized Joel LeQuire when he dropped a Medusa-like coil of black rubber hoses onto the counter. "Sweetie, I need y'all to check these for me and make sure they're reading right. They've been showing my blood pressure's normal, but I'm pretty sure it's real high."

I poked at the jumble of blood pressure cuffs and asked, "How many of these have you got?"

"Four," he said. "I like to keep them spread out through the house so I can get to them quick and check my pressure whenever I feel like it's jumping up."

Joel's neighbor, Mary Alice Reed, was sitting in the waiting room. When she heard Joel, she said in a loud voice, "Honey, if you want to keep something around the house that'll do you some good, you ought to get rid a *them* things and get you some *guns*. I keep me an equalizer beside my La-Z-Boy, by my chair at the kitchen table, next to the john, and beside the bed. And, of course, I keep one in here," she patted her purse.

Here was a very pretty, demure lady who kept five loaded guns in her immediate environs. Wow. You just never knew who was packing heat around this part of the country. Well, actually you did. It was pretty much everybody.

"What makes you think your pressure is high if all four cuffs are telling you it's normal?" I asked.

181

"Cause I been having these headaches and my scalp's itching and my sinuses have been hurting. My eyes keep going all bloodshot and my tongue's got this funny looking gray stuff on it." He stuck it out so I could see what he was talking about, but it looked fine to me.

Joel seemed to be at the front end of a long list of hypochondriacal symptoms that were proceeding from head to toe. At the rate he was going, I'd end up slapping him before he got past his chest. "Okay, okay," I said. "Just have a seat, and I'll get Alma to take your pressure with one of our cuffs and then check these out."

Joel selected a seat as far as possible from Mary Alice, but she simply turned around and resumed her talking. "Listen, Joel, don't let anybody sell you no automatics neither. They'll jam on ye. Get six-shooters. They'll never let you down."

I swept the pile of cuffs into my arms and carried them across to the lab area. When Alma was free, I pointed at them and told her what Joel wanted. She rolled her eyes. Joel heard me talking about him and popped back up at the counter like a jack-in-the-box.

"Honey, I brung a list here of my pressures I took this morning to help you out. At 7:00 it was 130 over 85. At 7:15 it was 128 over 80. At 7:25 it was 132 over 82. At 7:30—"

Alma cut him off. "Come on back and let's get your pressure."

Joel darted forward eagerly. She gestured toward Room 1, but Joel pulled up in surprise and said, "Aren't you gonna weigh me?"

"I just weighed you yesterday," she said.

"But I think my scales might be a little off from yours."

Alma gamely weighed him and said, "A hundred and forty-seven. Same as yesterday."

"But I got on different clothes!" Joel said.

Alma said in a resigned voice, "Are you ready to come back and get your pressure checked yet?"

"Just a sec," he said, pulling out a little spiral-bound notebook. He jotted something in it, recording his weight, I assumed.

According to Alma, Joel's blood pressure was normal and all four of his cuffs matched ours. He was devastated. He latched onto Daddy when he passed by the door of Room 1. "Doc, I don't understand it. I feel all light-headed and dizzy when I get up out of a chair quick or when I work outside for a long time in the heat. And the sun's been hurting my eyes when it's real bright, and when I get real hot I feel awful. My legs have been giving me a lot of trouble too. And my ankles. Do you think they look swole?"

Daddy went in the room with Joel and closed the door. He came out forty-five minutes later, looking exhausted. Joel, on the other hand, emerged looking fresh and happy. Alma flashed me a thumbs-up, indicating that I should charge him more than usual. I mouthed, "Forty-eight?"

She gestured again with her thumb and I mouthed, "Fifty-two?" She kept her thumb pointing up and I said out loud, "Sixty-two?" That was the most we'd ever charged for an office call in forty years.

She nodded. Then Daddy made eye contact with me and nodded wearily. I hadn't realized he'd ever noticed our hand signals.

Soon afterwards Mary Alice Reed was finished too. I talked guns with her as she paid her bill. "I've been shooting since I was three," I said. "My eyes don't work right. I can only see out of one at a time, but Daddy figured that was perfect for shooting, so he started me out young, so kids couldn't tease me about being no good at sports."

I asked her how long she'd carried a gun on her person. She said she'd carried one as long as she could remember, but recently her husband had made her get legal by applying for a license, since carry permits were getting harder to come by all the time.

"They made me take a damn test to prove I knew how to handle a pistol," she said with a grin. "I had to shoot at these little pieces of white paper."

It turned out she'd hit each one of the seventy-five little pieces of white paper that they'd put up. She'd made a perfect score. No one had ever done that before, even the police.

"The cop said, 'Lady, I had no idea you was gonna shoot that good.' I told him, 'Hell, neither did I. I ain't never shot at anything that wasn't moving before!' "

Michael came back in on Tuesday because of his increasing fluid retention. He'd adjusted his medicine the way Daddy had suggested, but he wasn't doing well. Alma weighed him and his weight was up nine pounds. That was a very bad sign. Retaining fluid was deadly for someone in congestive heart failure.

While Michael sat in a room in the back, Daddy stood next to me at the counter and reviewed his chart and the PDR, a giant reference book for medicine dosages. He closed the huge red book and said, "He's at the limits of all his medicines."

"What does that mean?" I asked.

Daddy's eyes filled with tears.

I realized what it meant. My eyes filled too.

Daddy shook his head slowly and said, mostly to himself, "I've got to go back there and tell him."

He didn't move, though. He stood there for a few more moments and then looked at me. "There's one more thing to try."

"What is it?"

"A heart and lung transplant."

God in heaven. I sat a moment, contemplating the person who would be in a position to donate the entire contents of their chest to someone else. It was a rough way for Michael to be saved. Of course, the heart-lung donor wouldn't be in a position to notice or mind the loss. And the donation would help a good man stay alive.

With nearly zero hope I asked, "Can that work?" What I meant was "How can something that gruesome possibly work, and how could a man as sick as Michael live through such a gigantic operation?"

Daddy just looked at me, frustrated, desperate.

He took Michael's chart and went into the back to talk to him. They came out together about fifteen minutes later. Michael looked sober, but not sad. "Don't worry about me, Doc," he said. "I've never been depressed a day in my life."

Michael saw how upset I was too. "You know, Carolyn, I never even knew I was handicapped till I was eighteen years old!" he said.

I struggled to smile.

"I know it sounds crazy, but the thought had never crossed my mind. Then, when I was eighteen, some fellow said something to me about being 'handicapped.' I wondered what he was talking about, who he was talking about, and then I realized he meant *me*."

He looked at me, holding his arms out in front of him, twisting them, looking at them. "I knew something was different, but I'd never realized I was 'handicapped.' "

Michael looked thoughtful. "A few years ago I was standing on a crowded street corner in New York City, on vacation, waiting to cross at the light when a little kid said real loud, 'Momma, what's wrong with that man's hand?' The kid's mother said, without missing a beat, 'Why, *nothing's* wrong with his hand. It's just made different from yours. That's all.' I loved her for that."

Michael had the same heroism that terminally ill children had. He spent all his time looking *out*. He plunged right out into the world with confidence, hope, and joy. He hadn't even registered that there was something to overcome.

I prayed things would work out, but I couldn't picture how that could happen.

This was another good reason to become a specialist. They not only made more money and had easier lifestyles, but they didn't get to know their patients like a family doctor did. Knowing your patients well was a guaranteed heartbreak. You knew in advance that the patients you'd come to care about the most were the ones who were on their way out the fastest, because you saw the sickest ones the most often.

The phone rang.

"Dr. Jourdan's office," I said.

"I can't stand these spasms . . . I mean headaches." This slip of the tongue confused Langston so much he just hung up without continuing.

Then he called back a few minutes later, as if it had never happened.

"Dr. Jourdan's office."

"This is Langston Stuffel. I got my headaches

again. Do you reckon he could give me something for it?"

"What do you think would help you?" I asked, toying with him.

"Oh, I don't know. Whatever he thinks."

"I can't remember what he gave you last time. Was it . . . ah . . . What was it?"

"I think it started with a *D* or something like that . . ."

"*D* . . . Was it Deltasone?"

"Noooo."

"Was it Diabenese?"

"Nooo."

"Was it Demulen?"

"I think it might have been something like Darvon or Darvocet or something like that."

"No," I said, "that doesn't sound right. Could it have been . . . ?"

"No it was Darvocet. It's coming back to me now. I'm pretty sure it was Darvocets."

"Well, okay, if you think that's what it was, I'll ask. Are you sure?"

"Yeah. Bye."

I hung up and dialed Frank.

"Frank, it's Carolyn, would you check the computer and let me know what kind of narcotics prescriptions Langston Stuffel's showing up with lately?"

"Sure. Let me see . . . uh, oh, . . . Langston's been busy. He's got Darvon from you, Lorcet from Dr.

188

Andrews on 1/3, 2/10, 4/15, Percocet from Dr. Brandon on 6/2, 6/23, 7/20 . . ."

"That's about what I figured," I said. "You know he's trying to go for disability on his back now?"

"Well shit, he'll probably get it too," Frank said. "You know I broke my back years ago and it still hurts when I've been standing for a long time, but I'd never get a damn dime! I'm lucky to get time to take an aspirin."

That afternoon Jason Wolfe burst through the door and stood in the middle of the waiting room flailing his right arm and making garbled swearing sounds. I looked up from reading my horoscope. Jason said, "I got a splinter in my hand."

"Okay," I said, "I'll put you down," and went back to my reading.

Jason was the owner and boss of a local construction crew. He had dark brown eyes, dark skin, and high cheekbones that marked him as part Cherokee. He wore his long straight black hair tied in a ponytail.

I heard another incomprehensible burst of sound. I looked up again, perplexed, to see Jason swinging his arm around wildly. It seemed like quite a production over a splinter.

He saw my expression and brandished his right hand, first giving me a look at the back side where there was a strange lump over one knuckle. Then he came closer and brought his hand level with my eyes. Then, with a flourish, he flipped it around to expose the palm side.

Good God. He had a piece of wood the size of a steak knife driven through his hand like a spike. His entire palm was impaled on it. One jagged raw end of it protruded at least three inches from the palm. The splintered stick was slightly triangular, with the pointy end stabbed into the flesh of his hand. About an inch or so of it seemed to be trying to emerge from the back side of his hand, but it had stopped before it pierced the skin, just raising it like a tent pole over the knuckle of his middle finger.

The stick wasn't driven straight through either. It took the long way, angling at about thirty degrees. About three inches of it was buried inside his hand. I looked at the thing in shock.

Jason shook his hand in my face for a second and then resumed his flailing and said, "Yeah. Right. I need some *help!*"

I agreed. I hopped off my chair and said, "Come on back."

I could hear someone saying, "Somebody needs to *do* something. Somebody needs to *do* something about this." Then I realized it was me. I went toward the back to get somebody, anybody, to help him.

Daddy met Jason halfway down the hall, took hold of his wrist, and began to examine his hand. Daddy flipped the hand back and forth, first looking at the raw end of the piece of wood and then at the nauseating tent of skin over the knuckle. He flipped it at least a dozen times. I guessed he was trying to evaluate its trajectory, trying to visualize what bones, muscles, tendons, ligaments, blood vessels, and nerves might be involved. The sight was just hard to take in. It was almost like one of those silly trick arrows that people wore on their heads at parties. Daddy kept flipping the hand. He too seemed to be looking for the trick.

"I pulled on it," Jason said, panting, "but I couldn't get it to come out. Then Wormey tried. He pulled on it *hard,* but he couldn't get it out either. It's *killing* me."

"Come on back here and lay down, and we'll see what we can do," Daddy said.

He led Jason down the hall by his wrist and had him stretch out on the surgical table. He said over his shoulder, "Alma, get him fifty milligrams of Demerol."

She went away to draw up the pain medicine while Daddy laid out the surgical instruments. He draped a stainless steel tray with a sterile moisture-proof sheet and then arrayed an assortment of sterile bandages, gauze, and gold-handled stainless steel instruments atop it.

Alma gave Jason the injection, and Daddy resumed his flipping, carefully studying the situation. "How'd you do this?" he asked.

"We're building an extension on a horse barn. I was up on a scaffold. The board I was standing on broke. I tried to grab hold of something to catch myself. Whatever it was I grabbed hold of broke off in my hand."

Jason's forehead was beaded with sweat. Rivulets began to run down his temples and into his hair.

"Turn on the fan," Daddy said.

Alma adjusted the fan so it would blow across Jason's face. At least this was part of a recognizable routine. It was common for people who were hurt to need the fan while Daddy worked on them. Cooling them off reduced their nausea. And mine too. I got several squares of gauze and swabbed Jason's face to comfort him and divert his mind.

My swabbing and the fan seemed to help a little, but when Jason looked at me his pupils were hugely dilated. They were so large I could make out only the thinnest band of brown iris around the edge of the black. No way had one shot of pain medicine done that. Especially since the pain medicine didn't seem to be working yet.

"Well, there's no point in x-raying you, because wood doesn't show up on an x-ray," Daddy said, then he left the room. He went into his private office next door, where I could hear him fiddling with something. Alma could hear him too, and she looked worried. What was going on? Whatever it was, she knew, and didn't like it. Maybe this would be a good time for me to leave. I tried to sneak out, intending to return to the reception desk. I glanced into Daddy's office as I tiptoed by and stopped dead. He had a toolbox out and was rummaging around in it.

It wasn't some sort of fancy Neiman Marcus toolbox for doctors, either. It was an ancient grungy battered metal toolbox. He pulled out a pair of pliers. Oh shit. I turned to take off, but Daddy saw me. "Carolyn," he said, "come here, I can use you for a second."

Apprehensively, I followed him back into Room 3. He rolled the instrument tray around behind Jason's head so he couldn't see it and then laid the pliers on it. Then he looked at Jason's eyes and checked his pulse. The pain medicine should have kicked in by now, but even I could see it wasn't working. Daddy told Alma to get him another twenty-five milligrams of Demerol.

"We're gonna get you another shot of pain medicine. That'll help you relax a little bit," Daddy said. I raised my eyebrows and bugged my eyes at him to ask why the pain medicine wasn't kicking in and he mouthed, "Adrenaline." Oh, the fear and pain were flooding Jason's system with adrenaline and this was offsetting the pain medicine.

The bright surgical lamp was turned on and adjusted to shine on Jason's stomach. Then Daddy took Jason's hand and placed it atop his stomach in the middle of the circle of light. Daddy gestured for me to go around to the far side of the table, then he began to pull on his sterile surgical gloves, a wisp of talcum powder escaping from each glove as he tugged at it.

Daddy swabbed the entry wound with bright orange Merthiolate. I appreciated this because the bright orange disinfectant made the red of the blood and the pink of the torn flesh much less noticeable.

Then he said, "Carolyn, you stand on that side. Alma can help me keep this hand in position."

It didn't take a genius to know what he meant. He wanted me to hold down Jason's left side and Alma his right.

Daddy looked at Alma and me. "Once we get started we're not gonna stop until this is out," he said. Then he looked at Jason. "This might hurt. I'll be as quick as I can."

Might hurt? I felt sick.

I already had Jason's left hand in both of mine, holding it so the back of it was against my chest. I adjusted it so it was against a breast, hoping that would distract him. He swiveled his head to look at me in surprise. I leaned over him and wiped his dripping forehead. His eyes were bulging and his chest was heaving with each breath. He was terrified and in a lot of pain. I saw Daddy turn and reach for the pliers and decided to go for broke. I kept a strong grip on Jason's left hand with my right one and then placed my left hand on his thigh, high on the inside of his thigh, you might even say on his groin. I asked, "Are these hot?"

Jason's wild eyes swung away from Daddy again to look at me in shock. He croaked, "What?"

"These overalls," I said plucking at the fabric in a particularly sensitive area. "Are they hot to work in?" I asked as innocently as I could manage.

Just then Daddy crushed the splinter in the jaws of the pliers and pulled so hard he lifted Alma onto her tiptoes. Jason sucked in a huge breath and his feet came off the table. Then, in the space of two seconds, it was over. Daddy brandished a seven-inch-long piece of bloody wood, still clamped between the jagged, slightly rusted, jaws of the pliers.

Jason's dilated gaze fixed on the gigantic splinter and then rolled to the pliers. It was obvious he was having to work hard to focus his eyes.

"Damn, Doc, that looks like a pair of pliers you used on me!"

"It is," Daddy said as he dropped the stick into a plastic bag and laid it on Jason's chest for a souvenir. Then he handed me the pliers. "You can put these back in the toolbox now."

"Doc," Jason said, "them's cheap Chinese! I had some Craftsmans out in the truck!"

His voice was starting to slur. Now that his adrenaline rush was over, the large dose of pain medicine was kicking in. Wormey would probably have to carry him home.

The next day Jason came in to have his wound looked at and have the dressing changed. On his way out, his hand swathed in a bulky white bandage cradled against his chest, he dipped his head to whisper, "You tricked me!"

"What?" I said, trying to act innocent again.

"I went home yesterday wondering if maybe you liked me, but when that dope wore off I realized you were just trying to keep me from seeing them pliers coming." His expression was a mixture of embarrassment and amusement.

"I was trying to help you," I said, smiling.

"It was a dirty trick."

"Worked though, didn't it?" I said.

"Yeah," he said. "It sure did. You're getting to be a hell of a nurse, Carolyn."

Spring

FIFTEEN

I looked out the window and stared at the pale green leaves on the trees. Redbuds bloomed at the edge of every patch of woods. Farmers had begun to roll slowly around their fields on tractors, tilling and sowing.

It was April. I'd been on leave for six months and longed to get back to my real job, my real life. I congratulated myself on my ability to imagine that my job and life in Washington were the real ones. I clearly had the famous family determination.

Momma was no longer fragile, but because she was seventy-two and couldn't quit smoking, the doctor didn't think it was a great idea for her to return to a stressful full-time job. And anyone hired to replace me would have to go through a significant training process because the Medicare and insurance coding systems were truly complex. I wasn't sure whether Daddy was up to breaking in another person or not, but I knew Alma wasn't. The more insurmountable challenge, though, was that there was no way the office could afford a person who already knew how to navigate the system. Daddy could never compete with the offers that groups of specialists could make to such people. If the new receptionist needed to be paid much at all, Daddy would have to start charging more people. I, fortunately and unfortunately, could live with Momma and Daddy and do the job with a minimal increase in overhead.

I was calling in a prescription when Oreda Brogden said, from the middle of the waiting room, "I've brung Chandler in to see the doctor."

I nodded and waved so she'd know I'd heard her and wrote Chandler's name on the day sheet. When I finished my monolog to Kmart Pharmacy's answering machine I stood up and leaned out across the desk smiling broadly. It was early morning and I was feeling good. I called out, "Hey!" Only then did I notice that Oreda looked exhausted.

Chandler was sitting in the front row of seats and had his back to me. He was slouched forward with his elbows resting on his knees, hands clasped tightly together. He was wearing his usual white V-neck undershirt and blue jeans. He angled himself around slightly to respond to my greeting with an attempted smile, but he didn't quite make it. He looked distressed, though there was no obvious reason why. I pulled his chart and stamped the date in red on the left margin of a yellow, dog-eared page. He'd been a patient for a long time, but he didn't come in very often. He apparently didn't have any chronic health problems.

Then I heard him mumble loudly, "I got monsters running up and down on me."

I smiled at what I assumed was a joking way to describe some itchy rash or something.

Daddy was standing at the counter and heard the same remark. He abruptly stopped writing notes in a chart. He went through the connecting door into the waiting room, sat down next to Chandler, and talked to him in a low voice for a few moments. When he returned, he closed the door behind him, and looked at Alma and me. "Watch out now, Mr. Brogden is having hallucinations."

The warning, a real rarity from Daddy, alarmed me, but when I glanced at Alma, she was going right on with what she was doing, apparently unconcerned. I supposed it was because we'd all known Chandler for years. Chandler wouldn't hurt a fly.

"Bring him on back now," Daddy said quietly. He never stood around waiting while Alma went through the preliminaries unless there was an emergency, but this time he remained standing in the hall as Alma called Chandler back and asked him to step up on the scales.

Now I got a good look at him. His eyes were extremely bloodshot and his nose was dark red, but otherwise I couldn't see anything much different from his usual self. He was in his fifties, had a pendulous potbelly, and a year-round deep purple sunburn from decades of laying asphalt for a living. His whole face sagged, giving him the look of a hound dog.

He turned his head to talk to Daddy over his

shoulder as he was being weighed. "Doc, you gotta help me. Somebody's *got* to help me. Them monsters is *breathing* on me. On my *neck*. I can *feel* them."

Daddy said in a light, comforting voice, "We'll see what we can do, Chandler. Let's go get your temperature and blood pressure first, like always, okay?" Then he nodded to Alma to take him into the first examining room.

When Chandler was out of earshot, Daddy asked Oreda, "How long has he been like this?"

"It started getting bad last night," she said. "We sleep in separate bedrooms on opposite ends of the trailer. I didn't notice anything until he came running through the house screaming for help in the middle of the night. By the time I got out of bed and went to see what was wrong, he'd beaten all my houseplants to shreds with a stick, shouting that the monsters was after him and they was crawling all over him and breathing on him. He begged me to stay with him so he could sleep. He said he was afraid to sleep unless I was watching over him so nothing could get him. I waited up all night with him on the couch in the living room till you got open."

Daddy went into the examining room with Chandler, but left the door ajar. We could all hear the questions and answers.

"You been drinking any, Chandler?"

"No."

"Been taking any kind of drugs or pills or anything?"

"No."

"Anybody in your family ever had any kind of mental problems?"

"No."

"Have you been using any farm chemicals?"

"No."

"Fertilizer, bug killer, weed killer?"

"No. Well, I did spray the tobacco for suckers and put some fertilizer on it."

Maybe he'd gotten poisoned from that.

"You wait here for a minute, Chandler. I'll be right back." Daddy came out to talk to Oreda. He asked her all the same questions he'd just asked Chandler and she confirmed what we'd all heard Chandler say.

"This is a real mystery," he said. "Schizophrenia generally runs in families and it doesn't show up for the first time this late in life." Daddy looked stumped.

He went back in the examining room. "We're gonna take a little blood now and that'll help us figure out what's going on here. Okay?"

He told Alma to draw a comprehensive panel of blood tests and then whispered to me not to charge the Brogdens anything. Neither of them had a job.

When Chandler came to the counter to pay, I told him there was no charge for today. He looked at me with his heavily bloodshot blue eyes. His lids drooped and the edges seemed runny. They were a bottomless pit of fear and need. I'd never seen such eyes. Even though it was painful to see, I couldn't look away.

To cover my staring, I said, "You've got the prettiest blue eyes."

"They're all red cause I hadn't slept in three weeks," he said.

"Three weeks!" Oreda said, startled. "Chandler, you didn't tell me this'd been going on for that long!"

"Well it has," he said.

"Well, you still got pretty blue eyes and Daddy'll get it figured out for you. Are you gonna try to go to sleep when you get home?"

"I'll try."

I handed him his prescriptions. Daddy had written him some powerful tranquilizers and antipsychotic drugs that surely would give him some relief.

He continued to look at me with his bloodhound gaze and said, "Y'all are just *good* people. You're just so good. I thank ye."

He remained standing in front of me, his eyes locked with mine. No one had ever looked at me with such desperation. I reached out and took his hand. At the same time Oreda latched onto his other side and began pulling him out the door. I didn't let go and neither did he. As he walked around the counter I lifted our clasped hands to clear the stacks of files and books and keep hold of him as long as I could. It was like a dance.

Then he began to cry.

"You call us if you need anything," I said, and I started crying too.

We got the results of his blood work back the next morning. Daddy'd asked for more than thirty tests that he would have to pay for out of his own pocket. The test results were all perfect. Every value was within normal range, a remarkable feat for a former heavy drinker who ate a high fat diet.

I called Oreda to tell her about the test results. Then I said, "How's he doing?"

"Well, he slept on the couch all day while I sat with him, but he had to stay up all night again because of the monsters," she said. "He didn't want me to leave him even for a minute, but I told him the doctor needed me to go out to the barn and see what he was using on the tobacco."

She told me the names of the products he'd used to spray the tobacco, but she had only the brand names, not the actual chemical contents.

"Should I call poison control?" I asked Daddy. "They'll know what's in these sprays."

He said, "No. Ask Oreda again about the possibility of any drinking or drugs or poisons he might have taken."

I did and she said, "No. Nothing. Just nothing."

"Well then," Daddy said, "let's wait and see if the antipsychotic drugs help."

* * *

First thing the next morning, before I'd even sat
down to eat my breakfast, the phone rang. It was
Oreda. She was crying. "Chandler died last night,"
she said. "He died in his sleep. I went to sleep for
just a *little* while, for just five minutes, and when I
woke up, he was dead!"

"Oh no, Oreda. I'm so sorry."

"I didn't watch out for him like he needed me
to," she said. "I went to sleep and he *died*."

"Oh Oreda, it wasn't your fault. Hang on a second.
Let me get the doctor. He'll want to talk to you."

I ran down the hall to tell Daddy. His jaw dropped
for a second and then he closed his mouth and
covered his shock with a neutral expression. He
picked up the extension phone in his office and I
heard him say gently, "Oreda? What happened?"

He listened to her for a few minutes and then I
could hear him trying to comfort her: "There was
nothing you could've done. Your dropping off to
sleep wasn't what killed Chandler. There was
nothing you could've done. These things just happen sometimes and we don't know why, but it certainly wasn't anything you did."

Chandler had come to us for help. He'd needed
us, desperately, and we hadn't known the right thing
to do, hadn't been able to do a damn thing to save
him.

When he hung up, Daddy came out to my desk
and stood for a moment. "Where do you think

206

Chandler is now?" he said. "I mean, do you think he went to a bad place?"

I looked up in surprise and saw that my father looked lost and afraid. I'd never seen him look like that before. I was also startled by the enormous significance of the question. I was surprised that he would look to me for the answer.

"What?" I said, buying time.

"You know he saw monsters and felt them breathing on his neck," Daddy said, looking haunted. It was the look of a man whose first nineteen years of life had been colored by the ranting threats of rural Southern religion and then amplified by an eighteen-month tour as a Marine in the Korean War. He'd been on the first boat in and the last boat out of Korea.

"Do you think Chandler got a glimpse of what was coming, like a vision of something? Some *place?*" he asked, clearly caught up in some horrible imagining.

"No," I said firmly. "I do not." I added, "I do not think Chandler had a vision of hell. I don't think he *went* to hell. There isn't any such place. I *know* it."

"You *wish* you did," Daddy said.

I knew what the church had told him, but I'd never know what he'd seen in that war. "God wouldn't make such a place," I said, trying to help him. "There's no sense in it. He loves us. I know He does."

When he remained silent I went on even more firmly, "People's ideas about God are the clearest projection in the world of the inside of their own heads and hearts. When I hear somebody describe what they think God's like, I know what they think *everything's* like. Visions of God come straight out of our deepest selves. I'm an optimistic person, so I figure God's good, and that there must be some sort of plan that'll explain all this. I don't know what it is. But not knowing the plan doesn't bother me. I don't *need* to know. I trust Him. I sure don't think I'm a pawn in some sort of game. While you live, you try to be the best person you can, do the best you can for everybody around you; and when you die, you go back to wherever you were before you were born. And it's not a burning fiery place with monsters breathing on your neck."

Daddy continued to stare at me. "I wonder," he said.

Then he turned and walked back to his office where he stayed for a long time with the door closed.

That evening Fletcher came over to try and diagnose the reason for a loud squealing in the engine of my Mercedes. "I can't see what's making that noise, Carolyn, but leave off driving it till I can figure it out. You might tear something up."

"Okay," I said. "I'll drive the old pickup." I kicked at one of the tires in frustration. "You know,

I've decided to face it: I'm just a redneck. I was out of my mind to ever think any different."

"Don't worry, Carolyn," he said as he packed up his tools, "things'll work out."

"I might've gotten carried away in Washington, but I was doing what I thought I was supposed to do. I was trying to be a success. I was raised to be *successful*. Now I don't know what that means anymore."

Fletcher said, "Anybody you ask around here would think your Momma and Daddy are a success."

"But what would they say about their daughter?"

"That she was a good daughter and helped her family take care of the people around here."

"Take care of people?" I said. "I can't take care of anybody! I just sit on a stool and watch them die. Didn't you know that?"

"I heard about Chandler."

"How can anybody stand to go back to a place like that day after day? It's one thing to have a fantasy about saving people, but when you can't sustain that anymore, what's the point?"

"The pitiful truth," Fletcher said, "is that sometimes the best thing, the only thing, we can do for another person is just show up. We might not know how to do anything for them, but at least we can show up. And that takes guts. But *everything* takes guts. It takes guts to care about people. But what else are you gonna do?"

In that moment I realized Fletcher had just given us a motto for a family coat of arms: We Show Up. Every day, no matter what, and maintained a stoic silence to boot. I'd have to keep going back to work, without complaining, because it was expected; and Daddy and Momma wouldn't be gushing any thanks. In other families my going or staying would have been talked about openly, but we never would. It wasn't the way we did things. We'd each keep up our pose for as long as we could stand it. I stared at Fletcher in hopeless frustration.

He said, "There's another way, you know."

"And what would that be?"

"You know how in Bible stories whenever an angel shows up, first thing he always says is, 'Fear not!' "

"Yeah."

"Well, it took me most of my life, but I finally figured out that he's not trying to comfort us when he says that. He's giving us an order. It's a command given more than 300 times in the Bible. The Lord's telling us not to let ourselves be afraid. We can't afford to be scared. It just gets in the way of us doing whatever it is that we're supposed to be doing."

I was stunned. Such an interpretation had never occurred to me and it sure wasn't what they taught in church. Fearlessness didn't come from being comforted, being patted on the back by God, and having our fear reduced. It meant making a conscious decision not to indulge ourselves. We had to intentionally turn things around, like when Virgil convinced Dante that the best way out of hell was to climb up the hairy-legged devil himself.

I said, "I don't know if I've got that kind of courage."

"But, that's just it," Fletcher said. "Everybody gets scared. It's okay to feel scared. But you can't let it run your life. If you'll just mind the Lord on this *one* thing, you don't hardly need any courage—or even faith.

"Just mind Him in the one thing," Fletcher said.

Sixteen

So I showed up again the next day. When Kermit shuffled up to the reception desk looking like he'd been at ground zero when a bomb went off, I mumbled to myself, "Fear not!"

He was skinned up all over. His clothes were dusty and torn and his hair was standing up in spikes all around his head. Extreme dishevelment was becoming a typical look for Kermit. "Have you been digging postholes again?" I asked.

"Hell no. Nobody ain't hanging this one on *me*. This one is *his* fault," he said, pointing at his friend, Obie Snyder, who had brought him in. Obie stood off to the side with a shamefaced look.

I waved them on back and told Kermit to go to his usual room. Obie went with him. Daddy passed them in the hall. "Good afternoon, gentlemen," he said, nodding to them both.

"What now?" he whispered to me.

"Got no idea," I answered, "except you can rule out posthole digging."

I desperately wanted to hear what was being said in the back, so I did something a little shameful. I put both phone lines on hold to prevent any annoying interruptions, and went to stand in the doorway while Daddy examined Kermit.

Daddy dabbed at the hundreds of red scratches with Merthiolate, methodically working his way from the head down. Every inch of exposed skin was scraped raw, like Kermit had been dragged through a briar patch.

"Doc, this is all my fault," Obie said. "I was trying to help Kermit lead his new little Black Baldie back home."

It seemed that Kermit had bought a new calf that had wandering ways. It refused to stay home in its own perfectly nice pasture. It usually didn't go far when it got out, but it had been missing for two whole days this time. Kermit had looked everywhere for it, but couldn't find it until Obie had called him saying the calf was in his yard.

"I knew there was no way Kermit could lead that calf back home by hisself. The little thing ain't halter broke and it's over a mile. So I got an idea that would save him a lot of steps."

Obie told Kermit he'd drive his car real slow and let Kermit lie in the trunk, holding onto the calf's lead rope. That way they could get the animal home easily. Unfortunately the little 500-pound calf either didn't understand the plan or just didn't want to go along with it. He hadn't been trained to lead, nor did he have the natural inclination to follow along closely behind an automobile. A dog will chase a car without training, but apparently a calf will not.

Kermit had wound the lead rope around his hand and wrist so as to keep a good grip on the calf. But this also gave the calf a good grip on Kermit. A calf, even when small, is quite strong and can get incredibly firm traction when it digs all four shiny, pointed hoofs into the ground. I wouldn't be surprised if cows weren't the original inspiration for four-wheel drive. Or maybe it was a goat, but the principle is the same.

Obie put the car in gear and went creeping down his gravel driveway.

"It might've been the smoke blowing in its little face—Obie's car burns a lot of oil—or it could have been the gravels he throwed up when he took off, but something scared that calf," Kermit said. "And it balked. Wouldn't move a step. I didn't wanna holler at Obie to stop, cause that would've spooked the little feller worse, and Obie couldn't see what was going on because the trunk lid was up. So he kept on driving and the calf kept on balking."

The result was that Kermit got jerked out of the trunk of a moving car. When Obie saw Kermit lying in the road in his rearview mirror, he stopped. But these were not men to be easily discouraged, so they decided to try again. This time the calf realized what they intended and ran away before Kermit could even get close to the car, dragging him up the gravel road. Skiing face-down on rocks.

The calf was probably ecstatic at getting to play. I could well imagine that when its load suddenly lightened as Kermit tore free, it probably kept right on running and bucking for miles. By now it was probably back in Obie's driveway, hoping to do it all over again.

When things quieted down, I called Jacob, hoping to hear something uplifting. Big mistake.

"What am I missing now?" I asked.

"I'm afraid to tell you this time."

"Oh no," I said warily. "What?"

"You know that nuclear submarine trip the Navy invited the Senator to go on?"

"The one where they're gonna cruise underneath the polar ice cap?" I said with a feeling of foreboding.

"Yes. Well, he doesn't want to go. He said, 'Let me get this straight. They want to seal me inside a metal can with a hundred guys, no women, and no liquor, and dunk me in ice water for a week? They're out of their minds.' "

"So he said you could go in his place."

That trip had been a dream of mine for years. "Oh God," I said. "What am I doing here?"

"I've been asking myself the same question," Jacob said. "Why can't you just help them hire someone and come back here? Is it some kind of *Deliverance* thing?"

"No," I said. "It's more than that."

"Carolyn, are you going to come back? Ever? Please come back."

I couldn't respond.

"I miss you," he said, "World domination is simply not as much fun without you."

"I miss you too. You can't *imagine* how much. At least you've got the rest of Washington to talk to. Nobody here cares what happened on *Washington Week in Review*. Haute cuisine is barbequed pork. *Nothing* I do here is *ever* gonna be on C-Span. I could save somebody's life and it wouldn't even get *covered!*

"But I can't just walk out of here either. I've got obligations, responsibilities—to Daddy, to Momma, to these people. I *want* to come back, believe me. But there's something about this place and what I'm doing. I don't know."

"It's absurd for someone like you to stay in that ridiculous job."

"If I don't step up to the plate here, I'll be leaving two seventy-year-olds to take up the slack and one of them's clearly not up to it. If I don't sit in this chair, the office will close. This place is an icon. And if I leave, it's gone forever. Daddy's grandfathered in on so many laws, no one else could ever operate with such low overhead. And if the price goes up, hundreds of people—the good ones, the ones who work, the ones who don't qualify for the state's charity medical care because they have jobs and yet they don't have any insurance where they work—won't be able to afford to go to the doctor."

I hadn't realized all this was going on in me, but I seemed to be on a roll.

"If I don't step up, I'm saying that I pick what *I* want over what hundreds of other people need. You know who I'm talking about too—all those people the politicians pretend to care about—the so-called 'working poor.' People who work their asses off and still don't make enough to live. Let me tell you, that kind of decisionmaking would be really frowned on by my parents." I paused, and then added, "And by me too."

There was a long and painful silence. Then I repeated one of our favorite quotes from *Henry V*, but this was the first time I'd ever said it without cynicism. "And what have kings that privates have not too—save ceremony—save general ceremony?"

Jacob remained silent. We were both thinking about how much we enjoyed the pomp and thrice gorgeous ceremony that King Henry had been referring to.

Then I added, "Here's the really scary part, Jacob. You know how we always talk about wanting to be in public service so we can help people."

"Of course," he said.

"Well, in this place I feel sometimes like I really *am* helping people. Actual people. It's not just an idea. I can't help them *much*. I know it's not glamorous, but sometimes I think maybe I'm doing more good swabbing up body fluids and being a friendly face here than I ever did working in the Senate."

There was an even longer silence. Then Jacob said, "It's embarrassing to have to admit it, but you may be right. Yesterday one of the Members brought a professional baseball team to the Hart Building. People came out of their offices and stood along the atrium balconies to see them. I joked to the guy standing next to me that the government had halted its productivity to watch a group of baseball players mill around and I wondered how much it was costing the country for us all to be idle. He said I had it backwards: that it was cheaper and better for the American people when Senate employees were on break."

I laughed.

"Maybe he was right, Carolyn. But I still wish you'd come back. I love you, you know."

"I know. And I love you too."

I hung up and burst into tears. The best friend I'd ever had, the best job, and the trip of a lifetime were being stacked up against my father and mother, who desperately needed me, along with the opportunity to really help the people I'd grown up with. I felt like I was dying from the strain of being pulled in both directions.

"Dr. Jourdan's office," I said.

"It's Langston. I need my Darvocets. You called in something else, something called Ultram. I went to pick up my Darvocets and they give me this stuff. I'm taking it back. I'm not paying for this."

"Why not? It's a new nonnarcotic pain reliever."

"Have you read the list of side effects? I can't take something with them kind of side effects. I'll just stay with my Darvocets."

In an attempt to introduce an important but futile insight, I said, "Langston, do you ever think you might be getting hooked on Darvocets?"

"No, I ain't hooked. It says on the bottle you can take them every eight hours, but I only take them every twelve hours."

"But, Langston, it doesn't mean one every eight hours for *life!* It's only supposed to be for a few days right after an injury."

"But I'm in *pain,* terrible, terrible pain."

So was I.

I was swiveling back and forth in my architect's chair, wearing my telephone headset, while Walker Eskridge gave me a minutely detailed description of his perianal dermatitis. Phone calls like this were a normal part of the job and I usually didn't mind them. Then I swiveled a little more widely and realized someone was standing at the waiting room counter. My one hazel and one green eye locked with Matthew's matching sky blue ones. He looked mightily amused. My voice trailed off in the middle of a rather graphic question.

Matthew was struggling not to laugh out loud. I felt my face grow hot. I nodded to indicate that I had seen him and would put his name down. He nodded back and sat down to read an issue of *Farm and Ranch* magazine.

I sat slumped in my chair trying to recoup my dignity when I found myself befuddled by a loud and persistent buzzing sound. I looked around for the source until I realized the buzzing was Walker's voice still coming through my headset. Preoccupied with my awkward social predicament, I'd drifted away from Walker's itch.

Daddy came out of an examining room then and I realized I was going to have to tell him Walker's symptoms to find out what should be done. I put Walker on hold, swiveled so my back was to the waiting room, and tried to keep my voice down as I said, "I need to ask you something about Walker Eskridge's skin rash."

"Okay," he said.

"He's tried a bunch of over-the-counter creams and powders but nothing is helping. What should he do?"

"Where's the rash?" he asked as he turned away and walked over to his microscope.

"It's, ah, on his rear end," I mumbled.

Daddy snapped out over his shoulder in an impatient voice, "What are you whispering about?"

"It's on his hiney."

"What?"

I gave up then. "Walker Eskridge's got a rash on his butt that won't go away. What should he do?"

Daddy said calmly, "Oh, he's had that same

problem for ages. Nothing seems to give him relief for very long. Call Dr. Davis and set up a dermatology consultation for him."

Perfect. Now I had to call Dr. Davis' office and repeat the high points to his receptionist. I snuck a peek at Matthew. He kept his face tilted down toward his magazine. The articles about advanced manure spreading techniques were probably engrossing, but I could see the side of what looked like a grin.

I got an appointment for Walker and then called him back to tell him when and where it was. He insisted I give the same information to his wife, as well.

Why was God punishing me like this?

When I hung up, Matthew said, while still pretending to read his magazine, "Where's your car?"

"Up on blocks," I said.

"What?"

"It's rolled off into the high grass!" I said.

Matthew closed his magazine and looked at me. "Tough day?"

I nodded.

We sat in silence for a few moments, then I said in a surly voice, "It's not running right, and I'll be damned if I'll take it back to Knoxville Mercedes. They're thieves. Home of the $600 oil change."

He continued to look at me with a sympathetic twist to his lips.

"I can't keep showing up here in a car like that

anyway. I need something a little less pretentious."

He raised his eyebrows, asking a question. "Like maybe a tractor," I said.

"Maybe I can give you some help there," he said.

"You got an extra tractor?"

"I got more tractors than you would ever believe, but that isn't what I meant. When do you get off work?"

"About 4:30."

"I'll be back at 4:30 then." And he left.

"Hallelujah!" Alma said from behind me. I hadn't realized she'd been standing close enough to hear Matthew. I turned and looked at her with a bland expression.

"Finally," she said.

"What?"

"A date."

"Don't be ridiculous," I said, in denial. "I've known Matthew all my life."

"Then you been stupid longer than I thought."

"He didn't come here to ask me out," I said, confused.

Alma looked at me like I was a dunce. "Did he act sick? Did he ask to see the doctor?"

He'd come in, talked to me, then left. Maybe Alma had a point. A tiny one. I erased his name from the day sheet.

Matthew came to collect me in his antique BMW at 4:30. It took him about three and a half minutes to cover the five miles between the office and his

222

farm. He blasted down the road at eighty miles an hour and then suddenly, without perceptibly slowing, made a ninety-degree turn onto a nearly invisible dirt path. He floored the BMW down a narrow track that wound around the edge of his farm, through a blur of forest, and then splashed across a creek without the aid of a bridge.

"That's where I live," he said as we tore by a tin-roofed cabin tucked back into the edge of the woods.

"It's pretty," I said.

"Built it myself."

As we passed the house a pack of dogs dashed out and raced along behind his car barking joyously. Matthew shot across an open field and passed a couple of beautiful bored-looking horses. He slid to a stop in a cloud of dust at the closest of three large metal buildings that sat in a row.

We got out and he shoved against the edge of a fifteen-foot door and rolled it slowly to one side. As daylight flooded inside, it first illuminated a cloud of dust motes and then, like a sunrise on the surface of the moon, the contents of the building. The building was jammed completely full of something, but I couldn't make out what. I stepped over a high sill and into an alley so narrow I had to turn sideways to move down it. It took a moment to understand what I was seeing. The bodies of five very old military jeeps were stored vertically in a row, slightly tilted, like a set of olive drab books on a shelf. The tires and motors were missing.

Then there was a full-size fire truck, brilliant crimson with gold lettering, and an ambulance, no, *two* military ambulances, both with old-fashioned green canvas tops painted with red crosses. I continued down the aisle, entranced. There was another antique jeep, this one intact and sitting in a normal position. It was about half the size of a normal jeep.

"I like this one," I said.

"That's real rare," he said. "It's a special Marine jeep called a 'mouse.' An M-422 Mighty Mite. It's little so they could drop it from a helicopter. It was only meant to run 500 miles and then be thrown away. It's got an aluminum body like a Land Rover, but it's a magnesium alloy, so if you try to weld it, it'll catch itself on fire and burn up."

"Sort of like a *Mission Impossible* car," I said. "What's that?" I asked, pointing to a vehicle with no body at all, just a seat and pedals and steering wheel on a bare platform.

"That's rare too. It's a special Marine truck that was made for Vietnam. It's called a 'mule.' It'll haul 1,000 pounds of gear anywhere. The steering wheel will lay over so you can drive it while you walk along beside it, or hide behind it if people are shooting at you. It'll climb a sixty percent grade, even in reverse. It'll crawl up a hill you can't climb on foot."

How strange, a motorized mouse and a mechanical mule. Then we came to a huge metal monster so odd looking I couldn't tell which end was the front. "What's this?" I asked.

"An armored personnel carrier from World War II. This one runs on wheels. The other one over there," he said, pointing into the gloom, "runs on tracks like a tank."

"Good Lord, Matthew! What are you doing with all this crazy stuff?"

"Do you like it?"

"Yeah! I love it. It's fabulous. But it's sort of spooky too. I've never seen anything like it."

"This is just the military stuff. Most of it was a mess, in pieces, when I got it. I put them back together. The next building's mostly German cars, BMWs and Mercedes, and then the other one's for farm equipment."

In the corner of the building sat a small square postal jeep. It was in pretty bad shape, but still had the red, white, and blue decal around it like a belt. It looked sort of jaunty. And spunky. "Sell me that jeep," I said.

"No."

"Why not?"

"Cause it's a piece of shit."

"Sell it to me, *please*," I said.

"What do you want it for?"

"I want to drive it to work."

"You got a $50,000 car, the best touring sedan in the world, and you wanna drive that instead?" He shook his head. "I used to think you was smart," he said smiling.

Something about that scrappy little jeep said "can do." It was the perfect vehicle: a red, white, and blue car that would remind me of Washington and yet poke fun at my pretensions at the same time.

"Hell, that's a right-hand drive, Matthew. You can't get a right-hand drive car for less than $30,000. It's a poor man's Land Rover! In fact," I said, "that car right there beat out the Land Rover Defender on incline pull tests."

He stared at me, surprised. I'd impressed him with that little tidbit. He knew who he was dealing with now. Another car nut. "Okay," he said, sighing. "You can have it."

"How much?"

"We can just call it even for the goat x-ray."

"You can't give a car away!"

"Carolyn, look around," he gestured widely with both arms. "Take it. You'll be doing me a favor."

"Thanks, Matthew."

"You wanna drive something fun?" he asked.

"What'll run?"

"It'll all run."

"Goodness," I said. "I don't know. I can't decide. What's the funnest thing?"

"Well, I like the amphibious armored personnel carrier the best. It'll go sixty miles an hour across the pasture and then we can run it through the pond. It won't float, but it's waterproof, so you can lock down the hatches and run along the bottom and then climb up the bank and out on the other side."

I thought he must be the strangest man alive.

He lifted up the gull wing door of the carrier and a set of steps was revealed by a matching lower wing. He pointed at a round platform suspended from the roof inside the middle of the carrier. It had a small seat in it. "You can ride in the gunner's seat if you want to. You can stick your head out the top and the chair will rotate 360 degrees. Sorry, the gun's gone. They won't sell them to you with the gun on them."

I hopped onto the bottom step and poked my head inside. I felt claustrophobic just looking inside the thick-walled metal container that had only two narrow slits for eyes. "How about a ride in the mouse or the mule?" I suggested. "Something a little less ferocious. And you drive."

"Okay," he said.

We rode around his farm in the mouse jeep. He stopped atop a hill with a beautiful view of the Smoky Mountains. "I come up here a lot of times at night with the dogs and build a campfire. I like to sleep up here," he said. "Or sometimes I park the pickup in the middle of the creek and sleep in the back. I like the sound of the water."

We sat for a few moments looking out at the mountains. "Do you like pears?" he asked.

I nodded.

He restarted the jeep and made a wild run through some steep woods. Riding in the small open vehicle, zigzagging through the trees reminded me of running through the woods as a child, but this was at five times the speed. We were completely surrounded by green and continuously whipped across the face and torso by small branches and leaves. He headed toward an open field with a single huge tree in the center. He pulled up to the tree and stopped. He got out and studied the pickings and then jumped up to snatch a pear about eight feet up. He came to stand next to me and carefully peeled it with his pocketknife. And handed it to me. It was delicious. Matthew certainly gave an interesting twist to the concept of eating out.

He took off again for parts unknown and we bounced and swerved across the green hills. "What do you want with that postal jeep?" he said.

"I like that jeep," I said. "I like it because it's square. It's anti-aerodynamic. To me, that jeep's got a real high frequency beauty that's beyond most people's ability to perceive, like a dog whistle—or a flower that looks plain white to us, but that looks great to a bug that can see infrared."

"It looks pretty rough to me," he said.

"I'll call it Old Paint."

"You need to put some *new* paint on it so it won't ruin any worse than it already has."

"I don't know how to paint a car."

"Wanna learn?"

"Yeah," I said, stunned that any man would offer to bring a woman into the secret and sacred, fiercely protected, all-male world of fiddling with cars. It was unprecedented. I said with real conviction, "I'd *love* to know how to paint cars."

"Then I'll teach you," he said, smiling at me. "Michael and I will. You know Michael Mayshark, don't you?"

"Sure."

"Well, he's the best custom car painter there is. Taught most of the street-rodders in Knoxville. I'll talk to him. He's got a great place to paint too."

I wanted to say, "We'll have to paint fast," but I didn't, because I didn't want to reveal any medical confidences. I suspected Matthew knew there wasn't going to be much time for this project, but he didn't mention it either.

"What color do you like?" he asked.

I thought about it a minute. "There's an antique Land Rover color I love more than anything. It's called Marine Blue, and when it fades it's the exact blue gray color of the haze on the Smokies. That's the color I'd like to paint it. So it'll just blend into the landscape, like camo. You won't even be able to find it out in the yard."

Matthew nodded. "Then Marine Blue it is. But you gotta let me take a look at the Mercedes too."

"Deal," I said.

229

SEVENTEEN

On Friday afternoon a complete stranger came in. He was a tall, dark-haired man who brought his wife in to be seen. He had a black patch over his right eye and a beautiful smile. He looked like a pirate.

When his wife went back to see the doctor, he was the only person left in the waiting room. I was curious about the patch, but I didn't want to embarrass him with prying questions. I've always had to struggle mightily to be discreet, but as the minutes ticked by with just him and me sitting there, my natural curiosity won out.

"What happened to your eye?" I asked him. He mumbled that it was an old war injury and looked out the front window toward the parking lot, his face turned away from me. I studied his profile. It must've been Vietnam. "Vietnam?" I said.

He nodded.

"Shrapnel?" I was really being a pest.

"No," he said turning to look at me, to try to figure out why I was asking him all these questions.

"I don't mean to bother you," I said, "but I've had two eye operations myself and I've had to wear an eye patch off and on all my life. My eyes're still crooked and I can only see out of one at a time."

He nodded at me and then turned his head away again. After a few seconds he said, "I was gonna shoot a fellow . . . but he got his shot off first. His bullet hit the scope of my rifle and exploded it in my face. It put my eye out."

I couldn't think what to say. Then I realized he'd said his rifle had a scope on it. Everybody around here knew what that meant: he hadn't been a regular soldier. He'd been a sniper. For many generations and many different wars, this area had provided most of the snipers to the military. Locals were renowned for an amazing proficiency with guns that came from handling them extensively from an early age.

I felt sorry the man had lost an eye, but I couldn't really blame the other guy for shooting too. And I had to admire such a beautiful shot. So I just sat there imagining the incredible drama of two snipers holding each other in their sites simultaneously until one of them squeezed the trigger.

After a few moments he turned and asked, "Do you wanna hear about it?"

"Yeah," I said, standing up and leaning over the counter so I could see and hear better.

"Being shot in the face put me in a coma. The Army doctors tried everything they could think of, but they couldn't get me to wake up. They flew me all over the place to different VA hospitals, but I stayed unconscious. They finally got tired of fiddling with me and told my family I never would wake up. Then they just discharged me and sent me home."

I got an image of a piece of lost luggage that suddenly showed up on the doorstep. Except in this case the package was a body bag that they couldn't quite zip up.

"My wife and I hadn't been married but less than a year when I got shot," he said, "but she stayed and took care of me anyway. Even though they told her there was no hope. And then one morning while she was standing beside the bed where I'd been laying for months like a stick of wood, all of a sudden I asked her, *What time is it?*

"It must've scared the fool out of her when I started talking all of a sudden like that, but she told me it was 7:30. Then I said, *Oh no! I'm gonna be late for work!*

"And she said, *No, you're not.* I said, Why not? She said, *Cause you don't have a job no more.* I asked her, *How come?* She told me, *Cause you've been in a coma for more'n two years!*"

The man and I laughed and then sat looking at each other, considering this amazing thing. Then he said, "Do you wanna hear something weird that happened to me?"

I thought to myself, *More weird than getting shot by someone you're trying to shoot, or more weird than waking up suddenly after two years in a coma raring to go to work?* I said, "Sure."

He said, "Jesus come to me while I was sleeping."

"He did?"

"Yeah. I used to dream just like everybody else before I got hurt. But when I was in the coma, I never had one dream the whole two years. And I never have had one in all the years since. But I did see something while I was sleeping."

"What?"

"Jesus. He come down and sat on a three rail fence and talked to me. I can't remember what He said, but I remember Him very clearly and I knew who He was and He just sat there on that fence and kept me company till I woke up.

"Do you believe me?" he asked. "Most people don't believe me."

"I believe you," I said. "What'd He look like?"

"He just looked like a man, but I knew who He was anyway."

The man and I sat in a companionable silence, thinking. He was smiling to himself at the memory. Then he took a deep breath and said, "If it wasn't the good Lord sitting on that fence, I know I wouldn't be here today talking to you. That's for sure."

I was inclined to agree.

As I thought about the strange mystery of coma and the blurred line between life and death, I remembered a night when I was a young teenager and I'd suddenly woken up in the wee hours of the morning. It took me a moment to realize that I'd been awakened by Daddy's phone ringing. His muffled, sleepy voice was barely audible through the wall. I listened to the indistinct sounds, trying to judge if he was going to be able to handle the problem over the phone and get to go back to sleep, or if he would have to drive into town to admit someone to the hospital. He often had to go to the hospital during the evening, sometimes more than once during a single night. He'd let me go with him if the next day wasn't a school day.

I opened the door so I could look across the hall. Suddenly a crack of light appeared underneath Daddy's door. I rushed to get dressed in the cold and was ready in less than five minutes. It took Daddy a little longer because he had to put on a tie.

I loved these trips to the hospital. We'd get up in the dark and go out when the truckers were the only other people on the road. We'd play country music on the radio and Daddy, who has a great baritone voice, would sing while I chattered nonstop.

Things were just different at night. We did things we couldn't do during the day. We could stop at Krispy Kreme, the only place open all night, and get a box of chocolate covered doughnuts still hot from the oven. And on clear winter nights sometimes we would stand out in the yard for awhile looking up at the brilliant display of stars, trying to call their names.

That particular night I went along when Daddy

had to go see a patient who had been taken to the hospital with chest pain. I followed him to the nurses' station in the Cardiac Unit where he was handed a chart. He glanced through the pages and then we went down the hall and into a room.

There was a man in the room, lying in bed, with a sheet pulled up to the middle of his chest. He didn't have a shirt on. He had a tube down his throat and was hooked up to a respirator. I'd never heard the sound before, but I recognized it immediately and was certain that I would never forget it. It was very loud and very sobering. *Whoosh. Click. Whoosh. Click.*

I stood back in one corner and watched Daddy examine the man. He held the man's eyelid open with his thumb and shined a little penlight into first one eye, then the other.

He murmured a request to the nurse. Did I hear him right? Ice water and a pin?

Ice water and a pin? I would have liked to ask him what they were for, but I didn't dare say anything. He had never let me come with him into the Cardiac Unit before.

I looked at the man carefully. His skin was a pinkish brown against the bright white bedsheet. His chest was moving up and down. He didn't seem to be conscious, but otherwise he looked fine. The nurse brought in a small clear drinking glass of ice water and a straight pin like dressmakers use and set them on the nightstand beside the bed.

Daddy walked to the foot of the bed, flipped the sheet up to expose the man's feet, and pinched down hard on a big toe. That didn't wake the man up. Next he picked up the pin and used it to prick the man's palms and then the soles of his feet, but again got no response. Then he gently turned the man's face to one side and poured a little bit of the ice water into the man's ear. Nothing happened. I was baffled.

Daddy stood looking at the man for a moment and then he walked around to the far side of the bed and flipped a switch. The room was suddenly quiet. I realized that he must have turned the respirator off!

I looked up at Daddy in surprise. I thought, *You've killed him! How could you turn off his air like that?* But since I never said a disrespectful word to my father, I said, "Can he breathe now, by himself?"

Daddy said, "No."

"Is he . . . ?"

"He's dead."

I was becoming panicky. I asked, "Why'd you cut off his air?"

"Because it wasn't doing him any good. His heart isn't beating. They couldn't get him restarted. They shocked him eleven times. He's been dead for almost an hour. They just won't let a nurse turn off the respirator. It's against the rules. A doctor has to come do it."

A surge of horror and revulsion went through me and I thought, *He's dead! I'm standing next to a dead man!*

I gaped at the body in confusion and backed up until, with a jerk, I touched the cold tile wall. I was trying to figure out what this thing "dead" meant. That was the first dead person I'd ever seen up close.

For the first time I noticed the tiny red marks in the middle of his chest where the cardiac needles had punctured the skin. Part of me was vaguely aware of what this meant. Less than an hour ago he had been surrounded by noise and equipment and people who had repeatedly pricked, pounded on, and shocked him.

But they and their tools had been cleared away, leaving him looking so peaceful. He looked dignified and graceful as he lay there—even beautiful.

Daddy asked the nurse, "Does the family know?"

She shook her head.

He pulled the sheets up to the man's shoulders to cover his exposed chest and straightened the bed. He brushed the man's hair with his fingers, tidying up the body in preparation for it to be seen by the family while he prepared himself to break the terrible news to them.

I followed him out of the room, stopping just outside, and watched him walk down the corridor to speak to the frantic little knot of people who were waiting for him in the family lounge.

I could hear them. "How is he? Is he gonna be all right?"

Daddy paused for a moment with an expressionless face and then said gently, "He has expired."

There was absolute silence for a moment.

They were trying to understand this word. They looked at Daddy in confusion, trying to interpret what he had told them.

Not "dead," or "fine," but "expired," like a parking meter. Like a coupon. Like a warranty.

I couldn't fault him. "Dead" would have been so graceless, so abrupt. Let them sidle up to the notion in their own time.

I waited in the hall while Daddy comforted the family, not wanting to stay in the room with the dead man, or go near the grieving family. As I stood there, shifting my eyes around in an effort to avoid seeing anything upsetting, I noticed a chart taped to the wall. It was entitled "Evaluation of Coma" and listed a series of six tests to determine the level of brain activity of a patient in a coma. *Ahhh . . . this* was the odd ritual Daddy had been performing.

I saw that he'd skipped Number 1, "Subject responsive to voice," and had gone straight to Number 2, "Pupils reactive to light." He'd progressed through them one at a time from memory.

Pouring cold water into a person's ear was the sixth and final test. If the person had any vestiges of life left in them, the ice water was supposed to make their eyeballs flick back and forth in a primitive nervous reaction. How *strange,* I thought, and how *crude.*

On the way home that night we didn't play the radio or stop for doughnuts. We didn't discuss philosophy or theology either. But when we got back to the house, before we went inside, we stood out in the yard for awhile looking up at the brilliant display of stars, trying to call their names.

EIGHTEEN

Momma was doing well in her recovery. She'd cut way down on her smoking and her Goldfish cracker consumption, but she wasn't well enough yet for me to have more than a virtual job in Washington. It was strange. I wasn't fully in either Tennessee or Washington. But I wasn't quite gone in either place. I was a ghost in two worlds.

In an effort to participate in a normal local lifestyle, I took the postal jeep to Michael, so he could see if there was any major mechanical work that needed to be done before we started on the cosmetic part. When I drove up to the house on wobbly, dry-rotted tires, there was a group of men standing with Michael, looking toward the jeep with poker faces.

"Let's torture test it, Carolyn!" he said with what seemed like an excessive amount of glee. But of course Michael was all about excessive glee. He was dying and we both knew it. I also understood that, because of his condition, it was hard for him to find someone to have fun with. He needed someone who understood medical problems but also shared his manic response to frustrating situations. Together we could have a full-bore wild time.

He got into the driver's seat with an unlit cigar clamped between his teeth and a lidded cup of distilled water. He looked around for a place to put the cup and, finding no cup holder, handed it to me. "Is this seat adjustable?" he asked.

"Not technically," I said, "but it's not bolted in very well, so it'll move around enough to keep things interesting."

"Perfect," Michael said. "Get in."

"Where?" I asked.

There is only one seat in a postal jeep. The rest is just open space for stacking boxes of mail. It had never occurred to me that I would have to ride along while he test-drove the car.

Michael looked over his shoulder into the cargo area. "Just a minute," he said. He went into his garage and came out with a red plastic storage crate. He tossed it into the back of the jeep. "You can sit on that."

I could tell Michael was taking some sort of a mind-altering substance. He was a bit too high, even for him. But I was happy to play Thelma to his Louise. He was a street-rodder and had been a race car driver on dirt tracks, so I trusted his driving. I also knew he wasn't looking to die just yet.

I'd never been involved in a "torture test" before. I scooted on the hard plastic cube, positioning myself in the middle of the open storage area. Not too comfy. Not only was the jeep itself a rolling hazard, but I was going to ride on a plastic crate with no seat belt and no way to keep myself from sliding around. I faked a level of cool I didn't really feel, trusting myself to Michael's considerable driving skill and the benevolence of the universe. The fact that a woman in my position, hanging out with a dying man, could still imagine that the universe was benevolent should have been a tip-off that I wasn't in my right mind.

"Here we go!" Michael said, and floored the jeep. It took off like a rabbit through the yard and I went flying over backward.

"Oops," he said by way of apology.

I struggled to get back onto my crate. It was a challenge to match the bouncing of my butt with the bouncing of the jeep, which didn't seem to have very good shocks. It went jouncing down Michael's driveway with all the finesse of a covered wagon.

He laid rubber as he pulled out onto the highway. "This little rascal's got power!"

I fell off the crate sideways this time. I didn't even try to get back on it. I didn't say anything because I was holding on for dear life and didn't want to distract the pilot. I tried several positions and then crouched on the balls of my feet behind Michael's seat. He was apparently trying to see what the jeep's top speed was, though I knew square cars were notoriously unstable at high speeds. The wheels hardly tracked at low speeds. Michael was motoring along a two-lane highway and was flooring the jeep on a stretch of road that rolled across a series of steep blind hills.

I moved to squat directly behind his seat so I could hold on with both hands. The back of the seat was tall, so I had to get on my knees to see over the top. Just as I got into my new position Michael said, "Hold on, we're gonna test the steering."

He got to a place where he could see that no cars were coming and slammed on the brakes as he jerked the oversized steering wheel to the left. He was doing a high-speed U-turn in the middle of a highway in this piece of shit. I tried to hide my face behind the seat, but got my head bounced hard off the right wall instead.

Michael shouted over his shoulder, "Carolyn, I gotta tell you, your taste in cars sure is hard on a one-armed man."

That explained the left turn. He couldn't have gone right because he didn't have a usable hand on that side. I didn't want to picture how he was steering with half of one hand on the slick steering wheel. And this wasn't a regular steering wheel with a normal turning radius—it had a huge diameter like the wheel on a pirate ship. It took an extravagant movement to get a small result. What was a good design for postmen who needed to sidle up to a mailbox at five miles an hour, was a very bad design for high-speed highway stunts.

The entire situation was so ridiculous there was no point in being scared. I might as well let go and enjoy myself. Soon both of us were whooping and screaming like fools as he raced the little truck up and down the hills and carved doughnuts in the highway. He at least had the excuse that he was on pain medicine and dying anyway. I was just a fool. But God, it was fun.

By the time he pulled back into his yard, I was lying sprawled in the back, breathless. The men hanging around the garage looked amused. Michael pulled to a stop in front of them and I called out, loud enough for all to hear, "Let's do that again. This time I'll drive."

Michael grabbed his water cup from the floorboard where it had rolled and got out of the jeep. "You're outta your mind if you think I'm ever getting in that thing again. We were lucky to get out with our lives." Then he winked like the lunatic he was.

We hadn't discussed the mechanical condition of the jeep, so I suppose it must've passed its road test. In fact, as I drove back home, I wondered if the road test had been strictly for the jeep. Maybe he'd been testing *me* in some sort of vetting ritual for wannabe car painters. To see if I had courage and stamina. To see if I had what it took to make the best of a bad situation. Looking on the sunny side of things was a highly prized trait in an area where life had been grim for as long as anyone could remember.

Or maybe he just wanted to be sure I knew how to

die and have fun at the same time. That was certainly something everybody needed to know how to do, since, whether we thought about it or not, we were all in the act of dying. And yet, most of us did everything we could to forget it.

I was beginning to understand, and even adopt, Michael's philosophy of life. Anything that didn't kill you wasn't a problem.

I was going postal. And I was taking Matthew and Michael with me.

"Carolyn, you gotta paint three cars before you really learn how to do it right," Michael said. "Then you gotta get rid of those first three cars quick before anyone sees them. The fourth one will look good."

Matthew walked around the jeep, studying it from all angles. "Those red, white, and blue stripes have gotta go," he said.

"But," I said, "that's the best thing on the car!"

"I don't know what she sees in the damn thing anyway," Matthew said. "It's got over 400,000 miles on it."

Michael looked at me with a slight smile and said, "It's what they call a 'special-interest vehicle.'"

"What's that mean?" I asked.

"It's what the car collectors call the cars that don't fit into the regular categories. Like in *Hemmings Motor News*, the fancy car collectors' magazine where you can buy exotic automobiles and hard-to-find parts. That jeep's a special-interest vehicle, like three-wheeled trucks, meter-maid cars, French minis. There's several different small trucks in the same category. Postal jeeps are sometimes sold in *Hemmings*.

"You don't have to apologize for what you like," he added.

I looked at the dented, square vehicle with pride.

Michael had a fabulous place to paint cars. It was a special superimmaculate concrete block room built onto his garage. A seepage system installed around the edges of the ceiling continuously dripped water down the walls, coating them, to capture dust. A splendid Packard was currently occupying the center of the main bay. My humble postal jeep was parked a respectful distance away from the fancy garage, on the grass.

Matthew and Michael had laid out an impressive array of equipment. There was a set of what looked like blacksmith's tools, hammers and metal-shaping gizmos for fixing dents. We were going to give those items a pass during this introductory lesson. In addition to the metal-forming tools, there were all sorts of sanders, grinders, and saws. We donned masks and goggles, Matthew flipped on the air compressor that powered the tools, and then he began to show me how all the tools worked. Lord, what a racket. Even working outside, with the compressor six feet away, the noise was deafening.

Once our work began in earnest, we wouldn't hear a bomb explode, we couldn't see farther than the length of our arms, and breathing was almost out of the question. It was loud and violent and creative. It was like making a 2,000-pound piece of jewelry.

Matthew and I sanded the devil out of the left front fender. The topmost coat had obviously been slopped on from a can of flat paint using a wide brush. We sanded through it and what appeared to be half a dozen more coats of white paint, finally reaching the lovely, shiny, original red, white, and blue enamel. In some places we went all the way past the dull gray primer, exposing and polishing the bare silver metal beneath. It was like an archaeological dig. The fender became a rounded rainbow, with bands of the different colors looking like an oil slick on wet pavement.

Michael had been sitting to one side, watching us while we sanded, but when we were ready to prime a small area of bare metal, he loaded the primer gun himself to show me how to use it. He used red oxide primer the color of dried red clay mud. This wasn't the best choice since it would clash with the topcoat, but because this was a practice vehicle, I got cheap leftovers. I didn't mind. The color of local dirt seemed appropriate somehow.

Even though I was standing right next to him, I couldn't understand how Michael was able to operate the paint spray gun with such delicate precision. He'd periodically pass me the gun and I'd clumsily imitate his movements. What he made look easy was not. It was like getting to stumble along with a companionable Olympic athlete.

We each wore respirators, but I could still feel myself inhaling paint. I liked it. I'd always known that I could have been a paint huffer if I'd been the recreational drug type, because the smell of fresh paint made me high. I said something about it to Michael and he said, "It might be fun now, but it'll hurt tomorrow. When you wake up in the morning, your chest will be burning."

Michael couldn't stand up for very long and soon had to paint from his motorized wheelchair. After we finished priming the fender, he did a jaunty little jig in the chair. I wasn't the only potential huffer in the crowd.

By the time we were done I was exhausted. I sat in a folding chair and untied my head rag, then peeled it and the mask and goggles off my face. I could feel a coating of primer on the skin I hadn't covered carefully enough. I hoped I didn't look as goofy as Michael and Matthew did. I ruffled my helmet-hair and said, "I didn't realize how much equipment it took to restore a car."

"I've made a fortune in the junk business," Michael said. "Two, actually. I lost the first one trying to act like something I'm not. I let a man I thought was my friend screw me out of millions in a Cadillac dealership. I only went into it because I thought it would be something classy. When I was

younger I wanted to be high class more than anything. I got over the desire several million dollars
later and went back to the junk business."

He leaned toward me. "I had to face it. I'm a junk
man. Just a junk man. That's all I'm ever gonna be."

I smiled at him, still high on paint fumes. Then he
turned a couple of doughnuts in his wheelchair
and demonstrated how it would lay rubber.
"Maybe I'm just a junk man," he said, "but damn if
I'm not a good one!"

Some part of me understood what he was trying
to say. I just wasn't ready to face the reality of it.

I sat in the barn using an overturned bucket for an
executive office chair because all the hay had been
doled out to cows during the winter. I'd stored documents out there because I didn't want to be
reminded of Washington when I was in the house.
And I liked sitting in the barn.

There were stacks of boxes behind me and I'd
bought a couple of used filing cabinets to store the
stuff Jacob was sending me. I was supposed to be
helping him with a hearing on bribery and corruption in relation to nuclear power plant safety, but I
was of no real use. It was really only because he
was such a good friend that he kept pretending I
was still in the loop. Any other colleague would
have knocked off the charade months ago.

I couldn't help but compare the house and farm
outbuildings to the elaborate underground world of

the Capitol, the House and Senate Office Buildings, and the Library of Congress. To go from the house to the barn you had to brave wind, snow, rain, heat, and black cows standing around in the dark of night. No such problem in our nation's capital, where you could be lost for days in the subterranean labyrinth underlying Capitol Hill. Temperature was perfectly regulated to obviate the need for a topcoat or umbrella and no cruel wind or whimsical breeze could muss a coiffure that had to be maintained camera-ready at all times.

I could enter the barn without having to pass through a metal detector, and I no longer had to risk running in high heels. Now I was dodging cow patties. I'd gone from chatting with John Glenn on the anniversary of his historic space flight to commiserating with widows and calling in tranquilizers on the anniversary of their husbands' deaths.

I looked out at the sun to estimate the time, then thought of Jacob. He kept himself and the boss on a tight schedule with the aid of an elegant watch and a fancy leather appointment book.

Although I was now officially on leave from my job in Washington, I was trying to keep some sort of a grip on it. But my plan wasn't working very well, even with Jacob's valiant efforts to help. Earlier in the day he'd called to ask if I was available to appear on CNN. I'd had to say no, I wouldn't be available to pop down to the studio in Atlanta and tape an interview. Also no, I wouldn't be available to cruise underneath the polar ice cap. No, I simply wouldn't be available.

That night Momma must have sensed my wavering, because she said, "I appreciate you filling in for me. Your father and I need you, you know. There's nobody else to ask."

Later, as I lay in bed, I thought about how strange it was to find myself confronted with the same issue my parents had faced so long ago. I was presented with whether to stay at the office or go on to better things. The maddening distinction was that we came to the situation as totally different people in utterly different circumstances. For me, staying had radically different consequences than it had for them. My parents had gained independence, a respectable livelihood, and an honored place in the community by choosing to work there. But, forty years later, it felt like I was losing nearly everything by making the very same choice.

Summer

NINETEEN

Now that I'd been at the office for nine months I was in danger of being permanently taken over by my temporary identity as a receptionist. In an effort to remember what I'd once been, I rented *Mr. Smith Goes to Washington*. It was as close as I was going to be getting to Washington for the foreseeable future. I hadn't seen the movie in years. So when the part came where Mr. Smith was preparing to enter the Senate Chamber for the first time I watched in morbid fascination, realizing that just a year earlier I'd seen the real-life Jimmy Stewart walk past the exact spot where he was now standing in the movie. My sighting of Mr. Smith had occurred fifty years after the movie had been made, but Jimmy Stewart had been even more impressive in person—surprisingly tall and straight with brilliant blue eyes. He'd taken my breath away.

Jimmy Stewart was never going to walk by Daddy's office. Not ever.

Afterwards I lay on the couch and stared out through the patio doors into the yard. I thought about a hearing we'd had a couple of years before. The nation had been attempting to site a nuclear waste dump, somewhere, anywhere. Washington

State didn't want it. Nevada didn't want it. Nobody wanted it. Nobody except the tiny mountain town of Wartburg, Tennessee. Wartburg's desire for the nuclear dump had sent a wave of horror across the rest of the state, but the little community had refused to be deterred. They had been a one-industry town, and that industry had closed. The entirety of their economic base had rested on the Brushy Mountain Maximum Security Federal Penitentiary (former home of James Earl Ray, murderer of Dr. Martin Luther King Jr.).

Brushy Mountain was like Alcatraz in that any prisoner who managed to get outside the fence would never survive to reach civilization. The terrain was too dangerous, what with the steep mountains, miles of impenetrable thickets, and the whole place being a thriving rattlesnake habitat. But even its penally paradisical setting couldn't save it. When Brushy Mountain closed, it left generations of fierce prison guards in pristine isolation with nothing to guard. A nuclear warhead dump seemed like a worthy substitution and just the shot in the arm the Wartburg economy needed. I could certainly see their point.

Representatives of the various potential dump sites had traveled from all over the country, at their own expense, to testify at the hearing. Enflamed passionately for or passionately against the dump, they'd practiced for hours, bought new outfits for the occasion, and brought their families along to watch.

Unfortunately, the press didn't exhibit the slightest interest in the hearing, and the lack of media coverage had a trickle down effect. The number one law of politics is: no press, no politicians. Senators wouldn't watch their own mothers testify if there weren't any cameras there to film it. Without any press, they weren't gaining any name recognition. Without name recognition, they couldn't raise the money to buy more press. So, the various Committee Members ducked in to see what the press situation was and then quickly ducked out again to go try to find some cameras somewhere else. Eventually the buzzers sounded, calling all Senators to the Capitol for a vote, and suddenly none were left to receive the witnesses' testimony.

It was sad. What should have been one of the high points of these people's lives was being taken away from them. Not only were they *not* going to be on television tonight, but they were apparently expected to testify to a bunch of empty chairs. These people were not sophisticated about Congressional hearings and they didn't know what to do when the Members vanished. Actually, nobody would know what to do. Who could be expected to know how to act during a Senate hearing when there were no Senators there? There was no one to ask them any questions, no one for them to talk to. The poor schmuck who had been the lead witness was bravely soldiering on, clearly confused about whether to keep talking or not.

I watched the other staff leave and the audience thin out until I couldn't stand it anymore. The doors at the front and back of the room kept opening and closing noisily as people left and figured, in perfect Washington style, if *they* weren't there anymore, noise was no longer an issue. Sort of a reverse tree-falling-in-the-forest thing. I had to do something. I wouldn't have dared sit in one of the Senator's leather swivel chairs, but I scooted my heavy, straight-back wooden seat toward the front of the dais and made eye contact with the witness, nodding to urge him to continue his testimony.

When he finished I asked him several questions. I could tell he was disconcerted that I seemed to have an expert understanding of the issues. I guess he thought the Senators were the experts and I was just the lady who refilled their water glasses. Little did he know. It was a bit strange to be speaking at a hearing, but it saved unbelievable amounts of time not to have to write the questions down and pass them to the boss.

When the first witness seemed satisfied that he'd made his points, I called the name of the next witness. In a similar fashion I took the testimony of each witness. This sort of thing would never have happened in a movie; Mr. Smith would never have bugged out on a group of earnest citizens.

As they spoke, I contemplated the origin of the word *testimony*. Learning this little tidbit of etymological information had been the most riveting few minutes of my entire time in law school. The term *testify* had to do with male anatomy, specifically, with testicles. Back in the good old days, before "raise your right hand and swear after me," when a liege lord had an important question to ask one of his vassals, he'd take hold of the man's private parts and ask the question. That put him eye-to-eye with the witness. If the lord saw something in the man's expression that displeased him or made him doubt the answer, he'd squeeze and repeat the question. Things could get worse, but I won't go into that. This technique was thought to be a pretty effective precursor to truth serum. Since women clearly lacked the basic equipment, they were thought to be incompetent to testify. You had to see their point. That was one reason why, until recently, women couldn't testify in court or have any legal rights whatsoever. I kid you not. It took men thousands of years to figure out the raise-your-right-hand thing.

Eventually each of the witnesses had testified. I tried the best I could to make sure each of them had fully vented, really gotten their money's worth. Then I reached for the boss's gavel and banged the hearing to a close, formally intoning a cryptic-sounding ritual that I made up on the spot. The audience seemed to enjoy that part. I figured some of them would come up for a chat then and maybe we'd go to lunch together, but I'd underestimated the effect of the trappings. They treated me with cautious awe, shooting me discreet glances as they packed up. Then they left without saying anything further.

I moved my chair back to its usual spot against the wall and sat in the empty hearing room alone. I thought about how sometimes the *only* thing we can do for another person is simply pay attention to them. Then it occurred to me this might even be the *best* thing we could ever do for anybody. Maybe the ability to confer attention on another person was not simply common courtesy, but was the fundamental act of humanity.

When it came down to it, all we really ever had to give each other was our attention. Wasn't that what love was? Paying selfless attention?

Maybe the reception desk bore a closer resemblance to the hearing room than I'd appreciated. Maybe it was important to be a person who'd sit there listening to people, whoever they were, whatever they wanted to talk about, until they felt heard.

Lying on the couch, I decided I could keep listening for a while longer. It was not lost on me that, at the end of the movie, Mr. Smith had not stayed in Washington. He'd gone back home where he belonged.

The first thing next morning Miss Hiawatha was back. Her stomach pains would not go away. They were keeping her awake at night and she, in turn, was keeping her friends, her neighbors, and Frank awake. Something had to be done. Daddy tried to calm an exasperated neighbor by telling them they needed to pay attention when someone Miss Hiawatha's age continued to complain of pain. In his experience, even if people weren't otherwise in their right minds, if they persisted with a complaint about pain, there really was something wrong. He had a similar policy about mothers who said something was wrong with their baby. In both situations he'd learned to trust what he was being told and to keep looking until he found out what was wrong.

So he had me set up an appointment for Miss Hiawatha with a radiologist for tests. The tests showed gallstones, so next we got her an appointment with a surgeon. The surgeon said at the same time he removed her gallbladder, he'd also go ahead and repair her abdominal hernia and a bladder problem. This three-for-one operation seemed sensible to everyone.

But the surgery got put off. The first delay was because she had her chauffeur take her to the hospital on the wrong day. Then the surgeon went out of town. Various delays continued for weeks—and she continued to hurt.

Every time I called to give her the new appointment time, she'd ask me to pray for her. "Don't worry, Miss Hiawatha," I'd say in a cheerful voice. "This is an easy operation, and it'll get rid of your pain. You'll be glad you did it."

She'd agree and then remind me again to pray for her. "I will," I always said, but I usually forgot to do it.

Then one morning Frank called and said, "Carolyn, Miss Hiawatha's dead."

"Oh no!" I blurted.

"She died last night. They don't know why. She was in the hospital and was doing fine, getting over her surgery. But then she just died suddenly."

"Oh no. I can't believe it. I just can't believe it."

"You know, she knew she was gonna die," he said. "Every time she talked to me she'd say, 'Now Frankie, don't you forget to pray for me.' But I didn't do it."

"She always asked me to pray for her too. I bet I didn't do it but maybe twice. Lord help me, Frank, I made the appointment for her surgery!"

"You didn't kill her," Frank said.

We sat, sharing a miserable silence, and then he said, "Did you know she called me every day? But Lord Almighty, she'd call me in the middle of the night or whenever. You know she called me last week at 4:00 in the morning and said, 'Frankie, I need some bread and milk and Sprite.' I said, 'Hell, Miss Hiawatha, it's four o'clock in the damn morning!' But then I felt bad and told her I'd send it when I got to work, and I did.

"She kept telling me stuff about her funeral too. She said, 'Now, Frankie, you make sure they dress me in pink. Promise me you'll go to my funeral and look in the coffin at me and make sure they got me all in pink. If they don't, you make them change my clothes and put on my new pink outfit.' She *insisted* I promise to make them change her clothes if she didn't look good. And of course I had to promise not to let them take her to Barnfield's under any circumstances because she didn't like the way they did hair and makeup and then there was a bunch of other stuff about a woman falling into caskets, a hearse that wouldn't start, and a preacher falling in a grave."

"She *did* know she was gonna die," I said.

"I guess I'll have to go do what I said I would," Frank said. "The family'll have a shit fit, but I'll be damned if I won't do what I promised her. Do you know I bought all her groceries for her? She'd call me and put in her order and I'd get a kid who works at the Bi-Rite to take it to her on his way home. At the end of the month, when she got her social security check, she'd pay me back."

Frank was a saint.

"I'll miss her," I said. "She was my very favorite patient."

"I'll miss her too," Frank said.

Frank made sure they took Miss Hiawatha to Addison's mortuary instead of Barnfield's and then he went several hours before her funeral to check on her outfit. He made sure she'd been dressed entirely in pink: with pink rings, bracelet, necklace, and earrings. Even the lining of the casket and the flowers were pink. When I saw him at the funeral we agreed that she looked nice and would have been pleased with everything.

As she'd feared, a family member read a poem he'd written about her, but it was mercifully short and, actually, not too bad. And, as Frank and I observed from the back, the whole extended family milled around in front of the casket in a way that looked superficially casual, but was actually orchestrated with military precision to keep cousin Freda from getting close enough to the casket to fall in and mess up Miss Hiawatha's hair. Freda finally did get to faint but was instantly intercepted and forced to swoon into the first pew by a young man who was a star defensive back on the White Oak football team.

"What's wrong, Obie? Did you hurt yourself?" I asked from behind the reception desk as the wiry farmer came through the front door in a strange stiff-legged gait. What had he gotten into? Could Kermit's accident-proneness have become contagious? I worried that if Obie looked this bad, Kermit might be dead.

"I just need Doc to look me over," Obie said. "Them folks at the hospital told me to see my regular doctor when it come time to get my bandages changed."

"What happened?" I asked, and was immediately

embarrassed, because I didn't want him to have to explain something personal in front of everybody in the waiting room. Men could be limping for a lot of delicate reasons. But it was too late. Eight pairs of eyes had swiveled toward Obie, awaiting his explanation.

He mumbled, "Oh, I got hurt working on my hog lot."

"Did the hogs get you?" I asked, nosiness winning out over good manners yet again. But as all farm kids know, hogs are carnivorous if given the chance.

"Naaaw. It wasn't the hogs," he said. He glanced around, realized he had a rapt audience, and decided to come clean.

"I had a load of hog wire in my truck and was gonna patch some torn places in the fence. A little shower come along, so I had to wait a few minutes till it quit raining.

"When the sun come out, I drove down to the hog lot. The ground was still a little wet, but not much. While I was rolling out some of that hog wire, they come a puff of wind from nowhere and blowed a hundred-year-old poplar I was standing next to, right outta the ground. I never seen nothing like it. It wasn't even windy and this puff just come along and knocked a full growed healthy tree outta the ground."

"Did it fall on you?" I asked.

"No. It fell across a power line and kept a coming

on down onto that hog wire while I still had ahold of it. It shocked the fire outta me. It made my muscles grab onto that wire so hard I was knocked off of my feet onto my knees. It liked to killed me." His hands clenched at the memory.

"I was just getting over it and leaning on the wire, pushing against it so I could get up, when it happened again! I tried to let go of that wire for all I was worth and could not get aloose of it. That electricity had hold of me and had my whole body clinched up as hard as it could get. I was afraid it'd shock me again, but I couldn't do a thing about it. And sure enough, here come another one. And this time, and I'm telling ye the truth, when that shock went through me I looked down at my arms and hands and I swear I could see right through them! I could see the bones just as clear as a x-ray! It scared me to death.

"I don't know what happened after that, but when I come back to myself I was laying up in the bed of the pickup. I thought I must've been dead and was getting hauled off to the graveyard, but the truck didn't never move, so I figured out I wasn't dead. I must of crawled up in there somehow by myself. I managed to get into the cab and drive to the house. My wife took me on to the hospital.

"The electric company told me that power line carried 72,000 volts of electricity and it had ran down that tree and onto that hog wire to get me.

They showed me the glass water pitcher that I'd carried down there with me, and rested against the base of that tree.

"You wouldn't believe it. It was all melted into a gob. They asked me if they could take it back with them to show people. I let them take it, but maybe I should've kept it so people'd believe me."

He didn't need it.

He'd come in for follow-up treatments for the burns on his back and legs. He was branded in the pattern of hog wire all over the lower half of his body.

Daddy told Obie he was lucky to be alive.

"I know it, Doc. The good Lord won't never strike His lightning in the same place twice. But I'm here to tell ye that them devils at the TVA ain't so merciful.

"They put three circuit breakers in every transformer so they can strike ye three times afore letting ye go."

We shook our heads with him at the unfairness of it. Then he added, "Damn government."

TWENTY

"You look awful," I said to Alma. It was 7:30 in the morning on a Thursday in June and I'd just gotten to work.

"I feel awful," she answered. As we went inside together she said, "Mrs. Honeycutt passed away yesterday."

"Oh, goodness. I'm sorry to hear that. But maybe it was a relief to her after being sick for so long and at the mercy of her nutty family."

"You never saw such a mess. Mr. Honeycutt's so out of it, I doubt if he understands she's dead, or would even care. And that daughter. We finally come to blows. I found Mrs. Honeycutt dead in bed when I got there. Nobody'd checked on her. She was laying in her own mess. Anyway, I told the daughter that her mom had passed away, and she started cussing me and ordering me out of the house. I told her I wasn't leaving Mrs. Honeycutt like that. I'm sure the daughter wanted one last chance to search the house for drugs before I had time to clear things out. She went crazy, and I had to smack her and lock her out of the bedroom. She beat on the door and hollered and acted like an idiot while I washed her mom and changed the sheets. I fixed her hair too. She had such pretty hair. Then I waited till the funeral home come for the body."

"Oh, Alma," I said, amazed at her fortitude and determination.

"It was Barnfield's out of Luttrell. And it must've been old man Barnfield himself who come out to pick up the body. The man had to be at least eighty," she said. "And his helper," she sat, shaking her head in disbelief. "His helper was even older than him. Lord Almighty, what a crew.

"You should've seen them, looking like two scarecrows—all skinny and wearing old suits that just hung on them. They come shuffling into the house pulling a stretcher and had to stop and rest in the living room. Both of them just flopped down in the recliners to catch their breath. When I seen them two characters I knew things wasn't gonna go right. They sat there *forever*. Old man Barnfield couldn't even get up without help. I had to haul his ass up outta the chair."

I buried my face in my hands at the image.

"I wondered how in the hell these two old men were gonna pick up a body and load it into a hearse. Thank goodness Mrs. Honeycutt didn't weigh no more than sixty pounds. I watched them wrestle her onto the stretcher. Then they had to take another half-hour rest break in the living room before rolling her on out the door.

"Then, after I haul old man Barnfield out of his

chair the second time, he goes over to the stretcher and leans on the back of it like it's a walker. But he hadn't tied the body down with the tie straps and he'd also forgot to lock the back legs, so they give out. The head end hit the floor and Mrs. Honeycutt slid right out into the middle of the living room floor."

"How awful," I said. It was both horrifying and absurd to imagine.

"The daughter stood screaming and cussing, and Mr. Honeycutt sat on the couch watching TV the whole time. I helped the old men get the body back onto the stretcher. I tied the straps this time and then the three of us lifted the thing up. I locked the legs myself and helped them roll it outside and load Mrs. Honeycutt into the oldest hearse you've ever seen in your life. I have no idea if they found their way back to the funeral home or not. What a circus."

"You see the craziest bunch of stuff," I shook my head in disbelief. "Some of it, I don't know how you stand it, and the rest, I don't know how you keep a straight face."

"Oh, this was awful. It was funny as hell, but I didn't dare laugh. She was their momma after all. And she was a good woman."

Daddy's patients had grown older alongside him, and these days he saw a lot of elderly people. It was natural that people in their seventies and eighties would be dying faster than young people, but the recent surging death toll still worried me. It was beginning to look like heroic efforts to keep Daddy's office open would shortly be mooted by circumstances. A niggling suspicion came to me, probably because I'd taken a lot of math in college. I did a quick calculation on a McDonald's napkin estimating and then extrapolating the current mortality rate of Daddy's patients. Higher mathematics revealed that by next week all of his patients would be dead. Of course, it was just a rough estimate, but I still felt like the receptionist at the Alamo.

I was still ciphering when a large man came to the reception desk. "I brung my boy. He's got the punies and I want the doc to take a look at him."

"Okay," I said. Just as I said it, Daddy walked up to his side of the counter to write a prescription for someone in the back.

"Hey, Doc!" the man called out.

Daddy flinched.

The man said, "Do you remember me? Barlow France."

"I sure do," Daddy said cautiously.

"Oh, don't worry, I ain't here for myself today. I brung my boy."

"Oh," Daddy said with obvious relief. "How's your leg? Whatever happened to that cast I put on you? You never came back. Where'd you have it taken off?"

"Soaked it off in the river. No offense, but the thing was a nuisance. A man can't work with something like that on his leg. The leg's fine now," he said slapping his thigh.

Barlow looked at me. "Can't win them all! Doc fixed me up good once when I'd been working on some of my hemorrhoids though. I thought I could handle them myself. I'd bought a fresh blade for my carpet knife and I had a good light and I had my wife hold a mirror for me, but I couldn't get the job done right. So Doc took care of them."

He'd tried to operate on his own hemorrhoids? I felt ill.

"I decided to go to the emergency room," he continued, "when I chainsawed the top of my leg. It was bleeding pretty bad, and I figured Wal-Mart'd throw me out before I could round up the needles and thread I needed. But ye know what them nuts at the hospital did? They brung a ruler and measured that damn cut. I said, 'What are ye doing? Fixing to charge me by the inch?' and they said, 'Yeah.' Can you believe that?"

I didn't dare tell him this was the way the insurance companies insisted it be done.

"So next time I got hurt—when I cut my head open with the claw end of a crowbar—I just went straight to the Wal-Mart and got a upholstery needle, cause they're curved like the ones I seen ye use. I got some embroidery thread that was loud colored so I'd be able to find the stitches when it come time to cut them out. Then I got my wife to hold the mirror so I could see the top of my head."

I was really starting to feel for Mrs. France.

"My head skin was tough as leather. It surprised me how hard it was to get the needle to go through. I couldn't do it with just my fingers. I had to go get my needle nose pliers."

"Skin's tougher than people think," Daddy said. "Harder to sew than you'd expect. How'd you numb it?"

"I didn't. And I got ahead of myself and forgot to wash the cut off first, so it got all infected and took forever to heal. It made a scar. Wanna see the scar?" He reached up and began to part his hair with his fingers.

Daddy backed up a couple of steps. "No, no, that's okay. You don't have to show me." He turned toward the back and attempted an escape.

"Wait up there, Doc. I was wondering . . . Would you sell me some of that good thread—for next time? That embroidery thread doesn't wanna slide out easy like the good stuff. It snags up and ye have to yank on it. And it comes apart into lots of little threads. It's just a mess."

Daddy stared at Barlow. "Wait there," he said.

He went into the back and came out with a small stack of sterile packages. "Here's everything you need. Needles, sutures, and a needle holder." Then he explained how to use each of the items—as one surgeon to another.

Barlow was thrilled. "What do I owe ye for all this?"

"Oh, nothing. It's a gift. But do me a favor, will you?"

"What's that?"

"Next time wash your hands real good first and then wash the cut too before you start sewing on it. Okay?"

Barlow nodded. Mercifully he allowed the other members of his family to come to a doctor for medical care. Daddy gave his son a shot and a prescription and sent them on their way.

As if the Honeycutt debacle and Barlow & Son weren't enough punishment for one morning, before we broke for lunch, a former all-state football champion nicknamed Bullet Head came in walking with a strange gait, like the Tin Man. He sagged against the reception desk. "Paul, my gout's flared up on me again," he said to Daddy. "My foot's so sore, if I was standing on a dime I could tell you if it was heads or tails. And I think I'm getting the flu."

"The flu?" Daddy said with an admirably straight face. "You must have caught it up in Newport at the Cajun Weekend. How'd that go?"

The Cajun Weekend was an annual event of the Tuckahoe Rabbit Hunters' Association that had to be held out of town because of the exuberant nature of the revelry.

"Oh, you should've been there. Oh goodness, that Cajun boy sure can cook. You really missed a good one."

"What'd he fix?" I asked.

Bullet was as interested in food as I was. "Well, you get them weenies, them good weenies, them *real* good weenies," he said, looking at me for confirmation.

I had no idea what he was talking about, but I nodded.

"Then you get Polish sausage and a bottle of hot sauce and your corn and onions and peppers, and some ears of corn broke half in two, Red Pontiac potatoes, and a *big* bunch of onions. You cut them onions crosswise, so you can pick them out and eat them. And garlic. *Lots* of garlic."

I was already feeling queasy thinking of all that grease hitting all the alcohol that was being used to wash it down.

"You put all them vegetables in a pair of panty hose. You cut the legs off, then you put them taters down in one leg and the corn and onions in the other and tie them off. When you've cooked them all up, you take a knife and lay it open. But before that you've got to put it all on a low burner in a big pot on the ground and then you put your shrimps in. When it's all done, you pour the whole pot out on the table, cut open them pantyhose, add some more hot sauce and salt and pepper."

I was having a sympathetic flare-up of gout just

hearing about it. And they'd spent two days eating like this and alternating it with heavy drinking.

"Dobber and Hog Head was eating everything. And everybody in line behind the Brush Grinder couldn't get any of them good weenies cause he took them all.

"We got in a lot of fishing too. You should've seen what happened to the Old Man. He and Dobber thought they'd go fishing with some dynamite to get us some fish for that Cajun boy to cook out on the grill Saturday night. They waited till after dark, cause you know how some people is. Anyway, we was all standing alongside the river there watching them, and damn if Old Man didn't light up a whole stick of DuPont stick bait and throw it in. I thought to myself, 'They's gonna be a lot of fish tonight.' But he'd killed the motor when he got out there in the middle of the river and started fiddling with the dynamite. When he threw that stick in, he realized he better get that motor cranked right quick and get outta there, but he couldn't get it started! He was jerking the hell outta that little rope. I swear it was the funniest thing I ever seen.

"This orange ball of fire started boiling up under the water and it swelled up all big and red and come up under that boat like I don't know what. It threw the boat clear up on the bank with Old Man and Dobber still a setting in it. You missed a real good time. You got anything for heartburn?"

Less than an hour later Old Man himself came in

276

with "flu" and "chest pain." He was a pale gray green and asked for something for a stomachache. He didn't mention the dynamite incident and neither did we.

At the end of the day, Michael sauntered into the office, looked at me, smiled crookedly, and said slowly, "Carolyn, Carolyn, Carolyn."

I said, "Hey Michael? How're you doing?"

Daddy walked up to the counter behind me and said, "Hi Michael."

Michael looked at Daddy and said, "Paul, Paul, Paul."

Then he just stood in the middle of the empty waiting room, wobbling slightly.

He was seriously stoned on something.

Daddy said conversationally, "Taking some new pain medicine?"

"No," Michael said, shaking his head in a slow and exaggerated way.

I had to suppress a smile. I said, "Michael, have you got your medicine with you?"

He staggered over and emptied his pockets onto the reception desk. He totally emptied the pockets of his jacket and pants. Pens, change, wadded receipts, billfold, and one amber plastic pill bottle. I handed it to Daddy, who looked at the label and said, "Ah."

He looked at me and said, "Percocet. From the cardiologist."

Michael must have been experiencing pain during

the final stages of his illness. His heart specialist had written him some pain medicine, but the normal dose had totally looped him because his system was so fragile.

He was high on Percocet. And he was driving.

I dialed up Michael's son, Little Mike, at the junkyard and explained that his father was having an unexpected and unusually strong reaction to his pain pills. "He's stoned," I whispered, and then asked Little Mike if he and a friend could come to our office and pick up his father and his father's truck.

I talked to Michael while we waited for his son to come. It turned out that he'd decided to drop by the office because he'd "woken up" at a nearby intersection when the person behind him blew the horn. The intersection happened to be where two big highways crossed.

After further discussion it was revealed that a lot of people had been blowing their horns at him throughout his drive. He'd thought they were just being friendly, but when he'd woken up he'd begun to suspect he might be having some sort of problem, so he'd come by to get checked out.

"Michael," I said, "you know you probably shouldn't be driving when you're taking this amount of pain medicine."

Michael adopted a shamefaced look that was obviously feigned. His sham guilt lasted about ten seconds, then he tried to look sober. "The Lord loves a man with a broken heart," he said.

"Does he?" I said. I wondered how he felt about brokenhearted women.

"Yeah. Psalm 51. King David says the Lord loves a man with a 'broken and shattered heart.' "

I nodded, too choked up to talk to him openly about his bad heart.

"So, I figure he must really love me," he said with a wide sweep of his arms. "Cause I was born already halfway there!"

TWENTY-ONE

"Carolyn, guess what?" Jacob said. "They're going to talk about the investigation tonight on the *CBS Evening News*. They're going to interview the boss. They've had cameras here all day. And there's going to be an article in *Time*. The Senator's ecstatic. We finally did it. Our careers are made!"

"Congratulations! My God, the evening news. And you did it *by yourself.*"

I felt guilty and left out. I'd abandoned Jacob and missed everything.

"Now the other Senators are going to be trying to hire you away with all sorts of sleazy promises like more money and travel and French food," I said.

"I know. It's going to be great. But I'm not going anywhere without you, so you've got to get back up here. Now."

"Jacob, there's something I've got to tell you."

"Oh no."

"I've got to."

"Dammit, Carolyn."

"You don't even know what it is!"

"Carolyn, don't."

This was bad. It was already August. There was

no way to resolve this without causing serious pain to the people I loved most in the world. I had a virtual job in Washington. Jacob kept seeing me there and I kept imagining myself there, and yet I wasn't. I was in Tennessee. I was trapped. I had to make a decision and, no matter what I decided, people were going to get hurt.

"Carolyn, I'm going to pretend this never happened. I'm never going to mention it again as long as we live and I'm going to continue with our careers in your absence, just as I have for these last months, but I want you to come home. Your life is here. I want you back. I'm asking you to come back. Soon."

The next morning I woke up early. It was barely 6:00, not yet daylight, and a full hour before my alarm would go off, but I got out of bed anyway and went shuffling around in my pajamas getting ready for work. I heard the phone ring, but Daddy must have answered it upstairs, because it only rang once. I heard the wail of an ambulance siren through the open windows and then half a dozen dogs up and down the road howling along with it.

Just as I was leaving to go to work the telephone rang again, so I went back inside to answer it. It was Janie Lucas asking if Daddy was on his way yet. She'd just called him for help after finding Fletcher collapsed at the breakfast table. She thought he might be dead.

This made no sense. Fletcher was much younger than Daddy. He wasn't even sick, he was never sick. He couldn't be *dead*. What in the world did *"thought* he *might* be dead" mean? Why wasn't she sure? I was disoriented. I had to work hard, to bear down, to concentrate on what she was saying.

Realizing Daddy must have grabbed his bag and taken off after that first call, I said, "He'll be there in just a second."

I hung the phone up and went back outside. "Old Blue," the '71 Chevy pickup that I'd gotten when I'd turned sixteen, twenty-seven years ago, sat blocking both the Mercedes and the postal jeep. Either of them would be faster, but I wasn't sure either of them would run. Old Blue's top highway speed was only forty-five, but most of the trip was along narrow winding roads, so it wouldn't cost me any time.

The truck rattled and roared along. I was nearly there before I realized both windows were down and I was shivering from the chilly morning air blowing in on my thin scrubs. I was in a mental suspension. I didn't pray because that would have meant I was entertaining the thought that Fletcher might actually be dead. This all had to be an awful mistake. A panicked misjudgment.

The sun was coming up as I got to his house. Fletcher's new black pickup was there in the driveway along with his wife's and daughter's cars. Behind them was a huge rescue squad truck and a blocky ambulance with the lights flashing. Daddy's SUV was parked diagonally in the yard almost up on the sidewalk. I swerved over into the church parking lot across the road from Fletcher's house. I started to get out and then stopped. What was I doing here? I was no voyeur. And to boot I had a weak stomach, a highstrung panicky disposition, no medical sense, and a lifelong overwhelming morbid dread of being anywhere near a dead person. But this was Fletcher.

I slid off the high bench seat, crossed the narrow road, and went through the front yard. I could see Fletcher's only child, Hope, who still lived with her parents, through the glass door. I jerked both my hands palm up in a gesture of, "What?" She answered me by slashing one hand down sharply.

Oh, Fletcher.

I gritted my teeth hard and went through the door to her. "What—?" I said.

Hope said, "He said he was going to get the paper and I went to get dressed for work. When I came back in the kitchen he was just sitting there in his chair. His eyes were open, but already fixed. I think. I started CPR anyway. Was that right?"

I couldn't speak to answer. I could hear the emergency medical people just around the corner, but I stayed where I couldn't see anything.

"What was I supposed to do?" Hope asked. "Wasn't it too late? I don't know how long he'd been like that."

Oh, Lord. Mouth-to-mouth resuscitation on your own dead father. How did people do such things? Daddy'd once breathed for a dead body for over thirty minutes until an ambulance got there to relieve him. When I found out the man had never revived, I asked Daddy how he'd made himself breathe into a corpse for so long. He'd said he didn't let himself think about it.

Finally I marshaled my chaotic thoughts enough to say in a shaky voice, "You did good. You did right. You got to. Even though. Daddy always says you got to do CPR and keep doing it no matter, just in case. You did good."

Hope said, "His face was already cold! I could feel it." She was totally shell shocked, but not crying either.

I saw movement in the yard and turned to see David, Hope's boyfriend, coming toward the front door. When I saw his rigid, stricken face through the glass, I realized what my face must've looked like. He looked directly at me with wild and questioning eyes. I twisted my mouth into an I-don't-know-anything expression. I made a gesture with my finger to point to where Hope was standing. He went to her and gathered her up into his arms.

I moved slightly further toward the kitchen, just until I could see Daddy. He was the only person in the room who was standing up in the middle of all the confusion. He was standing still, watching the men work. I stayed back out of the way, listening, hoping for some encouraging news. Daddy's face gave away nothing. I stared at him, but he seemed not to know I was there.

I could hear the sound of a rubber bag being manipulated. That would mean they had a tube down and were breathing for Fletcher by squeezing the bag. Good. A bag was more effective than mouth-to-mouth. I stood absolutely still and silent, alert for any sound or movement I could interpret, and then I heard an eerie moaning sound coming from somewhere on or near the kitchen floor. It sounded biological, not mechanical, but it didn't sound quite human, at least not like anything conscious. It sounded like a long painful wheeze or maybe what people called a "death rattle." It was a pitiful whistling sigh.

This husk on the floor that I couldn't even make myself look at was a person who just two days before had come home after a hot, exhausting job repairing the inside of a toxic waste incinerator in Oak Ridge to find a message on his answering machine from Daddy. His truck had broken down in Talbot at the fertilizer plant. Fletcher had searched his garage for a spare fuel filter and made another hour-long drive to install it so Daddy could get home.

And now he was breathing courtesy of a stranger compressing an ugly black rubber bag while I just stood around.

The two ambulance attendants stood up together,

lifting a metal stretcher and locking its legs. I turned and moved down the hall to get out of the way. Then I saw Janie. She looked too stunned to even feel grief. There'd be plenty of time for that later, I supposed. Daddy came up behind her.

"You need to tell the ambulance people where you want them to take him," he said softly.

She looked up at him in confusion and said, "I don't know. Where do you think? Addison's?"

Addison's was a funeral home. Daddy said, "Which *hospital* do you want him to go to?"

"Oh. White Oak I guess."

I turned and looked back over my shoulder to get my first glimpse of Fletcher. He was strapped to the stretcher with what looked like three seat belts. He had a tube coming out of his mouth and a black rubber bag held up in front of his face by an attendant who was compressing it at regular intervals. There was an electrical device the size of a toaster tied beside one wrist. His color was good and he looked relaxed and comfortable. He didn't look like what I thought a dead person would look like, so I figured he must still be alive. His hands lay gracefully across his thighs. Nothing flopped or flapped around. He was neatly dressed in clean, new-looking blue jeans and black track shoes. He didn't have a shirt on, but he had his pager clipped to his waistband. Then he was out the door.

I turned to look back at the kitchen. The kitchen table and chairs were an exact match to the ones in our house. Fletcher'd been sitting in his regular chair at the head of his table at the same time that Daddy had been sitting in his. But what a difference at this house. The floor was littered with pieces of white paper and plastic, the wrappings from syringes and whatnot.

Daddy was explaining to Janie that a pacemaker was beating Fletcher's heart for him. He made some obscure technical comments, but I couldn't understand what he was talking about. The words "alive" or "dead" or anything else clearcut never came into the discussion. I was content to wait until somebody decided to tell me straight out what the story was. I wasn't in a hurry. Daddy finally looked at me. "Go on to the office and open up," he said. "I'll be along."

I went out of the house and walked back through the yard, stepping over the concrete sidewalk I'd helped make the wooden forms for, over the bronze leaf begonias I'd given Janie, past all the emergency vehicles with their garish colors and flashing lights, and went to sit in Old Blue. I waited for the ambulance to back up into the road, switch on its siren, and take off for the hospital. The rescue squad truck pulled out right behind it. When both vehicles were out of sight, I pulled out. Daddy stood in the front yard talking to the police.

I did as I was told and went to the office where I just sat, looking out the window into the parking lot. When Alma arrived I managed to get out a halting sentence fragment about what had happened and she sat on her stool to wait with me. At about 8:00, Cynthia Claxton came in with a stuffy head. I told her what had just happened and warned her that I didn't know when the doctor would be coming in. I offered to call her at home or work when he got in, but she said she understood and didn't mind waiting. She'd been a patient for more than thirty years.

Daddy came in a few minutes later with another patient right on his heels. This was going to be very strange. He called Cynthia to the back and then I heard him ask her to "Say aaaahhhh." And still we waited.

After Daddy had seen the two patients he told Alma and me that Fletcher's chances were almost nonexistent since he'd been gone ten or twenty minutes before he'd been found.

Finally the hospital emergency room called and said they'd like to speak to the doctor about one of his patients. My voice cracked as I asked, "Fletcher?" The emergency room nurse paused, I could hear her flipping papers and then she said kindly, "Yes, William Fletcher Lucas."

I held the receiver toward Daddy with a shaky hand, but he went into the back to take the call in his office.

Daddy came out after just a minute or so and said with amazing composure, "They weren't able to revive him."

I turned my back to everyone and went into a corner of my little cubbyhole reception area to cry.

Another patient registered and then another and another. I looked out the picture window and was amazed that the sky was still a beautiful blue. Cars were going up and down the highway as usual. The world was going on as if nothing had happened. How could that be? Fletcher had been alive at breakfast and now he was dead. He was only fifty-eight years old.

A drug company rep came in to hype a new pill and I told her the doctor's best friend had just died. She remained at the counter so I added that the doctor had just come from his friend's house and hadn't been able to save him. I asked if she would mind coming back some other time. Instead she kept her artificial smile fixed in place and proceeded to lay out her samples and brochures on the counter as if I hadn't spoken. I was horrified, but so emotionally overloaded I couldn't think what to do. So I just watched in sickened fascination.

My father came out of an examining room and walked toward the front counter. The woman called out gaily, "Hey there! How's it going?"

"Not too good," he mumbled and detoured over to the lab area. He kept his back to her and pretended to write in a chart.

"I'd like to talk to you about a great new urinary antispasmodic we're coming out with!" She went on in a loud and hearty voice that froze both of us.

We were both trying desperately to remain composed, and she pretended to take that for interest. It was the cruelest moment I'd ever witnessed. And for what? A pill to keep you from peeing in your pants?

It just highlighted the fact that pills hadn't helped Fletcher. Neither had the rescue squad, nor the ambulance, nor the emergency technicians with all their wonderful machines, nor Daddy with his forty years of experience and all the good will in the world. All of that, and he hadn't been able to help his best friend. He hadn't even been able to prevent the fuss and mess and give him a peaceful exit from his own house.

Finally the lady left.

About an hour later the phone rang. It frightened me to see "Lucas, Fletcher" on the Caller ID. I stared at the name, my muddled brain suggesting it was Fletcher calling from the beyond to say *bye* or tell us something important. I hesitated as long as I dared then picked the phone up warily and half whispered, "Dr. Jourdan's office?"

"Why'd he die?" It was Janie. She and Hope had come back home from the hospital.

Janie was still not crying. She seemed profoundly confused. She repeated her question the way a child would. "Why'd he die?"

I couldn't speak. I struggled for a desperate spastic half breath, holding the phone away from my face so she couldn't hear it. My eyes were swimming again. Time to punt. I said, "The emergency room doctor called and talked to Daddy. Do you want to talk to him?"

"I guess I don't need to. Do you think I could have saved him if I'd been there when he—?"

"No," I said firmly, decisively. "Nobody could've." I knew it was something she needed to hear.

Later, I asked Daddy the same thing and he shook his head. He stood at the counter staring out the window with me. When I looked at his face, I realized I was seeing what it looked like to have just lost your best friend.

Daddy, Alma, and I worked our way through yet another unimaginable day. I kept repeating to myself what Fletcher had said: "Just show up."

Neither Alma nor I could make ourselves perform the normal ritual of pulling out Fletcher's chart and writing "Deceased" across the name. Several hours later I saw Daddy do it. He made some quick notes on the inside too. I filed the chart with the other deceased files without opening it. I couldn't bear to see what he'd written.

At home after work Daddy told me he'd wanted to stop the emergency techs, but couldn't figure out how to do it with Janie and Hope looking on. He said the techs'd had a terrible time getting Fletcher intubated and he'd had to watch them jam the hard plastic pipe down his throat over and over without offering to help. He knew if they managed to restore breathing and heart action, they wouldn't have gotten Fletcher back, but they might have gotten a vegetable. He knew Fletcher wouldn't have wanted that. So he'd stood over the body of his best friend, tormented, unable to do anything more helpful than just try to be in the way and slow things down.

The next time I saw Fletcher was when I walked up to what looked like a poorly made wax dummy in a casket at the funeral home. I kept thinking they should have made a better likeness of him, that this didn't even look like him at all. While I stood beside the casket looking down at him I heard a woman say in the most cutting tone imaginable, "He died *young* cause he *give* hisself away." Then the voice of a man responded in a lazy drawl, "He *worked* hisself to *death*."

Fletcher had on a suit and tie. I'd never seen him wearing a suit before. He looked nice in it. And he had on a beautiful, heavy white silk apronlike garment. It looked like an extremely nice version of the apron carpenters wear to hold a handful of nails and a pencil. There was a small sprig of some evergreen plant I couldn't identify lying across the garment. I supposed these were part of the Masonic burial ritual. Fletcher had been a mason as a trade and as a spiritual practice.

Daddy and I sat in a pew near the back. We learned from people who came by to talk that death by sudden cardiac arrest ran in Fletcher's family. A parent, a brother, and at least one cousin had all died the same way: too early and with no symptoms whatsoever to give anyone a warning. It was probably a hereditary electrical defect in the heart. This comforted Daddy a little. There was nothing he could have done to prevent something like that. But it still surprised us that Fletcher had never mentioned it to anyone. Maybe that helped explain the way he lived. He'd lived with a heightened awareness of his own mortality. Knowing his heart might give out early and suddenly, he ran full tilt and used to the max whatever time he had.

As we drove home I wondered if Fletcher knew all the answers now, to all the great mysteries. I knew he'd come back to tell me and Daddy the interesting stuff if he could. I wouldn't mind if he came back for a visit. I didn't think his ghost would scare me too much. Another first.

Monday morning he was buried at Caledonia, his family's 200-year-old cemetery. There were lots of flowers and overlapping layers of bright green artificial turf rugs under a dark green awning emblazoned with the name of the funeral home.

That evening, an hour before sunset, I went back to the graveyard with some vague notion of seeing if it felt like Fletcher was there or not. When I pulled up I could see Janie, Hope, and Sarah, Fletcher's sister-in-law, standing under the awning in casual clothes. They were dismantling and rearranging the various flower displays. They said people had told them to go ahead and take whatever they might want to keep because human scavengers would surely raid the flowers the first night after the burial. How macabre, I thought, but I didn't doubt it was true. They asked me if I'd like a flower as a keepsake.

"No thanks," I said. I didn't say what I was thinking—that a flower was not something I associated with Fletcher, or that I didn't really need anything more, since our whole farm was a keepsake. The rooster weathervane, the fences, the farm machinery, the lawn mowers, the outbuildings. There was nothing we had that Fletcher hadn't had something to do with at one time or another.

They seemed disappointed. "Well," I said, "I don't want to take something y'all want to keep, but, only if nobody else wants it, I'd like to have that green pocketknife that's a match to the one he gave Daddy." I knew Fletcher had carried it with him all the time because he'd used it frequently to help me with one task or another.

Hope said, "He had that in his pocket when he died. The hospital gave it back to us in a big envelope with the rest of the things he had on him." She looked at me, tired, and said, "They even gave us the clothes they cut off him. Why in the world do they give you back a pair of blue jeans and underwear they've cut off somebody?"

I shook my head.

The ground over the grave was already perfectly flat, with the sod so well matched that I could barely tell where the hole had been dug. Fletcher's beautiful sheltie dog, Bandy, was lying with uncanny accuracy on the center of the grave. One of my childhood friends, Sandra, was the local grave digger. She'd carefully removed the sod, dug Fletcher's grave, filled it back in, tamped the dirt, and replaced the sod. Then she'd hauled away the extra dirt. She'd done a good job.

The cemetery occupied the lower half of a large field amid rolling farmland. The far end of the field grew steep as it rose to the top of a ridge. This was where the cemetery would expand in the future. The far end had been mowed recently with a bush hog and the concentric rings of tall grass were still lying where they'd fallen. The sun was sinking, lighting everything with a yellow glow that I'd come to associate with Fletcher's departures. A perfect half moon was visible in the light blue sky.

We talked about how Fletcher, Ebert Davidson, and Daddy had cleared the upper half of the field and cut up the fallen trees for firewood several years before. Of the three, only Daddy was still alive. Sarah pointed up toward the top of the ridge saying her husband had once made her walk up to the very top of the clearing and sit beside him while he checked out the view from the plot he intended to buy.

I couldn't think of anything to say except that I hoped Janie would bring me any documents she didn't understand, so I could help her figure them out. I walked back toward my car, across the cemetery, having forgotten why I came, when I heard quite clearly a man's voice call my name. I smiled as I turned around to see who it was. But there weren't any men anywhere. There were only the three women left in the whole wide field. And none of them were looking my way.

TWENTY-TWO

I stood in the barn, kicking angrily at the loose hay on the floor. My stint as a receptionist was only supposed to last for a few *days*. But then it had grabbed hold of me and stretched into *weeks,* and then *months*. And now what?

My schedule for the life expectancies of the people around me wasn't holding up. I knew patients would die. But it was supposed to be in some sort of bearable order with the sickest and oldest going first. Things weren't going right, though. Miss Hiawatha hadn't been sick enough to die. And Fletcher hadn't even been on the watch list. How was I supposed to live in such an unpredictable world? Key people got snatched away willy-nilly and there was nothing I could do about it.

What was happening to my life? Where did it go if I wasn't there to live it?

I couldn't continue to try to hold onto both worlds. I got in Old Blue and backed the rattling, rusting hulk through the front yard faster than I should have, trying to make the bald tires spin in the wet grass. I backed right inside the barn. Then I started heaving file boxes into the bed of the pickup.

First went the files from the previous series of Congressional hearings: seventeen matching plastic containers with their Federal Express shipping labels still on them. They didn't give much satisfaction on impact as they'd been heavily taped for the trip from Washington to Tennessee. Then I tossed in a few of the Rubbermaid containers of records from my Senate office. The lids popped off these and papers spewed out. A flock of Senate logos with their gold leaf eagles went flying, still determinedly clutching their arrows. One landed near me and glinted in the light.

When the bed of the truck was full, I drove through the yard, across the hollow, up to the top of a ridge opposite the house, and stopped at a red clay mud hole scraped out by a bulldozer that we used as a burn pit. I dropped the tailgate and got up into the bed of the truck. I shoved the whole mess off into the burn hole, papers flying everywhere. Stationery, correspondence, transcripts. I got back in the truck and went for another load.

Next came the contents of the two filing cabinets from the current investigations. First in loose armloads, then whole drawers, one at a time. They were heavy, but I was mad, madder than I'd ever been in my life.

When I'd emptied the entire contents of my office into the hole I stood looking at the mess. Damn. I didn't have a match. I drove to the house to get some and then came back and lit the mess, but the paper wouldn't catch on fire, because the pages were too close together.

I drove across the road to the tractor shed. There was a single two-gallon metal can of gasoline with "Flammable" written across the front. Good. Flames were what was wanted. Wait a second. White trash was always getting immolated starting fires with gasoline. I decided to use diesel. Hell, everybody knew that was the safer way to go. There were ten gallons of that in two knee-high five-gallon red plastic jugs, each weighing about forty pounds, so I had to strain and twist like an athlete doing a hammer toss to sling each of the jugs up onto the tailgate. I shoved them back toward the cab and took off again heading for the burn hole.

I poured the whole ten gallons on the rubbish of my career, lit a match and stepped back, tossing it onto some of the pooled fuel. I didn't get the satisfying whoosh of a gas fireball as the flames licked their way along the fuel atop the paper. It was a leisurely trip. But the smoke was tremendous, dense and black. It went straight up for about twenty or thirty feet and then it was carried along by the wind sideways down the hollow. A stinking, choking cloud of dirty-looking smoke soon hung over the whole valley. That suited me just fine.

I was now living, not in my condo in the arts district of downtown Washington, D.C., but in the basement of Daddy's house. I'd gone from nearly $100,000 a year to zero. First my plans for the next few weeks had been scrubbed, then my plans for the rest of my life. My whole life had been scrubbed.

The sun began to set as I stood watching the fire. The smoke brought an eerie stillness and silence to the valley. It was a strange blanketed silence, just like when it snowed. Indeed, a fine mist of ash was falling. Ha, *black* snow.

The fire smoldered for two days, and a pall hung over the entirety of White Oak Hollow Road as the flames slowly worked their way through fifteen years of my life.

It was time to face facts with Jacob. I dialed his number with a shaky hand.

"Jacob, it's Carolyn."

"Where are you? I thought you'd be here by now. What's the problem now?"

"The problem now is that I'm not coming back. I just can't. I'm sorry."

"Oh Carolyn. Please don't. I can wait. But you mustn't do this. It doesn't make sense."

"I know it doesn't make Washington sense, but I think maybe it makes sense here," I said.

"Jacob, life with you is wonderful. It's like a movie, a high-budget political thriller where we get to dress in great clothes and move around in beautiful sets. But here, there's something I'm needed for. The truth is, as a Senate Counsel, my job is to be just one more person hyping a guy who's already famous. How meaningful is that? And we both know he won't really miss me for very long. Things are quite the opposite here."

Jacob sighed.

The next day as I stood in the yard looking out over the panorama of trees and hills and mountains, I heard a car coming up the driveway. It was Matthew in his white BMW. The top was down and he didn't seem to have any animals with him.

He got out of the car and stood looking at me. "I thought you might like to go for a ride," he said.

I nodded.

He opened the passenger door and held it as I got in. He went back around to the driver's side and got in and we drove off without speaking. He cruised the winding roads at what was, for him, a sedate pace. Occasionally he'd stop atop a high hill and we'd look out over miles of farmland or he'd follow narrow roads that ran along sheer bluffs that had been carved out over eons and we'd look down on the green river.

He drove for a couple of hours and ended up near his family farm. We turned off the main road onto the narrow dirt path that I now knew led into the woods, through a stream, and to his cabin. But instead of going to his house, he stopped the car in the middle of the shallow stream and turned off the ignition. We'd hardly spoken during the drive and neither of us spoke now. Then I burst into tears.

He gripped my left hand tightly. "It's okay Carolyn," he said. "It'll be okay."

"How?" I said.

"I don't know," he said. "I don't know how. But somehow it all always comes right in the end. You'll see."

"How long does it take to come right?" I asked.

"I don't know," he said. "I don't know."

For a while Daddy had seemed to be totally exhausted by the end of the workday. But now, with Fletcher's death, we all wondered if he'd be able to go on. The office was a grim place, but nobody could figure out what to do for him.

It was Harley who came up with something. He knew Daddy needed a big win to counteract his depression, so he decided, for Doc, he'd stop drinking. Avon came in to deliver the news.

For years whenever Daddy'd begged Harley to get treatment for his alcoholism, he'd refused, saying, "I believe in your headshrinking about as much as I do haints and ghostez." But now Avon said he was ready to go.

He had one condition though. Harley said Sarge would have to take him. Harley and Momma had a special relationship ever since she'd wrestled a loaded gun away from him when he was drunk. He always called her Sarge after that, and the name had stuck. I guess he knew it would take Momma's special kind of determination to get him sobered up.

Daddy called Momma and together they decided to call Harley's bluff. "Tell Harley he's on," he told Avon. "We'll be by to pick him up tomorrow morning. First thing."

Harley was going to the dry dock now whether he wanted to or not. Momma and Daddy asked me to go too and ride in the backseat on the other side of Harley, sandwiching him between me and Avon, in case he tried to escape en route.

It began to storm during the night, and the heavy rain caused a landslide on I-40 near Waterville. This posed a significant problem, because the sanitarium Daddy had selected was across the mountains in North Carolina. But the landslide only stiffened Momma and Daddy's resolve. There was an unspoken desperate agreement between Daddy, Momma, and Avon that come hell or high water— or in this case, a wall of rocks and mud across the Interstate—Harley was going for treatment.

Early the next morning we all piled into Daddy's SUV. Momma, me, Daddy, and Avon—all surrounding and strong-arming a blotto Harley. He'd apparently been drinking continuously since he'd decided to quit, in a sort of last hurrah. The trip was harrowing. At one point the road was closed, deemed impassable by the Highway Patrol. But Daddy drove for miles down a one-lane gravel road and through the middle of someone's peach orchard to get around the roadblock.

When we arrived at the sanitarium, Daddy asked

me to go in and tell them we were there. Then, before anybody could stop him, Harley made a drunken lurch for freedom and fell out of the car headfirst onto the asphalt parking lot, cutting a gash in his scalp.

Daddy got out and went around to the passenger side. He stood looking down at Harley lying bleeding, and said, "Go right ahead Harley. You can crack your head all over this parking lot, but you're still going in there."

These sorts of arrivals must have been commonplace because a stone-faced orderly came out immediately. He and Daddy wrestled Harley into a semistanding position by each grabbing one of his arms and draping it across their shoulders. Then they dragged him into the sanitarium and, I suspect, tied him to a wall somewhere inside.

So Daddy, Sarge, and Harley each did their part. And Harley's instincts had been right. Weeks later when he came in sober, for the first time since Fletcher's death, Daddy began to find some happiness in his work again.

"Hey Doc!" someone shouted. "Wait up!"

We'd been caught crossing the parking lot, trapped on open ground halfway between a locked office door and our cars. It'd been a long day and we all wanted to go home. I looked around and spotted Wormey hanging out of the passenger side of a new pickup truck being driven by Jason.

"I got something to tell you," he called out. "You won't believe this."

"What is it, Wormey?" Daddy asked.

"Got my throat cut, that's what. Look," he said patting the thick white bandage that circled his neck.

"How'd you do that?"

"Car wreck. Damn drunk pulled out in front of us. You know the Saddle Horn down on 11E?"

Daddy nodded.

"Some idiot pulled out of there right in front of us. No way Jason could get stopped, so we T-boned him. Throwed me through the windshield."

"Weren't you wearing your seat belt?" I asked.

"Hell no. Never wear them. Those things'll kill ye. They make it so they have to cut ye out of the car."

"Yeah, it's quicker to just go on out through the windshield by yourself," I said.

"Well anyway," Wormey said looking at me with narrowed eyes, "the damn windshield cut me like you wouldn't believe. Blood was running all over the highway. Jason saved my life."

"How?" Daddy said.

Why? I wondered, then felt a pang of remorse for the thought.

"He wadded up his shirt and put it on the cut, but that didn't work too good. So then he put a turkey neck on me."

"A what?" I asked.

"A turkey neck. He took my belt and wrapped it around my neck over the top of his shirt and pulled it real tight. Then I passed out."

He'd pulled a belt real tight around Wormey's throat?

"They said I cut my juggler vein. They said I should've died. But I didn't," he beamed.

"Well it finally happened," Daddy mumbled. "I've waited forty years and somebody finally did it."

"Did what?" Wormey asked.

"Put a tourniquet around somebody's neck," he said. "I knew it was just a matter of time."

"His face and lips did get pretty blue on the way to the hospital," Jason grinned, "purple really."

"You're a real hero," I said to Jason, meaning it. "I don't think I could've done what you did. I wouldn't have been able to think so fast and so clear with so much at stake."

"Aaawww hell, there wasn't much at stake," he said, winking, "just Wormey."

Fall

TWENTY-THREE

I stood in the middle of a green field that extended for miles along the edge of the French Broad River, covering hundreds, thousands of acres. The leaves were at the peak of their fall brilliance and the smoky blue haze of the mountains edged the horizon. Here and there along the banks of the river stood old white farmhouses, elegant in their plainness, with tin roofs, wraparound porches, and wooden barns nearby.

It was a chilly October morning, and I was standing on Eddie's porch with Matthew in a crowd of people waiting to see my first English-style foxhunt, with brass trumpets and red coats and all sorts of gorgeous, pretentious paraphernalia. The event was being hosted by a group of Anglophilic horse people who had moved to West Knoxville from other, more sophisticated places. Appalachian style was the opposite of Washington. East Tennesseans generally tried to avoid making a spectacle, but if somebody else, particularly a Yankee, would give it a go, they couldn't resist watching, hoping for a foul up.

It was pretty obvious that the foxhunters would have preferred to avoid all contact with the natives, but since they needed miles of picturesque land-scape to prance their horses across, they'd been forced to make a treaty with some of the local landowners. Then to their horror, they'd been unable to prevent these same landowners from inviting a few of their friends over to watch the hunt.

Matthew had been invited to observe the festivi-ties as part of the indigenous riffraff section. A childhood friend of his owned the 600-acre farm where the hunt started. So we stood watching as straggling heirs to nationally recognizable fortunes struggled to mount their horses. Heirs putting on airs. I'd never seen anything to compare with it. It was the most expensive collection of horses, tack, clothing, cars, and horse trailers I'd ever seen— juxtaposed with some of the worst riders in the world. It was a rodeo of the absurd.

There was something else odd about it that it took me longer to put my finger on. I scanned the crowd several times until it finally hit me that many of the members of the rough-looking audience were millionaires too. The rich people on horses had no idea that the party crashers were themselves rich. How could they? The contrast between the rich people riding and the rich people watching couldn't have been more extreme. The visitors were wear-ing silly-looking stretch pants. The locals were dressed in ripped flannel shirts and old blue jeans or worn denim overalls and stained baseball caps. Most of them were chewing tobacco or dipping snuff, spitting everywhere. These were men who'd startled themselves and their families by getting rich from unglamorous jobs like wood butchering (logging hardwood), hog butchering, or by owning a farm coveted by an outlet mall.

One of the wealthiest still lived in an old single-wide trailer. Most of the others lived in modest clapboard farmhouses like the ones they'd been raised in. It just wasn't part of southern highland culture to make a flashy show out of having stumbled onto some money. Most of them had scruffy beards, and the rest of them looked like they hadn't shaved in a week. Well, it was Saturday, so they were probably holding out until Sunday morning when they'd have to shave for church.

A man in a stunning red jacket, white riding pants, and tall shiny black boots rode by on a white horse with a braided and beribboned mane and tail. He was dragging a scent lure past the area where the pack of foxhounds were milling around.

"Look at that," someone said. "They don't even have a fox. All this mess and they don't even have a damn fox."

Another man said, "I'm going home."

"Maybe I should leave too," I said to Matthew. "It's pretty bad to be at an event where my hairdo can't compete with the horses'."

"Don't worry," Matthew said. "They can't pull this thing off as high class as they're pretending. Andy told me there was a big row last year because so many of the members can't ride well enough to stay on an English saddle. Only a few of them can jump anything. The local families' kids are really the best riders and they wanted permission to go along. The hunt club couldn't say no to the kids straight out, or they wouldn't be able to ride here. So they had to make a deal. The deal is: the ones with the fancy English saddles and outfits get to take off first. They're divided into the ones with the red jackets who're supposed to be the ones that can ride good and the ones with the black jackets who are still learning. Nobody in a black jacket is supposed to pass anybody in a red jacket or they get thrown out. Then the ones with the western gear have to wait a half hour before they can leave out. Then the local kids can go last."

We stepped down from Eddie's porch, walked across his lawn, passed a couple of tumbledown cow and tobacco barns, and then out through a field to where the hunt club had built a pavilion that looked like something out of the Tournament of the Field of the Cloth of Gold. It sat impressively amid what used to be fifty acres of pumpkins.

A thick bank of early morning fog was still hovering over the river and it enveloped the field. It swirled around the horses and riders making them look like something from a dream. There were half a dozen tall bonfires scattered around the field in front of the pavilion. You could warm yourself in their intense heat, if you were brave enough to stand close to them. A man in a white robe with a long purple cloth draped around his neck, like a tie he'd forgotten to knot, stood with an open book amid the pack of restless hounds and prancing horses.

"They call this 'the blessing of the hounds,' " Matthew whispered.

One of the hounds cocked up a leg and watered the back of the man's robe. The crowd guffawed. "Look, Otter's hosed off that feller's dress," someone said.

"What's he doing wearing a damn dress anyway?" someone said.

"He's a priest, ye idiot," someone else answered.

"A *bishop*," another voice corrected.

"A Catholic? Out here?" the man said, amazed. Even I got an involuntary shiver at that. Stories had been handed down in my family about Catholics burning my Huguenot ancestors on log pyres like the ones in this field.

"Hell no, it ain't Catholics, it's Episcopalians."

Someone shushed loudly and the ritual proceeded. Then just as the bishop stopped talking, the fog lifted. Waiters walked among the mounted riders, handing up small glasses of hard liquor. Some of the riders had more than one. Most of them had additional liquor in monogrammed silver flasks mounted behind their handmade saddles.

A red-coated rider identifying himself as the "Master of the Hunt" shouted to the crowd from atop his tall black horse. He waved a short leather crop around to indicate the circular course the club would be riding. He introduced another guy in a red coat as the "Master of the Hounds," who had a bullwhip that he could crack with great accuracy to keep the pack of foxhounds in order. Looking at that whip, I couldn't help but hope that one of the hounds would put teeth to him before the day was over.

A man blew on a curled up bugle and the first group of riders bolted away, red jackets clustered toward the front of the stampede. Moments later they arrived at the first jump. It was a low wooden structure built into the fencerow. The jump proved to be a bottleneck, so riders were forced to mill around, circling, while others built up their nerve to take a run at it. Some of the riders were so inept they'd actually fallen off their horses during the canter over level ground to reach it. Nearly all the red jackets and a few of the black jackets made it over the first jump. But some of the horses wouldn't jump. I assumed these were the smart ones. And some of the riders couldn't stay on the horses that did jump. Some fell off on the near side of the jump and others on the far side. Either way, bodies lay strewn across the field and the riderless horses raced off ecstatically, silver flasks glinting.

Somebody in a black jacket got tired of waiting around and took the jump (and made it) before a fellow in a red jacket had gotten across. The red jacket had already tried a couple of times, and his horse didn't want to do it. But the breach of the rules provoked a shouting match that we could hear half a mile away. So, in less than ten minutes there were already a considerable number of casualties and a complete breakdown of decorum.

After about forty-five minutes the second group got the signal to go. This group was made up of people with nonregulation costumes and/or horses: western saddles and cowboy hats on Tennessee Walking Horses or mules.

"Oh wow," I said, pointing to a mule taller than Matthew. The tips of its ears were at least seven and a half feet in the air. "Look at that brown and white mule! That's the cutest animal I ever saw in my life."

"He ought to be. That mule cost $26,000," Matthew said. "He's a spotted mammoth racking mule. His momma was a white Percheron draft horse. That's why he's so big. And it's real rare to get one to rack as smooth as a Walking Horse like he does. He'll jump too."

"A fence jumping mule?" I asked.

"Yeah. But you do it different with mules. You gotta get off him first and let him go over the jump by himself. Then get back on him."

Mules were clearly smarter than horses.

Predictably, several members of this second group were drinking beer. One of them had tied a six-pack to the back of his saddle to mock the brandy flasks of the others. As they left, a group of nonregulation dogs were also let loose: redbones, blueticks, and a couple of feists. We watched them as they ambled across the field in a slightly different direction, toward a gate. They opened the first gate and rode through hooting to demonstrate what they felt was the more sensible way to proceed.

A considerable amount of moonshine was being consumed by the spectators. The longer the jars were passed from hand to hand, the more noticeable was the belligerence in the conversation around us. I became aware of the sound of poorly muffled motors being started, engines being gunned, and then saw that behind the authorized groups, another, totally outlaw group was assembling: rednecks with four-wheel drives. Signaling their departure by fishtailing in the grass, what looked like a lost contingent of Stonewall Jackson's men took off on a cluster of ATVs, a battered Suzuki Samurai, a jacked-up Jeep with huge tires, and a little Nissan pickup. They roared past us, spinning, knobby tires tearing deep ruts in the soft ground.

Uh-oh. The hunt club wasn't going to like this at all.

The *Mad Max* crew made a beeline for a fallen rider. They stopped in a circle near the inert form where four of them dismounted. They heaved him up in the air and tossed him into the back of the Nissan. Then they took off again. They zigzagged along the whole course, picking up fallen riders and rounding up stray horses.

By the time we started back to the car in the early afternoon, there were only two riders still left out in the field, both on foot, scuffing the hell out of their beautiful boots as they chased their horses.

Matthew and I stood amid the parked trailers and watched as people loaded their horses. There was a lot of snatching at each other's sleeves to steer someone out of the way of a horse charging through the crowd, its rider hanging on for dear life. Then, after all the horses had been loaded, the riders were transferred with noticeably less care from the beds of the pickups to the backseats of various German sedans and Land Rovers.

Observing the sullied opulence, I suddenly realized what it had been like to watch Jacob and me sprint through a bad neighborhood in search of a taxi, disheveled, but dressed in a tux and a ball gown on our way home from an inaugural ball.

"There can't possibly be another event like this anywhere in the world," I said. *Except maybe in D.C.,* I thought.

"I'd bet money that's the truth," Matthew said as he sped across the river bottom in the opposite direction taken by the rest of the cars, who were predictably heading toward the paved road. "I know a shortcut," he said.

We drove down a bumpy track beside the river. Then suddenly Matthew stopped. "Look at that," he said. Not 200 feet away, up on a rock ledge, was a red fox. He stood there majestically with his black stockings and black snout, his huge bushy tail held straight out behind him, calmly surveying the river bottom field where at least three dozen hounds milled about, baying as they tried to follow the trail of the scent lure.

TWENTY-FOUR

Henry Loveday had always held a special place in my memory as the most astoundingly accurate rock thrower I'd ever seen. When we were in high school he'd point out a particular nut on a hickory tree and knock it to the ground with a single piece of gravel thrown like a bullet. That had made a big impression on me. I've always been a fan of ultracompetence. Henry was now a perfusionist, operating the heart-lung machine at White Oak Hospital. Once he knew that I was home and we were both now in the medical profession, he'd made a point of checking in on me from time to time. Then one day he called to offer to take me to work with him so I could watch an open-heart operation. He apparently still enjoyed the idea of showing off in front of me.

"Henry," I said, "you don't need me fainting in the operating room while you're trying to work."

"Well, I understand, but if you ever change your mind, just call me," he said.

"Thanks. But don't hold your breath."

As a doctor's daughter, I had a great deal of experience with fainting, but I'd also learned that it didn't have to be a bad experience. In fact, I'd had some of my most profound insights about life while viewing things from the perspective of the floor. But fainting on cue in front of my own family and friends was quite a different matter from attempting to remain upright in front of a bunch of strangers through such a gruesome display as an open-heart surgery. That was a bigger statement than I cared to make.

I told Daddy about Henry's offer, and he said I should reconsider. "You'll never get the chance to see anything like that again," he said.

That was the same thing he'd said about that little girl with the heart on the wrong side. Maybe it was a sign. I'd been doing a lot of thinking about hearts lately. I couldn't get them out of my mind: Momma's, Fletcher's, Michael's, mine. Maybe I owed it to them to go take a look at a real heart. It was time I got over my squeamishness anyway. This would be a huge step: the polar opposite of anything that happened in Daddy's office. It would be *big*. I called Henry back.

The night before I was supposed to view the surgery I got only three hours sleep, as I obsessed over all the instructions I'd gotten on fainting from Momma and Daddy:

"If you know you're gonna faint, just go ahead and lay down in the floor so you won't hurt anything." "Remember, if you're gonna fall, fall backwards." "Try not to touch anything on the way down, but for sure don't grab at the instrument tray. There's knives on it." "Whatever you do, don't fall across the patient."

The next morning jogging across the parking lot I felt like a Marine, or a Samurai, prepared to look death in the face. Of course it wouldn't be *my* death I'd be looking in the face, but it would still be a trial: a journey to the heart of things.

I never suspected that the first ordeal would be simply to find Henry in the huge sprawling hospital. I'd never seen so many kinds of doors in my life. Just between my car and the operating room I encountered the glass front door of the hospital that opened with a push bar, metal elevator doors, wooden doors with regular knobs, glass doors that mysteriously disappeared sideways into the walls when a person approached, double doors that opened when someone slapped something on the wall several yards away, doors with odd brushed stainless steel paddles that you could open by pressing with your hands or elbows or side (or forehead). By the time I found Henry, I felt like Maxwell Smart.

Somewhere along the labyrinth I'd been tossed a set of scrubs, which I slipped on over my clothes. I pulled paper booties over my tennis shoes, covered my hair with an opaque shower cap, and fumbled with a paper mask that had a metal edge that could be bent to fit whatever size nose you had. Henry demonstrated how to tie the mask atop the head and then behind the neck and I copied what he did.

In the operating room Henry pointed to a battered stainless steel stool that sat next to a fancy blue padded one that I took to be his. I sat down and a door to my left opened and a blond-haired woman who looked to be maybe forty was rolled in on a gurney. Several masked people appeared and Henry hurried over to help them move the woman from the gurney onto the operating table. A man I took to be the anesthesiologist approached the woman, gently touched the side of her face, and spoke to her in a soft voice. She responded in a slurred mumble, but then he fiddled with some of his equipment and she stopped talking.

A door on the far wall whooshed open and two new masked characters entered. They peeled back the blanket over the woman, removed her hospital gown, and began to manipulate her body on the operating table. Each took a leg and bent it at the knee, rotated the knees and toes outward, laid the leg back down, and taped the woman's feet to the operating table. She bore an unfortunate likeness to a frog about to be dissected.

Someone hooked an extension into the left side of the table and the woman's arm was laid atop it and taped at the wrist. I could see a series of black magic marker lines drawn on the inside of her forearm and the insides of both legs.

I looked at Henry. "She's gotta have five bypasses and a dead part of her heart cut out," he said. "They're going to take the grafts from her arms and legs." I continued to stare at him, nauseated. "It's the best way to do it," he said. "Sometimes the ones they take out of dead people don't work as good."

I turned back to the woman to see the two attendants swabbing her chest, left arm, and both legs with yellow brown Betadine liquid. The dark liquid ran in rivulets down and around the sides of her body. They blotted her whole body with sterile towels, and then carefully covered her, one extremity at a time, with a sort of yellow Glad Wrap. When they finished this phase we had a totally naked woman tied down like a frog, drawn on with magic markers, painted brown, and wrapped in yellow plastic. My effort to appear casual was being badly undermined by the panicked thumping of my own heart.

Two more masked people came into the room and began preparing the instrument trays. They made several huge piles of blue cotton towels, each stacked about two feet high. Then they opened the glass cabinets and began to remove instruments from their sterile packaging. An enormous amount of trash began to accumulate.

They covered several large trays with an array of knives, saws, scissors, needles, and cautery tools. There were dozens of clamps and things that I couldn't identify and a particularly off-putting set of long wires with steel hooks on one end. I stood up beside my stool to get a better look, thinking this was a bit like Michael's car painting equipment, but when I saw the shark jaws of what had to be the chest spreader, I had to sit down and look somewhere else for a while.

My eyes came to rest on a large, perfectly ordinary looking clock on the wall. An official sign had been made of plastic and placed just underneath the clock that said CLOCK. I smiled.

The anesthesiologist and his assistant put something that looked like a shoehorn down the woman's throat and then put in a plastic tube. They removed the shoehorn and pushed another tube down. I looked at Henry. He said, "Sonar equipment. The first one was a respirator tube. It went into the lungs. It's hard to get a tube into there, so they have to use a guide. This one's easier. It goes into her esophagus to run the echocardiograph."

The anesthesiologist gently oiled the woman's closed eyelids and taped them shut. Then he oiled the area around her eyes. His assistant taped a pair of plastic goggles over the whole area. I looked at Henry and raised my eyebrows. He said, "She won't be blinking for a long time now and they don't want her eyes to dry out."

It was impossible not to feel the similarity to anointing the dead and placing coins over their eyes.

After about forty-five minutes no part of the woman was visible anymore. She was covered in layer upon layer of plastic, cotton, paper, and tape. Only narrow gaps in the blue towels over her chest, left arm, and both legs indicated anything at all was underneath.

Then the surgeon came in. He was dressed like everyone else except he had on fancy suede clogs and wore an especially heavy-duty shower cap. The surgeon adjusted the hydraulic operating table to a comfortable height. I saw why his shower cap was different when he put on a headlamp that looked like something straight out of a science fiction film. A small intensely bright light rested on the middle of his forehead just above a pair of glasses with magnification loupes on both eyes. He adjusted the three brilliant overhead lamps so that there was a tremendous amount of light on the woman's chest.

"That's why they have to overcool the room," Henry said. "Those lights put out a lot of heat and they have to stand right under them for hours." I just nodded, grateful that the room was cold because that would quell my nausea.

It looked like the operation was about to start, so I took a deep breath and stared at the floor. After a short silence during which I tried not to be aware of the incision being made, I heard the surgeon say, "Shit. She told me she'd quit smoking. Dammit, look at this."

I had a befuddled moment wondering if smoke had come out of her chest when he'd opened it, but I was afraid to look up. Then I realized he must be able to tell from the constriction of the blood vessels—from the reduced amount of bleeding coming from the cut he'd just made—that the patient had recently been smoking.

"Yeah, she quit smoking alright," one of the nurses said. "I caught her with a cigarette this morning and she said, 'This is my last one.'"

There weren't any sounds for a while, then I smelled something burning and involuntarily glanced up to see a haze of smoke over the woman's chest, the result of cautery to stop the bleeding from the incision. Then I heard the sound I'd dreaded: the buzzing of what had to be a bone saw. "Oh God," I said softly to Henry, "they're *sawing* on her," and grabbed his arm without looking up. I held his arm in a death grip for the few seconds it took the surgeon to cut through the woman's sternum.

I don't know how long it took them to dissect the arms and legs and remove the blood vessels that would be moved north or west of their former locations and restitched into the woman's heart to become coronary vessels. It might have been an hour or so. I glanced up again and saw the dissected vessels being held up and examined and trimmed with scissors to neaten the ends. The wounds in the arms and legs still gaped. *Breathe in, one, two, three, four. Hold, one, two, three, four. Breathe out, one, two, three, four. Hold, one, two, three, four.*

The sporadic conversation was so soft I could only catch the odd word here and there. But Henry seemed to understand it all because he'd periodically call out a number or fiddle with equipment in response to something I hadn't even heard.

Eventually it was time for the woman's heart to be bypassed with the heart-lung machine. A flurry of activity took place and the pumps on Henry's machine started turning, filling the clear plastic tubing with a strange bright orangey red fluid. It was such a startling orange red that I wasn't sure what it was. It certainly wasn't the color of any bleeding I'd ever seen. But when it continued, I realized that it must be the color of blood as it circulated inside the body—when it's not in contact with the air and not drying or clotting like it would in an open wound. I wondered if blood was this same color inside the darkness of the body.

There was another period of waiting and then a burst of mumbled conversation I didn't understand. Henry reached up and twisted a plastic stopcock valve on a small, clear plastic bag hanging directly in front of him and suddenly I felt panicky. I looked around the room wildly for an explanation of the awful feeling I was experiencing and scanned the various monitors for some sort of an answer. Then I saw that the woman's heartbeat had flatlined. Oh Lord.

I stared back at Henry with tears in my eyes and said, "What'd you just do?"

"I stopped her heart."

Oh God. He'd *killed* her. I felt tears begin to

stream down my face. I realized that Henry had to do it to help the woman; it would be much harder to fix her heart while it was still beating. But this was still utterly shocking. It had never occurred to me that this was how things were done, or that my friend would be the one who did it.

Henry said softly, "It's *okay,* Carolyn. You're just getting to see something most people never get to see. It's a medical sacrament."

I couldn't speak.

"I'm acting as a hierophant," he whispered.

"A what?"

"Hierophant. The priest who presides over initiation rites. Haven't you ever studied any mystical religious material, like the Kabbala or Rudolf Steiner?"

I shook my head.

"Well, what we're doing is taking a person who's your everyday kind of flawed normal mortal and giving them an experience of the afterlife, a taste of God, and then bringing them back into the world. It usually changes them forever."

I stared at him dumbfounded.

He continued, "It's like what John the Baptist did to Jesus when he baptized him in the Jordan. The real meaning of that's gotten lost over time. What people don't understand anymore is that John didn't just dunk Jesus. He held him under the water until he pretty well drowned him. He gave him a near-death experience, so when he came back he'd bring back a vision of Heaven with him. The fellow that came back wasn't just a human man, Jesus, anymore, but something more, he was the Christ."

I must have looked suspicious, because he added, "I'm hoping this lady'll come back different too and stop abusing her body with cigarettes or whatever."

"Well, no wonder my baptism didn't feel like anything," I said. "They just immersed me." I thought more about what Henry'd told me. "You know, I've heard that big operations like this changed people, but I thought it was fear causing the change. Facing their own mortality."

"Well, it's not. Seeing God's what causes it. Facing their *immortality*."

Wow.

But hell, I thought, having all the external indicators of success stripped off and being forced to work as a receptionist for nearly a year had changed me—and with a lot less fuss and expense. Clearly there was more than one kind of sacramental immersion that would do the trick.

Henry called out numbers intermittently, sometimes using a word that sounded like "pleej." "What's 'pleej'?" I asked.

"It's the heart poison I use to stop her heart. I'm letting the surgeon know how long it's been since I gave her a dose."

"Oh," I said. Then it became apparent why he had to call out the time. The medicine wore off after a while. As I watched, the woman's heart started tentatively beating again and the surgeon ordered Henry to give her another blast of pleej. And he did.

This was too awful to have to watch.

Every time I looked up Henry had another horse-sized syringe full of something he was giving the woman through the ports in his tubing. He also did frequent tests on her blood for various things like clotting time. He'd used so much medicine and equipment on her that finally his personal forty-gallon trash can got overloaded. He tossed a small plastic testing clip on top of the heap and it slid off into the floor. I picked it up and stuffed it into a gap in the trash.

When I drew my hand back there was blood on it. I looked at it, smearing the blood between my fingers. It was a slightly more normal color than what was running in the tubes, but it was thinner than any blood I'd ever seen before. It felt slick, like WD-40, and it wouldn't dry. I was wondering if that was what a massive dose of anticoagulant did when Henry saw the blood smears on my hand and covered them immediately with another sterile blue cloth. "You can go next door and wash that off," he said. He nodded toward the door that led to the room filled with sinks.

I shook my head. It seemed the least I could do to bond with this person I'd seen nude, dissected, and killed. It actually felt good to be making a bit of human contact with the woman by touching some part of her.

The surgical technician handed the surgeon a clean length of gauze string. He fiddled with it and handed it back to the tech. The tech measured the now bloody string with a ruler. Then the PA held up a piece of blood vessel, looked at it, laid it beside the length of bloody string, and cut it.

"They're cutting the first graft to measure," Henry explained. "They have to make sure it's the right length. And notice how they marked it when they took it out of the body. It's critical to know which end is which because the valves inside a blood vessel close under back-pressure—so if you sew it in the wrong way, it locks closed and won't work."

This cutting, measuring, and sewing went on for a couple of hours until all five grafts had been made. Never did any of the four people at the table show the least bit of restlessness or discomfort. Some time later I woke up with a start and realized that I'd been sleeping. I swallowed, sat up straight, and tried to figure out what was happening.

Things weren't going well. I looked at the only thing in the room I could understand: the tracings on the heart monitor. Oh hell. The woman's heartbeat was only on the top half of the line. And it was over 200 beats a minute. I knew enough to understand she couldn't live with that.

The surgeon began to manipulate the controls on the hydraulic table and it slowly rolled to the right. He paused, looked at something, and then slowly rolled the table in the opposite direction until she was on her left side. I glanced at Henry. "Looking for leaks," he said.

Then someone said something in a nervous voice about the left side of the woman's heart ballooning to the size of Texas. Henry was going to have to take back her heart functions while the surgeon regrouped and considered what could be causing the problem. That meant she had to be pleejed yet again. But this time it was almost a relief to see that awful-looking heartbeat disappear and go to a simple flatline.

I heard a bit of mumbling from the surgeon. I could make out "blood . . . positive . . . B."

I knew they might need to give her extra blood and I thought how handy it was that I was observing, because in a pinch I could give it to her. Her blood type was the same as mine, B positive.

Then I heard, ". . . probably HIV too."

Uh-oh. I strained my ears to hear the conversation. I'd misunderstood. Her blood type wasn't B positive, she'd been tested before the surgery and came up positive for type B hepatitis. And it sounded like they suspected HIV exposure as well.

Oh shit! I'd been rubbing her blood all over my right hand. I was an idiot! I looked at my hand, searching for any cuts or scratches, studying it for any minute breaks in the skin. After about half an hour I couldn't control my anxiety any longer and asked Henry, "That thing I picked up, was it sharp?"

"No. But go wash your hands."

"Too late now," I said, figuring that scrubbing would only reduce the thickness of whatever protection I had between my blood and hers.

I looked back at the surgeon. He wasn't happy either. He'd operated on the woman all day and was ready to be done with her. He continued to make remarks about her lifestyle. This time about cocaine use. I knew he was trying to get emotional distance in case he couldn't get her heart restarted. It was a tough time. Although everyone was doing their best, they'd taken a live person into the room and made a dead person out of her. However short her life expectancy had been that morning, if they'd left her alone she would've at least made it until the 6:00 news. Now she might not.

There was some back and forth discussion about blood and about ordering some more. The masks muffled the sound and made it hard to tell who was talking. I gathered that donated blood was still considered suspect and the surgeon didn't want to give the woman any unless it was absolutely necessary. I was surprised he was worried that a drug addict who already had hepatitis would get yet another disease from a transfusion.

This was so different from what Daddy did. He was one guy with a handful of Band-Aids who saw dozens of people every day. This was a dozen medical professionals—100 years of graduate school —working on just one patient using more equipment than I knew existed in the world. I tried to think about what all this effort meant to the woman. Was she even here anymore? Was she dead or alive? What did those words mean in a place like this?

"Where do you think she is right now?" I asked Henry.

Henry gave me a sideways look. "I usually don't talk to *anybody* about this kind of stuff. But you didn't run out screaming on the last one, so I'll tell you straight. I *know* where she is right now, because I can feel it. I been doing this for twenty-six years.

"She's not in her body right now. She's still here, but she's expanded to fill the whole operating room. The strongest part of the anesthetic, when they put the little mask on her face, made her leave her body. You can see it happen if you know what to look for."

I nodded, imagining I could just barely detect a calm presence filling the room. "Do they ever leave the room?" I asked.

"Sometimes," Henry said, "but they usually only go as far as the family lounge. They're checking on how their loved ones are holding up. Then they come back. Usually."

"Usually?" I said.

"Out of the twelve thousand of these operations I've been at, only six of them have left and stayed gone."

"Died?"

"Yeah."

"That's amazing."

"Maybe. Maybe not. I make it a point to keep in touch with them while they're out of their bodies, so they can understand what's going on. I always help lift them onto the operating table and then lift them off again when we're through. That's not part of my job. I do it because I wanna lay hands on them. Twice. I'm praying with them before I start and again after I'm done. And the whole time I've got their blood in my machine I never forget it's their soul I've got running around in these tubes. I meditate over their blood. I think it helps them if someone in the room stays conscious about what's really going on."

Henry was really out there. But everything he said seemed vaguely familiar to me. And felt right somehow, even though I didn't understand why.

Nobody could find where the leak was coming from and they couldn't finish the operation until they found it, so the surgeon decided to take a restroom break. This after six hours of unrelenting concentration. The instrument technician left with him.

I was so shocked and so exhausted I was numb. I decided that, despite what Henry said, the woman was basically dead now, so she probably wouldn't mind very much if I looked inside her. The least I could do was try to learn something from all this effort and sacrifice.

I stood up and walked out from behind Henry's machine to stand next to the large instrument tray that hovered over the woman's feet. I was at least five feet away from her heart and the table she was on was raised higher than my waist, so I couldn't really see much. I was glad. I could see a tool with huge metal jaws holding back the edges of the hole in her chest. The opening was as wide as my head. It was about as long as my forearm. Luckily sterile drapes and the yellow plastic skin-wrapping obscured every bit of human surface that I could recognize so it seemed like the hole might not be in a real person at all. There was something strange about the hole itself. It nagged at me, but I couldn't put my finger on what it was.

I stared at the gaping wound until I realized what was wrong: there was no blood. A live woman had a gigantic *not-bleeding* hole in her chest. It was unnerving. Then I realized the bloodlessness was Henry's doing. *He* had all her heart's blood. That was his job. He had it circulating in his machine and throughout her body, everywhere but her heart. Henry's machine was like the I-640 bypass around Knoxville. That must be why they called it bypass surgery!

I stretched up on tiptoe and craned my neck to try to see her heart, but couldn't see anything. All I could see was something that looked like a skinless breast of chicken lying in the middle of her chest surrounded by a jumble of pale yellow and pinkish stuff. I went back to my stool, disappointed not to have found anything heartlike to look at.

Henry said, "Did you see her heart?"

I said, "I'm not sure. I saw something that looked like . . . it looked like . . ."

"A raw piece of chicken meat?"

"Yeah. A skinless, boneless breast of chicken. What was that?"

"That's the heart."

How anticlimactic.

"If that's the heart, I gotta say, it don't look like much."

Henry smiled. "A lot of the most important things in life 'don't look like much.' "

Well I couldn't stand this. I *had* to get a closer look now. I decided to get up on the anesthesiologist's stool and take a peek over the curtain that hung between the woman's face and the hole in her chest. From that altitude I'd be able to see everything.

As I carefully eased sideways into a space the size of a phone booth with seven-foot high towers of monitors on three sides, I tried to map out the best direction for my fall. I took a deep breath and stepped up onto the stool. I looked straight ahead and then gradually tilted my face down in tiny ratcheting increments until I could see the incision. It seemed to extend to the far horizon. The cut was so long I felt I could see the curvature of the earth in it. I had an instant, vivid, nightmarish vision of my head breaking off and landing face-first in the ghastly hole.

I said, "Whoa," and got down off the stool. Little spots were dancing before my eyes.

"It's okay to look," said the nurse anesthetist.

I couldn't do it though, so I turned to go back to my stool. Henry intercepted me halfway. He took my arm and propelled me back, this time to the far side of the table where the surgeon had stood. He gripped my elbow in support. "Now what do you wanna see?"

"The lungs," I said. I wanted to see lungs so I could see what all Michael would be getting swapped out.

The PA bent over the woman's chest and gently poked around. He touched some fleshy things and then carefully took hold of a pale, lobular, stiff-looking thing with his thumb and forefinger. "Here you go. That's the lung," he said, pulling back on it very delicately.

I had expected the lungs to look spongy or fluffy —to be pretty pink cloudlike bags of air. What the PA had hold of looked like something to be avoided in the meat case at the supermarket. I bent closer and saw tiny flecks of black in the flesh. "It's got black specks in it!" I blurted out in shock.

"She lives in the city," the PA said. "Some of the damage is from smoking, but the big specks are from vehicle exhaust in town."

I resolved to race back to the farm as soon as the operation was over.

Henry must have felt my urge to bolt, because he increased the pressure on my elbow and said calmly, "What else would you like to see?"

"Henry," I said, "I've seen enough today to last me for the whole rest of my life."

We were both on our stools when the surgeon came back in to resume his careful scrutiny of the grafts. He found something to sew on and then stood and watched some more. The pleej eventually wore off again and the woman's heart stuttered back to life, zooming straightaway into a high-speed, chaotic rhythm.

The surgeon said something over his shoulder and a nurse left and then came back wheeling a cart with what looked like a fax machine on it. Henry came out from behind his console and went over to the small machine. He flipped the top open in a way that I hadn't suspected was possible, like a laptop, and revealed an exotic portable electronic device with a keyboard and monitor. Henry banged out something on the keyboard. There was a flurry of discussion about things like how fast the beat should be and where the "assist" should occur. Assist? Give me a break. What a euphemism. Assist like a parachute's an assist when you've just fallen out of an airplane. The woman was dead as a door-nail without the assist. I was shocked. It never occurred to me that they would roll a dead person out of the operating room and plug them in at the ICU and consider the operation a success.

Henry kept pecking away, checking the tracing on his small flipped-up monitor, confirming it with the anesthesiologist's big monitor. My God, he was programming the woman's heart.

They were finally ready to close. While three people closed the arms and legs, the surgeon and the PA closed the chest. The surgeon was handed the big wires with the ominous looking hooks on the end. I stood up to see what they were for. He had a pair of fancy pliers and was twisting the wires with a serious amount of physical effort. Ah, he was wiring the sternum back together. After each wire was twisted to the limit of his muscles, the PA cut the trailing ends with a pair of stainless steel wire cutters.

People were moving around the room everywhere now. The closing up process was nearly complete. Suddenly the resident, who was trying to leave his square foot of real estate for the first time in eight hours, tripped over something in the floor. The anesthesiologist's heart monitor flatlined and several alarms went off. Then, in an instant, eleven people turned their heads and looked toward the woman's chest to see if her heart was still beating.

It was. Thank God. There was a muffled burst of relieved laughter. This was downright spooky. Alive, dead, alive, dead. I was embarrassed to realize that I was losing the ability to feel any difference.

Orderlies came in with a very high-tech gurney and Henry helped them painstakingly move the woman off the operating table with all her trailing wires and tubes. Henry rolled his battery-operated heart-beating machine alongside her as she was taken down the hall to the Coronary ICU. I followed along, afraid to let Henry out of my sight, lest I be lost in the hospital forever.

As we walked down the hall I contemplated the phrase "died on the table." Now it had a whole new meaning. How could anyone "die" with all this equipment? What did death mean anyway in a situation like this? The woman's heart wouldn't beat on its own, so it seemed to me that she met the technical definition of "dead" right now. But she was plugged into a new set of electrical outlets in the Cardiac ICU and everyone behaved as if she was still alive. I hoped they were right.

There was something uniquely compelling about medical work that made it impossible to compare with any other profession. Although I'd had several jobs that were generally perceived as exciting and important, they were nothing like this. My befuddled and passive observation of this heart operation seemed somehow more valuable, more meaningful, than anything I'd ever done as a lawyer. And I'd been a good lawyer.

Henry and I returned to the operating room. He set to disassembling his machine, wadding lengths of plastic tubing and tossing them into a fresh trash can. He dropped a blue towel to the floor and kicked it back and forth across a pea-sized blood spatter. It was the only blood spatter I'd seen in the room the whole day and it had come from cleanup rather than the surgery.

He made some notes on a clipboard and then turned to me. "Ready to go?"

I nodded and followed him out of the room.

Henry said we could go grab a quick snack in the hospital cafeteria, but then he'd have to go back and do another procedure in an adjoining operating room.

"When do you get to go home?" I asked.

"When all the hearts are done."

"Do they keep you all day and then all night too?"

"Sometimes."

"Do you get the next day off if you have to do that?"

"Hell no. That's what medical work's all about. You do the best you can for as long as you can and then, no matter what happens, you keep coming back day after day and do it again."

Henry was a person who showed up too. And he was a sort of professional athlete. A step up from the rock throwing hall of fame.

"Henry," I said, "you have a hard job. An important job."

"So do you, Carolyn. So do you."

I went outside and blinked into the sudden brightness of the sun. In the Senate, I'd learned not to squint or flinch as I walked in and out of the series

342

of overlit news camera setups that lined the halls. In my old job, just going from one office to another, I'd flash through the background of half a dozen local news broadcasts across the country. I'd learned to keep my head up and eyes wide open to avoid looking like a criminal fleeing the court-house. Now I was learning a new skill: not flinching from surgical lights and the sights *they* illumi-nated. I knew I'd still feel as nervous as a gopher sticking its head out of a hole for a while longer. But I figured I'd get it right eventually.

I'd been back at the reception desk for a couple of days when the phone rang.

"Carolyn, this is Little Mike. I'm calling to give you some sad news, but I knew you'd want to know. Daddy's died."

I couldn't say anything. I made a sort of sighing noise, I think.

"Mom and my sisters want to tell you, we can't ever thank Doc enough. He kept Daddy alive for *years* longer than anybody ever expected. His heart doctor told us it was because of Doc that he'd stayed alive this long, and he couldn't understand how Doc did it. That's meant a lot. Especially this last year. It really made a big difference to us. And we thank you."

Momma and Daddy and I went to Michael's funeral. We noticed the crowd when we were still a couple of blocks away from the funeral home. Cars were lining the street, waiting to turn into the parking lot.

"Look," I said. "There's a line."

People were streaming out the front door of the funeral parlor and continuing down the sidewalk and around the corner. I'd never seen such a thing. But because my parents had been to far more funerals than I had, I asked, "Have you ever seen that before? Coming out of the funeral home and down the street?"

"Never," said Daddy.

Momma was shaking her head.

We parked and got in line about a block and a half from the door. The crowd was almost all men. The mood was respectful, but not really sad. Frequently quiet laughter would break out here or there and you knew it was some funny remembrance about Michael. One of the men behind me in the line said, "Are you Doc's daughter?"

I said, "Yes."

"You're the girl Michael was teaching to paint, aren't you?"

"Yes."

"He told me about you. He was awful excited to get to teach a girl to paint cars."

I nodded, "It's fun."

The men in line within earshot looked toward me and smiled. Michael had touched a lot of lives. Quite a feat for a man with only half a hand.

An hour and a half after the funeral had been supposed to start, we finally reached the casket and Michael's family. I looked at Michael and got a surprise. He looked handsome. I'd never noticed before that he had a handsome face. And I'd never seen him with his face still before. He'd always been moving and talking. *You rascal,* I thought. I'd tried so hard to avoid seeming to stare at his hands, I'd never noticed he had a beautiful face. There was a lesson in that. If he'd been alive to see my embarrassment, I knew he'd have barked out his good-natured laugh.

TWENTY-FIVE

It was mid-October and the leaves were turning. The view from the house was unbelievably beautiful. The fall colors in the Appalachian Mountains, the largest and most diverse hardwood forest in the world, were a sight people came from all over the world to see.

I'd been cleaning the office and spotted a box full of old-style medical equipment. There were a dozen glass syringes with large reusable needles. They were banded with a whetstone for sharpening the needles. I shuddered at what it had been like to get a shot in "the good old days." That's why they'd hurt. Now, with the tiny disposable diabetic needles, you could barely tell you were getting stuck. I found an adjustable headband that had a convex reflector on it. I put it on and looked at myself in the bathroom mirror.

"What are you doing?" Daddy asked. He'd caught me playing with his stuff for the umpteenth time, and now I was over forty! I asked him what the headband had been used for.

"It's a head mirror. It's used to reflect light, so you can see down people's throats. It comes with a smaller laryngeal hand mirror, sort of like what the dentists use. You lined up the head mirror with the overhead surgical light and then you bounced the light from the head mirror onto the laryngeal mirror, so you could see inside the throat cavity."

I dipped and tilted my head to try to get the light to shine on my hand. "This is pretty hard to use," I said. I couldn't imagine trying to use two of them in relay. It was like lining up a tricky pool shot where you had to bank off more than one rail.

"They were hard to use. The new hand light is much easier. Of course, nowadays you can do an MRI and see the whole inside of a person in incredible detail."

I nodded.

"I wouldn't ever want to have it done though," he said.

"Why not?"

"It'd be too upsetting."

"Why?"

"Because nobody's normal. You don't want to know what's not right in your brain or your heart or your kidneys. So if you don't let anybody look, you can't find out. You can remain in blissful ignorance."

"I guess modern medicine is gradually doing away with blissful ignorance."

"Yeah," he said. "And it's a shame. I'm all for making the diagnosis, but there's an awful lot of harmless abnormality that we're better off staying unaware of."

"What you don't know can't hurt you?"

He nodded. I knew I wanted to stay as oblivious as possible to my own abnormalities.

Daddy had scheduled the annual cattle vaccinations for that afternoon. He had his new cattle chute ready and the Rabbit Hunters had promised to come over and help him round the cattle up and run them through the device. He was worried all day that he wouldn't be able to get away on time. Come hell or high water he had to leave at 4:00.

Just as 4:00 finally rolled around, when Daddy was putting on his windbreaker, Joel LeQuire's enormous clattering diesel pickup truck pulled up in front of the office.

Daddy said firmly, "Oh no, not today. I can't be late leaving here today." But as he said it he was also removing his windbreaker. He noticed Alma's pained expression and said, "Well, there's no reason we *all* have to suffer. You can go on home. Carolyn and I'll handle this." When Alma didn't move he said again, "Go on." She took off like a shot, squeezing past Joel and Cheryl in the doorway without saying a word.

Gosh, I was startled and proud that Daddy trusted me to be his only assistant. I'd never helped him by myself before except in emergencies. But now I was getting a chance to work on a regular case. Of course I'd seen a lot during the last year.

Much of it I could have lived without, but it did give me a certain veneer of experience.

Daddy leaned toward me. "Let's get this over with as quick as possible. Don't ask him anything. Don't talk to him about anything."

"Are y'all closing?" Joel asked.

I nodded, afraid to speak.

"That's okay, Joel. What'd you need?" Daddy asked.

"Well Doc, it's sort of a private problem. Can we go in a room and talk about it?"

After a brief hesitation Daddy turned and waved for Joel to follow him. They went into Room 1 and shut the door.

Cheryl stood with her back to me, looking out the window. She looked lonely. I said, "You're Cheryl Piatt, aren't you?"

"Cheryl LeQuire now," she said in a tired voice with her back still turned toward me.

"Maybe you don't remember me. I'm Carolyn."

She turned and looked at me. "I remember you."

Daddy came back out after a mercifully brief interval. "Carolyn, go to Frank's and get me two Fleet's enemas. The prepackaged ones."

Oh, yuck, I thought. But I did as I was told. When I returned, I knocked on the door of Room 1.

"Here," I said as I stretched my hands toward the opening. I stood as far back as possible, where I couldn't see anything. The door opened fractionally and Daddy's gloved hands shot out and snatched the two small cardboard boxes. Then he kicked the door closed.

I wandered around my reception desk, idly tidying up my papers. Suddenly the door to Room 1 burst open and Joel marched smartly across the hall to the bathroom in an odd goose-step.

Daddy came out of the room and peeled his gloves off, turning them inside out. He dropped them into the floor in the middle of the hall. Well, that certainly made a statement. We stood waiting in silence, watching the sweeping second hand on the clock go round and round. Nothing.

"Carolyn, go get me a couple more of those Fleets," Daddy said, looking grim and determined.

"They only had two of the regular ones. All they've got left now is peppermint or something weird like that," I said.

"I don't care if they've got nitroglycerin in them, just bring me two more," he said. He seemed to be getting hysterical.

So I went to get two more and tried not to imagine what Frank thought I was up to.

When I returned, Daddy called toward the bathroom door, "Joel, come on out. I've got something else we can try."

Joel obediently goose-stepped back across the hall into Room 1 without making eye contact with anyone. Daddy followed him into the room in a rather menacing way and the door clicked shut. It was 4:30.

I turned to Cheryl and blurted out, "You know what pisses me off about seeing you again after all these years?"

"What?" she said.

"That the girls who were pretty in high school are *still* pretty. It doesn't seem fair."

"Well," she smiled, "the smart girls are still *smart.*"

She studied me for a moment and then said, "We didn't give you much of a chance, did we?"

"No," I said.

"You know, being a cheerleader was fun, but I never figured it'd end up being the high point of my life," Cheryl said. "Joel and I got married right out of high school."

"I didn't realize you'd been married to him for that long," I said.

"Oh, we didn't marry each other—at first. This is the third time for both of us. And right now things aren't looking too good. We both got kids with other people. It's tough."

She stood staring out the window at the highway.

"You know how when we were kids, we played that card game Old Maid?" I said.

Cheryl nodded.

"Well, there was something about that game that always confused me. I liked it. I sort of looked like the picture of the Old Maid. We were both tall and thin and had buck teeth and glasses. I never said anything to anybody about it, but I didn't understand why it was a bad thing to end up with the Old

Maid. I couldn't understand why nobody wanted to be like her. I still don't."

Cheryl looked at me and said, "Maybe nothing was wrong with her. Not a damn thing."

After a couple of minutes the door to Room 1 burst open and Joel crossed the hall to the restroom moving like a windup toy soldier. I really felt sorry for him. Daddy tugged the second pair of gloves off and threw them into the floor without bothering to turn them inside out.

He paced in a small circle for about half a minute. "I can't wait around here anymore. I've got to go. I've got things I need to be doing. Carolyn you're going to have to take care of him."

Then he left!

What was I supposed to do? Not anything that required gloves or handling anybody's butt, that's for sure. But this was the first case I'd ever been given lead responsibility on. Not just lead, but solo. I was a medical professional *alone* with a patient. It was a big responsibility. I had someone's health in my hands. I couldn't just leave him. Could I?

No. I had to stay and lock up, although giving Joel his own key might not be such a bad idea. I could have a copy made at the hardware store in a couple of minutes and leave it outside the bathroom door. But better not. I kicked the four loose gloves down the hall toward a biohazard container. No way was I touching them. After about twenty minutes of pleasant conversation with Cheryl, I shouted through the restroom door, "Joel, Daddy's gone. Do you want to try to go on home?"

"I can't," he said through the bathroom door.

"Are you having cramps?" I asked.

"No. Nothing's happening. I'm just scared to try to drive home. I just leased that truck two weeks ago and it's got velour seats," he said.

"Oh," I said, racking my brain for a solution. Then I got an idea. "Joel, how about if I give you one of those big Hefty Leaf and Lawn trash bags to sit on? They're waterproof."

He didn't answer, but after a minute the door to the bathroom opened and Joel came out and stood staring at the floor. I knew he must be mortified.

"Joel," I said, "I know this might be a little strange or embarrassing for you, but you've got to remember I grew up here. I've been hearing and seeing this stuff all my life. It's nothing weird to me. So don't worry about any of it. It's just everyday business."

That seemed to relieve him. He still wasn't talking, but I went to the supply closet anyway and pulled out a large black plastic trash bag. "You want me to put this across the seat of the truck?" I asked. He nodded.

"Better put two, cover the whole thing. And one in the floor," he said.

Cheryl and I went outside with three bags and prepared the truck. Then we came back in and I said, "Everything's ready."

He still wasn't moving. I think he was afraid to leave the immediate proximity of the bathroom. With four enemas in him, I could see why.

"Joel?" I said.

"Can I get you to tie one of them bags around me in case something happens on the way to the truck?" he said, still staring at the floor.

Couldn't he just've asked for a bag and tied it on himself? Or had Cheryl tie it on him? I waited a second. Apparently not. I went to the supply closet and got another bag. Joel stood in the hall helplessly while I tied the bag around his middle like a huge shiny black diaper. He looked ridiculous, but it gave him the confidence he needed to go get in his truck. I stood in the doorway and waved as they drove off.

Well, I'd done it. I'd handled my first case. I'd risen to the occasion, dug deep within myself, and done what it took to help someone, even though I didn't want to and had no idea how to solve the problem. I was proud of myself. I was proud that Daddy and Alma had trusted me enough to give me the responsibility. And I was happy I'd been able to help somebody. It wasn't glamorous, and it wouldn't be replayed on C-Span tonight, but I felt great.

I was shocked the next afternoon when Alma reminded me it was the first anniversary of my coming to work as a receptionist. That was a year ago? My God.

It was late on a Friday and Pup had brought Adron in. An ill-tempered cow (an actual animal, not Ms. Slimp) had butted him hard up against the rough boards of a barn wall. His left arm was scraped and looked like it might have splinters in it.

Daddy looked at the wound, cleaned it up, and painted it bright orange. Adron was typically stoic about his injury and hardly spoke while Daddy worked.

When Daddy finished rolling clean white gauze around and around Adron's arm it was nearly closing time. He explained to both Adron and Pup how to care for the wound and then we all stood at my counter looking out at the beautiful fall afternoon. It was a perfect day.

Adron, of course, had no money. He didn't really understand about money, but he was uncomfortable not having anything to give Daddy for fixing his arm. He fidgeted in his shy way, then said, "Doc, do you like squirrels?"

Daddy said, "Yeah," not sure exactly what Adron was getting at: hunting them, eating them, raising them, feeding them?

"I gotta lotta squirrels at my house."

"You do?" said Daddy.

"You can come look at them sometime."

"Do you like to watch the squirrels play, Adron?"

"Uh-huh. I got so many, and they run all over. They's funny to look at."

"When's the best time to see them?"

"You can come now if ye want to."

"That's a pretty nice offer. I might just do that. Where do you live?"

"Oh no," I said, interrupting, "please don't get started on this again. How about if we just follow Pup over there now?"

Daddy looked at me. "Would you like to see Adron's squirrels?"

I nodded.

So we put the instruments in the autoclave to sterilize over the weekend, turned off the lights, and locked the door. Adron sat on his knees in the backseat of Pup's car looking out the rear window to make sure we didn't get lost.

During the ride I thought about what a long, painful slide the changes in my life had been over the past year. Now that it was over though, I felt like I'd somehow landed in my rightful place.

That evening Jacob called. He'd also realized it was the anniversary of my new life as a receptionist. He filled me in on things in Washington, and then I asked, "How was your vacation?"

"Well, technically speaking, I'm sure it was fabulous. It must've been. The Asian Association toured a bunch of us around an endless series of gorgeous South Pacific islands for a couple of weeks 'promoting intergovernmental understanding.' "

"Sounds wonderful," I said.

"Yeah, well, on the last evening, in Fiji, the Chief

Counsel of the Energy Committee and I were stretched out side-by-side on lounge chairs on the porch between our private $700-a-night thatched-roof huts, watching a spectacular sunset when he turned to me and said, 'No offense Jacob, but wouldn't this be great if we were here with somebody we really cared about?' That sort of summed up my feelings about the whole trip."

I laughed. "A perfect fast-lane moment."

"Hey, I'm sending you a present. I had to write an op-ed for the boss that's going to run in this Sunday's *New York Times*. I put in, just for you, a reference to a groundhog. I was a bit afraid the boss would nix it, but he seemed not to find it out of place."

"Really? A groundhog. For me. You shouldn't have. Why a groundhog?"

"I'm not sure. I just wanted to put in a reference to something you might like. An animal. Are you pleased?"

"I'm honored. You know you're a maniac, don't you? You sneaked a groundhog into a *New York Times* op-ed as a secret present for your hillbilly friend."

"Another of my best creations and, as usual, it's got another guy's name on it.

"I've been reading a book for you too," he added.

"Oh yeah?"

"Yeah. It's called *The Angle of Repose*. It's about how everything has a particular characteristic way it will fall when dropped. A certain way it will land."

"Hunh. I've been thinking about something similar myself except my image was bugs on a windshield. So each of us has an individual splatter pattern. Like bird droppings. What does my angle of repose look like? Pretty good?"

"It's actually quite lovely," he replied.

"Thank you. You know, angle of repose, that's a wonderful image. Repose sounds so peaceful. But I hope only a *thing* has an angle of repose. A heart, a soul, a spirit, what do they have? I think they must fall in the other direction. Toward God, toward the heavens."

"We 'fall to rise.' You're right, of course. *Fall* isn't the right word for what you've done. For you the word is *climb* maybe. But climbing is only for the very strong. I don't know how you've done it."

"The only way to change your splatter pattern is to change your center of gravity," I said.

"You're talking physics to *me?*"

"I'm serious. I think I changed the center of gravity from inside of me to somewhere outside. I moved myself out of my favorite position as the center of the universe and decided to hang out on the sidelines for awhile."

"You know people tried to burn Galileo at the stake for talking about something similar."

I said, "I got another book for you." Then I quoted the opening lines of *David Copperfield*: "Whether I shall turn out to be the hero of my own life, or whether that station will be held by anybody else, these pages must show."

"Yeah. Exactly. Our lives are Dickens' tales and the central question is always whether we're playing a hero or a villain."

"I think so," I said.

In the early evening I sat on my bucket in the barn and fiddled with Fletcher's green pocketknife. I looked at each of the blades, testing them for sharpness, and wondered what he'd been doing when he'd made the various nicks and scratches in the metal.

I remembered how, in this same place, he'd talked to me about another pocketknife: the one that'd enticed Daddy into this community. It was a strange story that I'd never understood until recently. Until Henry had explained it to me. I'd never really believed that the man who'd woken up in the hospital was a *different man* from the one who'd died.

But now I realized it was true.

All my life I'd missed the real significance of the events. The fact that a country doctor'd had the courage and skill to save a man's life by doing open-heart surgery on him in a silo with a borrowed pocketknife wasn't the point. The point was that, by intervening in each other's traumas, we could utterly transform each other's lives.

The man who'd been electrocuted hadn't been able to read and the man who'd awakened in the hospital could. The man who had died had been reborn as someone else. No telling what else that new man could do that would never have been possible if he hadn't had his heart stopped by accident and then had it restarted through the selfless intervention of another person.

I'd always thought the story was about the astounding surgery. But it wasn't. It was about using the talents you had, whatever they might be, to the most constructive purpose. I'd thought the story was about the fact that a *pocketknife* had been used to open a man's chest. But it wasn't. It was about using whatever tools you had on hand to do whatever needed to be done. I'd thought it was about saving lives, about the fact that the man had *lived*. But it wasn't. It was about *how* the man lived, who he lived *as*. I'd thought it was about being seen doing good works. But it wasn't. It was about seeing what other people needed and doing it.

It was about the fundamental act of placing our attention outside of ourselves and onto other people who needed it. Fletcher and Michael had been really good at that.

Our whole lives were set up to give us every possible opportunity to do the right thing, to mature into good people. God didn't care how or where we did it, just as long as we did. He gave us a series of choices. We had to take what we *were* and what we *had* and do the best we could with them. There were no extra bonus points for visibility or magnitude. I'd always aimed for the big score, but now I understood better.

Like Henry had said, a lot of the most important things don't look like much. In fact, a lot of the most important things are downright invisible, and rightly so. We'd do them for the wrong reasons if they weren't.

Nobody'd been able to reach into Fletcher's and Michael's chests and fix their hearts. I guess they hadn't needed it. But both men had enough skill and concern to intervene with me. They'd steadied me at the critical moments and steered my life in a better direction. They'd saved me.

Pocketknives were powerful tokens of crisis and change, of growth, and of lives well lived. I wouldn't be operating on anybody or doing anything glamorous with one, but helping keep Daddy's office open seemed like a worthy task and maybe listening to people could do some good too. I walked to the door of the barn and stood looking out over the Smokies.

Harry, the wolfhound mix, bumped my hand with his huge scruffy snout to get my attention. I scratched his head and watched the sun set with him leaning heavily against my leg. When the last bit of light was fading, I said, "Let's go," and stepped out of the barn and into the rest of my life.

As I walked toward the house, I slipped Fletcher's knife into the pocket of my jeans, thinking I'd carry it for a while now and see what I could do with it.

ACKNOWLEDGMENTS

This book is dedicated with my deepest heartfelt thanks to the following people:

My father's patients

Paul L. Jourdan, M.D.
Elise G. Jourdan, Pharm.D.
David C. Jourdan

Deborah C. Grosvenor

Kathy Pories

Dan Berkovitz
Joe Willis
Chuck Jones, Ph.D.

Cheenie Rao
Jana Murphy
Yvonne Loveday
Mark Winegardner
Robert Snow

Edd Bissell
Wayne Wheeler
Virginia Allen
Jim Howell

And to all the millions and millions of people around the world who do good.

Heart in the Right Place

A Conversation with the Author
and
Questions and Topics for Discussion

A CONVERSATION WITH THE AUTHOR

What inspired you to tell your story?

I love my little community—the culture and the dialect—and I wanted to preserve a picture of what Smoky Mountain culture was like before it was overrun by new people moving to the area and by the effect of the increasingly pervasive presence of national media in our lives. I also wanted to preserve a picture of what family medicine was like at its best—before the business people got in charge of health care and when the doctor not only knew his patient but also knew four generations of the patient's family and all his cousins too.

You portray people and events so vividly. How were you able to accomplish this?

I like to jot down things I hear people say, just a remark or a snippet of dialogue. That's what truly interests me, the way real people talk. Most of the book originated on fast food drive-thru napkins and Post-its where I'd make notes to myself of things I'd heard. I used to be ashamed of that, that I didn't write by sitting at a desk and having deep thoughts but was inspired by listening to anybody and everybody around me talking about the most mundane aspects of their lives. Then recently I learned that most of the great country music songs originate the same way, so I don't have to be so embarrassed anymore.

The problem with working that way was that I accumulated huge stacks of ragged scraps of paper. When my desk got covered with them, I sorted them out and transcribed them. Finally I sprang for a palmtop computer and began making notes at the reception desk so I wouldn't forget what I was seeing and hearing. My note-taking gradually escalated into serious writing. I'd get up at 5:30 and write for ninety minutes before work, because that was the only time when I could do it. And I kept doing that for several years until, eventually, I shocked myself by having a book.

How did everyone in town respond to the book once it was published?

Really positive. All positive. Nearly every day I get phone calls or e-mails from somebody thanking me for writing the book. I've gotten amazing letters from the families of the main characters—they write because, like me, they find it hard to talk about the events without choking up. Over and over people have told me they're pleased by the careful detail in the recollections. A lady told me she'd bought a copy of the book for each of her children because her husband, their father, had such a prominent role in it. A few months later one of the children told me they'd bought copies for each of the grandchildren too, because by reading the book they'd have a way to know their grandfather. That was nice.

And how did you father respond? Was he surprised to find himself at the center of your book?

For a long time he couldn't imagine that his life was anything special or that it would be interesting to other people. In his mind he just did what he did and that was his job. Now he gets it. The newest development has the whole family bemused: Hollywood has expressed some interest in making a television series like *Northern Exposure* from the book. I can share in the befuddlement over that. But actually, everyone's life is worthy and riveting if it is observed properly.

So true, but how do you think we can observe another person's life properly?

By listening. But we don't listen to each other. This is a really serious problem in our culture nowadays. If we're polite we take turns talking in a self-absorbed way, but we rarely ever listen to what anyone else is saying.

When you do listen, things happen. You find yourself empathizing, developing compassion. It's hard work, though. Suddenly the world isn't "all about me."

If you don't listen, you miss a lot. You fail to realize that each of us faces very different, but equally trying, life circumstances. You don't discover that each of us is so deeply flawed that it's really tough for anyone to proceed through life with any grace at all.

Our whole culture is designed to cover this over.

To me the most significant thing in the world is observing the heroism of each individual's struggle to get on with life in the face of great obstacles.

If we can ever learn to control ourselves, to get still and quiet in the presence of another person, we can see that every person's life, no matter how modest or goofy looking, is deeply heroic. This is the basis of all worthy spiritual practices, learning to occasionally give up your seat at the center of the cosmos and move to the sidelines so you can observe another person as the center.

I learned that watching the show is more meaningful than being the show.

What was the most difficult challenge you had to overcome in writing about your experiences?

Writing a memoir like mine is very different from writing fiction. This book deals with really tough situations involving the people I love most in the world. And a lot of it didn't turn out so great. It's emotionally wrenching, and the minute details of those things aren't fun to focus on for the many years it takes to write a good book.

For some of the stories I did a hundred or more revisions and cried every single pass through them, reading or writing. I often wondered why I was doing that to myself. I suppose it was because I wanted to try to learn what I could from my life and the lives of people around me. I didn't want to just gloss over all that experience and say, "Next!"

Were there any surprises in the process?
The magnitude of the success of the book and the breadth of the audience. I never considered the material regional, but I wasn't sure how an insider's take on a rural area in the Smokies would be received by people in New Jersey and California. I worried that some convoluted notion of political correctness would make people uncomfortable with an accurate depiction of mountain folks being themselves. But they get it totally. And now it's being translated into foreign languages!

A friend of mine who's from Nebraska said, "Your work centers around the absurd, but effective, solution. And it works because you come from this community where no matter how awkward the circumstances are, nobody seems to possess the capacity to perceive humiliation." I love that. I hope that's right.

We tease each other all the time. Sick and dying people would tease each other in that office. We have a tremendous tolerance for eccentricity and ignorance. Situations that might cause humiliation or shame elsewhere are seen as a source of good-natured free entertainment in Strawberry Plains.

I understand that your father recently retired because of health issues. Whom do people go to see now that he's not practicing?

A young doctor who grew up in the area started a practice close by, so that's very lucky for everyone. The new guy can't get away with all the tactics Daddy employed, like improvising equipment by rooting around in a toolbox, but he's good.

Are you working on another book?

I try to write a little every day. I'm always working on several different things.

I've done a lot of work on a sequel that picks up where *Heart in the Right Place* left off. I just finished a small book of true bear bloopers, stories about times when tourists and bears have startled each other in Great Smoky Mountains National Park. That was a lot of fun to do, very comical.

And I'm on a third revision of an action-adventure novel about a very strenuous chase through the Smokies. Most people don't realize it, but nearly all of the National Park is a harsh and terrifying wilderness. One step off the trail and you're in a whole different world.

Do you have any writing advice?

Yes, I have formulated the Three Fundamental Laws of Writing:

1. Start the book.
2. Work very hard on the book for a long time.
3. Finish the book.

An old friend, whom I've know since I was nineteen and a student at the University of Tennessee, asked me these questions:

1. How many people do you know who want to write a book?
2. How many people do you know who've ever even started a book?
3. How many people do you know who have ever finished a book?

My friend bet me a million dollars that sheer momentum would carry any book I completed all the way through the process of getting an agent, getting published, and getting a movie deal if I would simply start and finish a book.

He was right. You don't need anything else before these two steps have been completed—not an agent, not anything.

What do you miss most about your life in Washington, D.C.?

I miss the clothes a lot, but actually they were a pain to wear because I was always worried about damaging something really expensive. Now I have a sort of shrine in my closet, a museum, where I store the really expensive pieces, like the Hermes scarves.

I also miss the restaurants, the ultra-luxurious travel, my friends, and being surrounded by people who were paid large amounts of money to create and maintain the illusion that I was a really special, interesting, and important person.

QUESTIONS AND TOPICS FOR DISCUSSION

1. Carolyn Jourdan must leave her glamorous, fast-paced life in Washington, D.C., in order to return to her small hometown to help her parents. What kinds of sacrifices have you made for your family? In what ways did those sacrifices affect your life? Were you, like the author, surprised by how you were changed by them?

2. Jourdan reflects on the differences between Michael and Harley's lives: "Harley had a death wish. He'd been graced with an extraordinary physique, and he abused his body and sought release from the world. Michael, who'd been born with a bad heart . . . struggled heroically to stay alive day by day". She then concludes, "If there was one thing I'd learned growing up in a doctor's office, it was that people's mood was rarely dependent on their external circumstances. Its origin was almost always internal." Do you find that this distinction holds true based on your own experiences? Are there people you know who reflect Michael and Harley's different approaches to life, and if so, in what ways?

3. Early on, Fletcher says to the author, "Your daddy's smart. He could've done anything, could've been any kind of doctor and got rich, but he came out here instead cause he wanted to help people." What are the trade-offs in being a small-town doctor versus being a doctor in the big city? What is gained and lost on both sides? What would we lose if small-town doctors disappeared?

4. When Jim Garrison comes to the office with a life-threatening emergency, the author thinks, *"Somebody's gotta do something about this."* She suddenly realizes that her father is the only person who can help. Have you ever been in a situation where you were the only person who could help, and if so, how did you manage it?

5. How would you characterize Carolyn Jourdan's relationship with her father? In what ways is it similar to or different from her relationship with her mother?

6. After Taylor Jackson leaves the office, the author thinks, "Every day in this place was spent viewing the most personal and critical moments of other people's lives. . . . I was inadequate to the experience." Do you believe that's true? How would you respond to the situations Carolyn Jourdan faces in her father's office?

7. During one of her telephone conversations with Jacob, the author says, "You know how we always talk about wanting to be in public service so we can help people. . . . Well, in this place I feel sometimes like I really *am* helping people. Actual people. It's not just an idea. I can't help them *much*. I know it's not glamorous, but sometimes I think maybe I'm doing more good swabbing up body fluids and being a friendly face here than I ever did working in the Senate." Discuss the different ways people help each other. How do you think caring for others informs who you are? Share an experience you had directly assisting someone.

8. Discuss the ways in which Carolyn Jourdan's view of her father and mother shifts over the year. For instance, early on she describes them as "stoic" and "utterly self-contained." How does she see them by the end of the book?

9. When the author catches a glimpse of a human heart during surgery, she says to Henry, "If that's the heart, I gotta say, it don't look like much." Henry smiles and says, "A lot of the most important things in life 'don't look like much.' " Can you think of other examples in the book for which this holds true? Does this statement reflect a situation you have experienced?

10. Near the end of the book, the author realizes the true significance of the story about performing surgery with a pocketknife: "I'd always thought the story was about the astounding surgery. But it wasn't. It was about using the talents you had, whatever they might be, to the most constructive purpose." Who else mirrors this sentiment and why? Historical figures? People in your own life? To what degree is this true for yourself?

A former U.S. Senate Counsel to the Committee on Environment and Public Works and the Committee on Governmental Affairs (now Homeland Security and Governmental Affairs), Carolyn Jourdan is an award-winning writer and documentary filmmaker. She lives on the family farm in east Knox County, Tennessee, and has seven stray animals (four dogs and three cats).

Center Point Publishing
600 Brooks Road ● PO Box 1
Thorndike ME 04986-0001 USA

(207) 568-3717

US & Canada:
1 800 929-9108
www.centerpointlargeprint.com